REMEMBER WITH ADVANTAGES

Also by Henry Keown-Boyd:

A Good Dusting
A Centenary Review of the Sudan Campaigns 1883–1899

The Fists of Righteous Harmony
A History of the Boxer Uprising in China, 1900

REMEMBER WITH ADVANTAGES

A History of the Tenth, Eleventh
and Royal Hussars, 1945–1992

by

HENRY KEOWN-BOYD

Old men forget; yet all shall be forgot,
But he'll remember, with advantages,
What feats he did that day.

Henry V, Act VI, Sc III

LEO COOPER
LONDON

First published in Great Britain in 1994 by
Leo Cooper
an imprint of
Pen & Sword Ltd
47 Church Street, Barnsley, South Yorks, S70 2AS

A CIP catalogue record for this book
is available from the British Library

ISBN 0 85052 382 6

Typeset by CentraCet Limited, Cambridge
in 11/13 Garamond

Printed by Redwood Books,
Trowbridge, Wiltshire

To All Those Who Have Served
in the Three Regiments

Contents

————

ICH DIEN – The Tenth Royal Hussars (PWO)

TREU UND FEST – The Eleventh Hussars (PAO)

ICH DIEN – The Royal Hussars (PWO)

Contents

Illustrations

Illustrations

Between pages 104 and 105

Between pages 168 and 169

Colour Plates

Between pages 152 and 153

The Trustees thank all those who kindly lent the photographs reproduced in this book.

Foreword

BY HER ROYAL HIGHNESS
PRINCESS ALICE, DUCHESS OF GLOUCESTER
COLONEL-IN-CHIEF OF THE ROYAL HUSSARS
(PRINCE OF WALES'S OWN)
1969–92
AND
DEPUTY COLONEL-IN-CHIEF OF THE
KING'S ROYAL HUSSARS

'Remember with Advantages' is the record of three English cavalry regiments between 1945 and 1992. The 10th and the 11th Hussars each thrived for over 250 years; following their amalgamation in 1969, The Royal Hussars existed for only 23 years before further cuts to the British Army at the end of the Cold War led in turn to its amalgamation in December 1992.

I have been connected with these three regiments throughout my life. Uncles, brothers and great nephews served in them and my husband, Prince Henry, was a regular officer in the 10th Hussars. He also served with the 11th before becoming Colonel-in-Chief of the 10th from 1937 to 1969. On the amalgamation I was greatly honoured to be appointed Colonel-in-Chief of The Royal Hussars (PWO) by Her Majesty the Queen, a position I held throughout its 23 year history.

This book explains how the events which followed the Second World War influenced the lives of those who served in British cavalry regiments, and describes the combination of sportsmanship, comradeship and service which were their enduring characteristics.

Foreword

I am confident that the same spirit will survive in the successor regiment, The King's Royal Hussars, of which I am pleased still to be associated as Deputy Colonel-in-Chief.

Alice.

Barnwell, 1994

Author's Note and Acknowledgements

Much which is contained in these pages is adapted or quoted verbatim from the spoken or written contributions, most gratefully received, of past members of the Regiments concerned. Many of the events and anecdotes recounted here took place decades ago and memory plays tricks. Thus, although based on fact and experience with no intent to mislead, some episodes may have lost nothing in the telling and I cannot guarantee total accuracy.

In the course of researching and writing this History I was in contact, one way or another, with about eighty former and serving members of the three Regiments, so it would be impracticable to try to mention all by name and invidious to refer to some and not others. That said, the unswerving support, especially in times of difficulty, given to me by the Colonel of The Royal Hussars, Major-General John Friedberger, and the Regimental Secretary, Lieutenant-Colonel Robin Merton, cannot be allowed to pass unacknowledged. Without their help, understanding and patience this History would never have seen the light of day.

Similarly, my grateful thanks go to the editor, Tom Hartman (himself a former 11th Hussar), who gave unstintingly the benefit of his professional and expert advice at all stages in the preparation of the book.

Historical Introduction

Before the dawn of recorded history cavalry came into being, perhaps somewhere on the steppes of Asia, when a shaggy man dashed from his rude shelter, sprang onto a shaggy pony and charged at another shaggy man throwing stones or brandishing a club.

The ancient Egyptians made wide use of the chariot but the Greeks and Romans fought mainly with infantry, regarding cavalry as an ancillary arm. In the Dark Ages the terrifying descendants of the shaggy man from the steppes conquered half the known world on their ponies and in Europe in the Middle Ages warfare was conducted almost exclusively by heavy cavalry, 'the Knights in Armour'. However, by the 14th century, with the emergence of the professional pikeman and archer, the battlefield dominance of cavalry began to decline. Nevertheless, *l'arme blanche* remained a powerful influence in the art and practice of war for another five hundred years until the invention of the magazine rifle and the machine-gun in the late 19th century.

British cavalry regiments evolved from the mounted nobility and their feudal followers but under the names and numbers which are familiar to us they did not begin to appear until the late 17th century. In this book we are concerned only with three Hussar or Light Cavalry regiments, the Tenth and Eleventh, and the robust but sadly short-lived child of their marriage in 1969, The Royal Hussars. Both parent regiments were formed in 1715 as Light Dragoons to suppress the Jacobite rebellion in

Scotland and redesignated Hussars (a Hungarian word meaning scout)* in 1806 (10th) and 1840 respectively.

The 'Shiners' and the 'Cherrypickers' took part in most of the campaigns which fill the pages of British history (see Appendix A for Battle Honours) and, as every school-boy used to know before the teaching of such deeds became unfashionable, the 11th rode with the Light Brigade at Balaklava, under the leadership of their flamboyant Colonel, Lord Cardigan. In this action the Regiment won its only Victoria Cross, awarded to Lieutenant Alexander Dunn, a Canadian. The 10th served with particular distinction in the Boer War winning two Victoria Crosses (Sir John Milbanke and Sergeant Engleheart), while the 11th had to content themselves with sending drafts to other regiments in South Africa. In the Great War of 1914–18 both regiments spent four years in the trenches on the Western Front, used mainly as mobile reserves and were spared the nightmarish casualties suffered by the infantry.

Since the turn of the century intense and often splenetic debate had raged in both military and political circles as to the future of horsed cavalry. As we have seen, in the First World War most of the regular cavalry regiments had been relegated to the role of reserve infantry. Even as early as the Battle of Omdurman in 1898 the classic cavalry charge against infantry armed with 'modern' rifles had proved to be not merely futile but almost suicidal. In the Boer War few such charges were made and fewer still were successful. It is true that Allenby used cavalry, mostly Yeomanry and Australian Light Horse, with some effect in the Palestine campaign of 1917/18, but even to the die-hards it was gradually becoming clear that the days (or, in some circumstances, the minutes) of a man on a horse on a 20th century battlefield were numbered. Paradoxically it was the internal combustion engine and its adaption for a warlike role which came to the rescue of the old British cavalry regiments and with remarkable speed and dexterity officers and

---

* According to Chambers Encyclopaedia the literal meaning of the word in Hungarian is 'twentieth', one Mathias Corvinus having in 1458 raised a body of cavalry against the Turks by ordering one man in twenty in each village to enlist.

troopers alike leapt from their saddles into the turrets and driving seats of tanks and armoured cars.

In the British Army mounted troops played little or no part in the Second World War but other armies were slower to modernize. The Poles used horsed cavalry during the German invasion of 1939, as did the Russians two years later, and the last cavalry charge faced by British troops was launched by Italian colonial horse at Keru Gorge in Eritrea in January, 1941. On almost all these occasions men and horses were mown down long before reaching striking distance of their enemy.

The 11th Hussars, who held their last mounted parade on 10 April, 1928, were in the forefront of mechanization and were re-equipped with Lanchester and Rolls Royce armoured cars. It was not until 1937, however, that the 10th lost their horses, only to be issued with a few 15-cwt trucks! A year later these were supplemented with some aged and decrepit tanks with which, in 1940, they were sent to fight the crack German Panzer Divisions in France. The sad story of that campaign need not be repeated here; suffice it to say that most of the Regiment was able to escape from France, without its vehicles, and served with great distinction through the rest of the war in North Africa and Italy.

Meanwhile, the 11th found themselves in Egypt at the outbreak of war, having served in Palestine during the Arab uprising in the 1930s. They soon acquired a reputation as the most desert-wise reconnaissance regiment in the British Army, fighting throughout the North African campaign, crossing to Italy, withdrawing briefly to England for re-fitting, landing in Normandy shortly after D-Day and remaining in action almost continuously until the unconditional surrender of Germany.

Thus both regiments achieved war records which each could claim to be second to none. For the next quarter of a century they were to play an equally important, if less spectacular, role in keeping the fragile peace of the Cold War in Europe, a role punctuated with occasional forays to more distant and exotic climes, such as Malaya and the Red Sea. This then is the story of those years and the years which followed after the 'marriage' of the two regiments and the birth of The Royal Hussars.

Germany

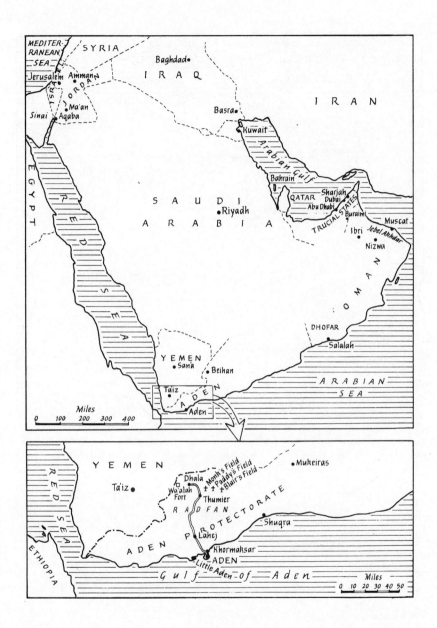

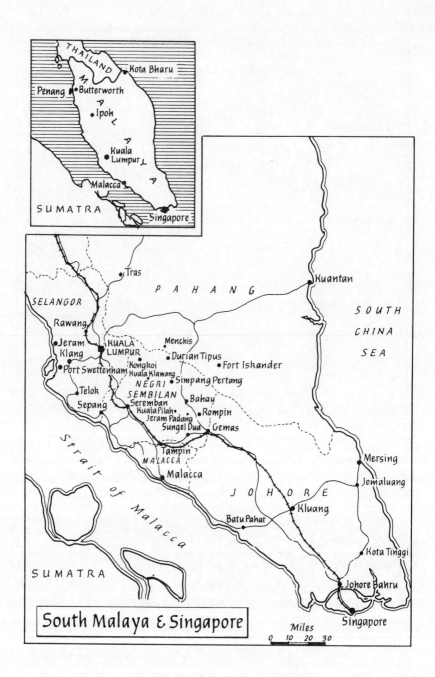

THAILAND

Kota Bharu

Penang • Butterworth

• Ipoh

Kuala Lumpur

Malacca

SUMATRA

Singapore

M
A
L
A
Y
A

• Tras

P A H A N G

Kuantan

SELANGOR

Rawang

• Jeram
Klang

KUALA
LUMPUR

• Menchis

Durian Tipus

• Fort Iskander

SOUTH

CHINA

SEA

Port Swettenham

Kongkoi
Kuala Klawang

Simpang Pertang

Telok

NEGRI
SEMBILAN

Sepang

Seremban

Bahau

Kuala Pilah
Jeram Padang

Rompin

Sungei Dua

Gemas

Mersing

Tampin

Jemaluang

MALACCA

J O H O R E

Malacca

Batu Pahat

Kluang

S
t
r
a
i
t

o
f

M
a
l
a
c
c
a

Kota Tinggi

SUMATRA

Johore Bahru

South Malaya & Singapore

Singapore

Miles

0   10   20   30

xxii

Northern Ireland

Londonderry
L·O·N·DONDERRY
ANTRIM
Larne
Lough
Neagh
Aldergrove
BELFAST
TYRONE
Cookstown
Pomeroy
Omagh
Coalisland
Dungannon
Aughnacloy
Castle Archdale
Lough
Erne
Enniskillen
FERMANAGH
Caledon
Armagh
HMP
Maze
Strangford
Lough
DOWN
Downpatrick
Gosford Castle
Upper
Lough
Erne
Rosslea
ARMAGH
Bessbrook
Newry
IRELAND
Miles
0   10   20

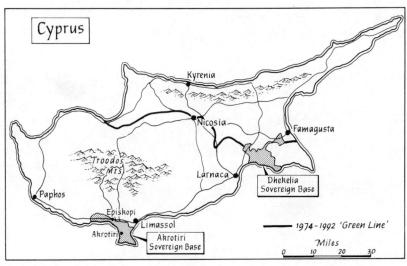

Cyprus

Kyrenia
Nicosia
Famagusta
Troodos
Mts
Larnaca
Dhekelia
Sovereign Base
Paphos
Episkopi
Limassol
Akrotiri
Akrotiri
Sovereign Base
1974–1992 'Green Line'
Miles
0   10   20   30

ICH DIEN

The Tenth Royal Hussars

(Prince of Wales's Own)

Chapter 1

EUROPE 1945-53

The Second World War ended for the 10th Hussars in Italy when Field-Marshal Kesselring surrendered to Field-Marshal Alexander on 2 May, 1945. The Regiment, under the command of Lieutenant-Colonel D. R. B. Kaye, had fought its last action of the war a few days earlier on the banks of the River Po in support of the 167th and 169th Infantry Brigades.

Immediately there developed that curious period which can perhaps be best described as 'the post-war Phoney War' when the Western Allies, principally the United States and Great Britain, found themselves locked in a potentially deadly game of military and diplomatic manoeuvres with their erstwhile Eastern Allies, the Soviet Union and Yugoslavia, over the control of Austria and north-eastern Italy. This tense period, virtually ignored by historians for decades, sprang into prominence in the later 1970s and 80s with a series of revelations, books and law suits relating to the enforced return by the British of thousands of anti-Communist Cossacks and Royalist Yugoslavs to Stalin and Tito and thus, in many cases, to a terrible death.

This is not the place to reiterate the arguments surrounding these contentious and gruesome events and, in any case, the Regiment was fortunate enough to have little or no direct involvement in them. However, by mid-May, in response to ambitious movements on the part of Marshal Tito's forces, the 10th had moved up to the Italian-Yugoslav frontier near Trieste, the control of which vital sea-port was one of the main bones of contention between the Western and Eastern Allies. But contact with the Yugoslav forces was minimal, being confined to the arrest of a few infiltrators and one or two football matches! By the end of 1945 the Regiment had moved to Austria and thence, via the Ruhr, to Lübeck on the Baltic and it was here that 'Regimental History' was resumed with the publication of the first post-war Gazette in 1947.

Curiously enough, in the light of a then unimagined event which was to take place nearly a quarter of a century later, the Colonel of the Regiment at this time and until 1949 was a former 11th Hussar, Lieutenant-General Sir Willoughby Norrie, who had succeeded Colonel V. J. Greenwood in 1946. In April of the same year Lieutenant-Colonel J. P. Archer-Shee succeeded Lieutenant-Colonel Kaye, who had commanded the Regiment thoughout the Italian campaign.

Lord Norrie, as he later became, was one of the outstanding figures of both regiments, between whom his affections were equally shared. He had joined the 11th in 1913 and took part in one of the few successful cavalry charges in France in the First World War, a description of which, and the controversy surrounding it, appears in the 11th Hussar section of this book. For his war services he was awarded the DSO, MC and bar. In 1931 he was appointed to command the 10th Hussars, apparently on the direct orders of King George V, to whose ears had come reports of the Regiment's low morale and standards of efficiency, a state of affairs which Norrie quickly rectified.

As the only 11th Hussar ever to reach the rank of Lieutenant-General, Norrie commanded 30 Corps in the Western Desert during the critical battles of 1941/2. After the war he was appointed Governor of New South Wales and later Governor-General of New Zealand.

In his absence, his duties as Colonel of the Regiment were taken over by his deputy, Brigadier C. B. C. (Roscoe) Harvey, whose career as a fighting soldier was as distinguished as that of his principal. He had joined the 10th in Ireland in 1920 and quickly established a considerable reputation as a horseman. He was second-in-command in France in 1940 and formed and commanded the 23rd Hussars, a 'hostilities-only' formation, before taking over the 10th in 1941 prior to its departure for the Middle East. In the course of the war he was awarded no less than three DSOs, having commanded 8th Armoured Brigade in North Africa and 29th Armoured Brigade in North-West Europe.

In June, 1946, a contingent under Lieutenant J. Verge with RSM Dunk and a veteran of the First World War, Corporal Tom Smith, travelled to London to represent the Regiment at the great Victory Parade.

In the same month a curious entry appears in the Regimental War Diary (a form which seems to have lingered on well into peacetime).

'14th June – Regt. is warned to stand by 3 troops in case of disturbance as shipload of POWs (Prisoners of War) Russian bound are (sic) due to dock at Lübeck prior to being handed over.

'16th June – Regt. provides 3 troops to patrol Lübeck area while the German POWs are disembarked from the ship and taken to the Russian zone by train. No incidents occurred and the operation was finished by the early afternoon.'

In the light of the controversy surrounding the return of prisoners of war mentioned earlier in this chapter, it is impossible to read these terse entries without a slight feeling of unease. Who were these unfortunates being returned to the tender care of Stalin over a year after the cessation of hostilities? Were they Germans, as recorded in the diary, and, if so, why were they 'Russian-bound'? Were they Russians who, having fought for the Germans, had been captured by the British or Americans? In either case, or whoever they were, it is clear that they were not returning eastward voluntarily, otherwise there would have been no need for precautions against disturbance. We shall probably never know but we can guess what fate awaited them.

On a lighter note, in the spring of 1947 a pack of hounds arrived at Lübeck from, of all places, Italy, with the 4th Hussars. The Master was the now famous 'Loopy' (Sir George) Kennard and the kennelman a German ex-paratrooper called Walter. The pack itself had an unusual provenance. Raised from various drafts in England, it was flown out to Rome from Croydon in a bomber and driven to Trieste in a 3-tonner. Perhaps for the first time in history the cry of English foxhounds was heard in the Italian countryside, but political and diplomatic consideration eventually brought this happy state of affairs to an end when hounds hunted a fox across the Yugoslav frontier where it promptly went to ground in a mass grave of Tito's victims!

Such gruesome finds were unwelcome to the local military administration, maintaining an uneasy 'stand-off' with the Yugoslavs, and the area commander, General Harding, ordered that hunting cease and the pack be deported. Fortunately, it so happened that the 4th were on the move and brought the hounds with them to the Lübeck area. By the end of September the pack, which had suffered considerably on the long and frequently interrupted train journey north, was fit to open the season in which both fox and deer were hunted.

It may be of interest to note in passing that Hitler had banned hunting in Germany soon after coming to power in the 1930s on the grounds of cruelty! But the allied occupation forces were very much a law unto themselves in the immediate post-war years and in terms of sport did more or less as they pleased. The pack was originally only five couple strong, but was gradually supplemented by drafts from England and when the 4th left for Malaya in 1948 the 'Lübeck Hounds' were inherited by the 10th. With Henry Bathurst as Master and George Errington as Field Master, hounds were also hunted by Tony Nunn, Tim Morley or Sergeant Philipson, depending upon who was available. One remarkable hound was Talbot, a draft dog from the VWH. After the move to Iserlohn (see below) Talbot went AWOL while hunting a buck into thick woodland and was still missing when hounds were taken home. Three days later he turned up at the barracks of another regiment in Dortmund, having travelled eighty kilometres across the industrial Ruhr!

In late 1948 the Regiment, still under the command of Lieutenant-Colonel Archer-Shee, moved to Iserlohn with some regret as Lübeck had, on the whole, proved to be an enjoyable and interesting station. Germany in those early days was still in a condition of semi-chaos and many varied duties fell to the British Liberation Army (soon renamed the British Army of Occupation on the Rhine or BAOR).* Relatively junior officers found themselves administering large numbers of half-starved and badly housed civilians. Swarms of refugees from the east, displaced persons (DPs) and released prisoners of war milled around without visible means of support and the principal role of the army was to bring some order and discipline to this shambles until the fighting troops could be replaced by the Control Commission Germany, known jocularly as Charlie Chaplin's Grenadiers.

When racing started up again in the British Zone of Germany after the war, it was organized by BAOR. Thus the 10th Hussars were put in charge of Dortmund racecourse, including the Tote, which came under the Quartermaster, Major Jack Garcia.

The 10th, like a number of other cavalry regiments with racing traditions, ran a successful stable. The string was based at Dortmund which, as Piers Bengough recalls, meant very early starts from Iserlohn to ride out and be back in barracks before NAAFI break.

It was almost impossible to keep track of the comings and goings of officers and men in and out of the Regiment, so many were departing on release or Python,† while others were being drafted in from elsewhere. Among the more notable departures were those of Major Bobby Archer-Shee, later Regimental

---

* At the end of the Second World War West Germany (the Federal Republic) was divided into three military and administrative zones, American, British (BAOR) and French, while the Russians occupied East Germany (the Democratic Republic). With the passage of time, civil administration was handed over to the West German authorities and the Allied 'Occupation' became a purely defensive arrangement under NATO. In East Germany the Russians installed a puppet Communist régime which endured until the reunification of the two Germanies in 1990. Throughout this period the strength of BAOR remained at about 55,000 men.

† A system of home posting or leave for those who had been serving overseas for a specific length of time.

Secretary, RQMS Hall and SSM Read, while WO1 C. Wass returned to the Regiment as RSM after several years service with the 23rd Hussars, replacing WO1 Dunk.

In the midst of all this feverish activity it was felt that the spiritual welfare of middle-ranking officers had been neglected and thus it was decided that squadron leaders and company commanders should undergo Christian Leadership courses. One reluctant 10th candidate hazarded a variety of guesses as to why the military hierarchy had so ordained. The officers, he suggested, were selected for their ungodliness; the Chaplain's Department was idle and underemployed; the C-in-C (Monty) was repenting the unnecessary deaths of some of his soldiers and wanted to make his mark with St Peter, or, more probably, simply wanted to take over from God.

'Thus reasoned George Errington and I', continued Alisdair Tuck, the author of these blasphemous thoughts, as we went to join one of these courses on the order of Jack Archer-Shee. He, like all other commanding officers, was told that he had to fill his allotment of vacancies, no excuses accepted. This particular course took place not far from the Danish frontier where lived two attractive sisters well known to George, Mike Pernetta and some others in the Regiment. They were known as the Great Danes. As we travelled back from this boring 3- or 4-day course I expressed the opinion that the whole thing had been a dead bore and an infernal waste of time, but, George replied, 'You know I thoroughly enjoyed that course, didn't have to listen to what the parsons were droning on about, snoozed through the day and spent every night in bed with one or both the Great Danes. I'm all for Christian Leadership courses. I wonder when the next one is!'

Soon after Christmas, 1948, Jack Archer-Shee handed over command to Lieutenant-Colonel Anthony Abel Smith. It had been Colonel Jack's second period of command, as he had led the Regiment for some months in the desert before being wounded at Alamein, and a difficult one during which, as we have seen, so many of the wartime soldiers had left and been replaced with drafts from other regiments who were themselves simply awaiting demobilization.

In the spring of 1949 B Squadron, which had been placed in suspended animation at the end of the war owing to the shortage of personnel, was re-formed as a training squadron geared to receive the National Service recruits who were arriving at a rate of fifty to sixty every two months. They remained with the squadron for four months before being trade tested and posted to the other squadrons.

On 15 May, 1949, the new panels commemorating the Fallen of the Second World War, one hundred and sixty-two officers and men, were unveiled, having been added to the First World War Memorial Gong. The Regiment was drawn up in a square on the parade ground at Epsom Barracks, Iserlohn, and the service was conducted by the Rev G. E. McNeill, Deputy Assistant Chaplain General of 2nd Infantry Division (the division with which the Regiment was serving at the time). Following the unveiling by the Commanding Officer, Lieutenant-Colonel Abel Smith, the regimental trumpeters sounded 'Last Post' and 'Reveille'.

In June Lieutenant-Colonel Sir Willoughby Norrie retired as Colonel of the Regiment and was succeeded by Lieutenant-General Sir Charles Gairdner. Originally a gunner, Sir Charles had served with the 1st RHA in the First World War and had been wounded. Transferring to the 10th Hussars in 1925, he commanded from 1937 to 1940. Later in the Second World War he commanded the 6th and 8th Armoured Divisions and in 1945 was appointed Churchill's personal representative to General MacArthur and Head of the British Liaison Mission to Japan. On retirement from the army he spent most of the rest of his life in Australia where he was Governor of Western Australia from 1951 to 1963 and of Tasmania from 1963 to 1968. When he died in 1983 a State Funeral was held for him at George's Cathedral, Perth, the capital of Western Australia. In his youth, despite his wound, he had been a considerable athlete; scratch golfer, cricketer, hockey and polo player.

The same year, 1949, saw the early death of a previous Colonel of the Regiment, Colonel V. J. Greenwood, who had joined the Shiners in 1910. After distinguished service in the First World War, during which he was wounded and awarded the Military Cross, he commanded the Regiment from 1927 to 1931 and was its Colonel from 1939 to 1946.

Another sad loss was the death in a traffic accident of the serving RSM, WO1 Cyril Wass, early in 1950. Mr Wass joined the Regiment in 1926 and had served with it continuously until the formation, under Roscoe Harvey, of the 23rd Hussars in 1940 when he was selected as one of its SSMs. In 1942 he was appointed RSM and fought in North-West Europe until he was wounded in Holland, returning to the 10th as RSM at Lübeck in 1948. A memorial service was held at Iserlohn and he was buried with full military honours at Sheffield.

In the summer of 1950 the North Koreans crossed the 39th parallel and invaded South Korea. Sixteen countries, including Great Britain, responded to the United Nations call to repel the invaders. The tide of war swung to and fro for three years, but, whereas the American-led UN forces were able eventually to check the Communist Chinese-backed North Koreans, they were unable to inflict a decisive defeat upon the enemy. An armistice was signed on 27 July, 1953, and a United Nations (in fact American) presence remains on the frontier to this day.

The first British armoured regiment to be sent to Korea was the 8th Hussars and, in order to bring it up to war establishment, reservists were recalled and some officers and men seconded from other regiments. In view of the nature of the enemy and the climate, both of which can best be described as thoroughly nasty, competition for this posting was far from intense, rather the contrary. Piers Bengough recalls returning to the Regiment from a course at Bovington with a less than glowing report and being told, 'You're for Korea, my boy!' However, his fellow subaltern, Walter Clode, had scored even lower marks and soon found himself on a ship bound for Frozen Chosen as Korea was known, in Bengough's place!

Once there he was involved in some heavy fighting. His squadron leader, Major de Clermont, has described the Battle of Maryang-San in 1951 in which two squadrons of the 8th were in direct support of the King's Shropshire Light Infantry, the King's Own Scottish Borderers and an Australian battalion. By dawn on the second day only three of de Clermont's fifteen Centurion tanks were still 'on the road', while most of the others were bogged down in paddy fields.

'It now became the story of "The Three Musketeers"', he wrote in *The Daily Telegraph*. 'Out of fifteen tanks just the three troop leaders were still in the hunt. For the next hour these crashed and cleft their way through virgin pine, parting the trees like Wagnerian monsters and pausing only for a foot reconnaissance or to pour death and destruction on to Pt 210 [one of the objectives]. Finally they burst into the open 200 yards short of the objective to crash high explosive into the bunkered hilltop. The murderous effect of the HE bursting in the pine trees at virtually point blank range was soon apparent, but the Chinamen in their holes shot on. Then, as our infantry worked to within 40 yards of the top, they called for the change from HE to Besa (machine-gun).

'Immediately the thunder ceased, to be replaced by that sustained crackle that is more blessed to give than to receive. Under that leaden umbrella A Company (KSLI) swept up the hill with bayonets fixed. Already some 40 dead or dying Chinamen were on the ground and the remainder got short Shropshire shrift.

'Within five minutes all three tanks were on the objective, eliminating the possibility of an immediate counter-attack. The KSLI had only 15 casualties and I have never seen infantrymen so elated.

'About 14.30 hours I met the company commander of A Company who was to take Pt 227. I said I would send my one (sic) troop tank up a spur as far as it could get and that my squadron headquarters would support from the road. The attack came in from the east at 16.30 hours. The tank got up the spur and was at once shot at by one of those disagreeable 57mm recoilless weapons. The troop leader, Walter Clode, 10th Hussars, was not amused and destroyed it.

'Finally at last light we got on Pt 227 and so ended the Battle of Maryang-San. Our division had got all its objectives for the loss of some 300 men. The co-operation of all arms had been the decisive factor.'

Later other members of the Regiment served in Korea attached either to the 'Skins' (5DG) or the 1st Royal Tank Regiment. These included Lieutenant John Cooper, Sergeants Burch and Cookson (who was wounded), Corporals Bowen, Nicklin, and Duggan, Troopers Liquorish, Wilkes, Truswell, Ford, Sinden, Gateson, Morley, Brookes, Chapman, Cookes, James, Bambrough, Tolson, Dickinson, Dunster, Harris, Hawkins, Tomlin, Robinson, Winton and Woodroffe, all with the Skins, while to 1st RTR went Sergeant Marshall, Corporal Thirst, Troopers Aukland, Darcy and Hopkinson.

Already with 1st RTR was Lieutenant Tony Uloth, who, some years later, was to transfer to the 10th. He recalls an incident, probably more amusing in retrospect than at the time, when his gunner fell asleep while on standing patrol at night. Surrounded by silence and blackness, Uloth and his crew sat nervously in their tank waiting for something unpleasant to happen. Determined to keep everyone awake, Uloth glanced down at the gunner sitting at his feet.

'And you, M . . .', he ordered, 'maintain a close watch on the caves in front using your six sight.' No reaction. 'M . . .!' he repeated in a louder and more urgent tone. Still no response, but a nudge with the foot galvanized the dozing M . . . into action.

'With a great shout of "Firing now!" M . . . squeezed the trigger,' Uloth remembers, 'and with the customary flash and a noise like a supersonic tube train a 20-pounder HE round soared away into the general direction of the Chinese, its trace making a perfect parabola through the night sky. The subsequent silence seemed even more total than before.

'Not for long. A crackle of small arms fire started it, then various calibres of machine guns all opened up, some in the vague direction where the shell had landed. Soon mortars and artillery joined in from both sides and a brisk exchange of fire developed.

'"Look what you've done, M . . .!" shouted Uloth through the din. "You were fast asleep, weren't you?"

'"Not on your life, sir. Honest I was wide awake!"

'However,' continues Uloth, 'the evidence of the obvious

truth was so clearly visible that I had to laugh. In the middle of M . . . 's chubby forehead was a large circular mark from leaning it heavily against the eye-piece of the gunner's sight, making him look for all the world like a rather aggrieved Cyclops. Eventually the racket dwindled and died away and I had to make some feeble excuse to the company commander's acid enquiry on the radio as to what I could see at 3,000 yards in the pitch dark!'

This incident did not prevent Tony Uloth from being Mentioned in Despatches for his services in Korea.

John Cooper, arriving early in 1952, found the Skins in static positions north of the 38th Parallel. The Regiment had landed at Pusan in December, 1951, shortly after the opposing sides had agreed a cease-fire line which would be acceptable to them both in the event of the remaining armistice terms being agreed. Although the 30-day time limit for such agreement had elapsed, the United Nations command considered that, its military objectives having been achieved, further offensive action on the part of its troops would contribute nothing towards eventual peace and would simply cause additional casualties.

'On the whole, things were fairly quiet,' writes Cooper, 'but towards the end of the summer one of our tanks was hit by 17 direct HE shells. The crew, battened down, lost their tracks, but were safe. Thank Goodness the Chinese did not use AP! The 5DGs were a marvellous bunch and one felt privileged to be with them.'

Back in Germany, the even tenure of life was disturbed by one major event annually – the Administrative Inspection.

In the 1930s, the humorous author of military tales, Anthony Armstrong, wrote a short story entitled (if memory serves) 'The SPADGAS'. An infantry subaltern, on checking his platoon's list of G1098 kit prior to the annual Administrative Inspection, is puzzled by the item SPADGAS. His platoon sergeant, a veteran of many inspections, is equally mystified and certainly no such piece of equipment is to be found in the storeroom or anywhere else. What is to be done? The absence of this item cannot be admitted to higher authority. But the subaltern and his sergeant are nothing if not resourceful and they resolve to *make* a SPADGAS. A fitter is pressed or bribed into service and a neat little contraption, workmanlike but with no obvious *raison d'être*, is designed and constructed.

When the Great Day arrives the inspecting officer scrutinizes the platoon's kit and seizes upon the SPADGAS. 'What's that thing?' he queries. 'Why, a SPADGAS, sir!' stammers the subaltern, while his sergeant stares fixedly to the front. 'Ah! A SPADGAS – haven't seen one of those for years,' murmurs the inspecting officer as he passes on to the next platoon, congratulating the subaltern on the condition and completeness of his G1098 kit as he goes.

Weeks later, the original of the list – the subaltern had been working from a copy – turns up in the company office. There, under s where SPADGAS was listed on the copy, was quite clearly typed SPADE GS.

Although fictional and rather far-fetched, this little story is not entirely divorced from the realities of an Administrative Inspection – or least one of the period with which we are dealing. *The Gazette* of February, 1952, for example, records that 'The Commander 5th Infantry Brigade, Brigadier R. Delacombe, CBE, DSO, carried out his annual administrative inspection of the Regiment on 10th and 11th December. We were all proud to receive once again an "outstanding" report.'

Of course any report other than 'outstanding' would have been unthinkable and inexcusable. Training for war in Britain's National Service army of the 1950s was strictly limited, but there were no 'ceiling mileages' on bullshit. Almost all the equipment was obsolete and, metaphorically, held together with sticking plaster. The purpose of the Administrative Inspection was to ensure that the sticking plaster was well concealed under several inches of paint. A game of double bluff was played between the inspecting officer and his staff and the regimental officers and senior NCOs. The inspectors were aware that to delve too deep would reveal a state of affairs which could lead to serious questions as to whether the British Army was in any condition to fight the Russians. The regiment under inspection knew this and the inspectors knew that it knew it. On the other hand, every effort had to be made on both sides to ensure that this charade was not too obviously a meaningless ritual. Therefore certain deficiencies and short-comings had to be discovered, but these should be minor and of no operational significance.

In one *Gazette* the editor bemoans the refusal of any significant number of National Servicemen to sign on as Regulars, but it is hardly surprising that they did not do so. The conscript's main complaint, particularly if he served his stint in BAOR, was that it was 'a complete waste of time'. From the point of view of an 18-year-old who wanted to get on in civilian life this was probably fair comment, but there can be little doubt that as a social exercise in 'house-training' (for which, of course, it was not intended) National Service was immensely successful and its abolition a grave set-back to the country. Even militarily it was undoubtedly of some value as it provided a large pool of semi-trained personnel who could drive a tank without colliding with the one in front or fire a rifle with reasonable accuracy.

So far we have paid scant attention to the most important item of equipment in an armoured regiment, the tank. We will therefore glance here at some of those with which the 10th were equipped during this period.

The Regiment ended the war with Shermans and at Lübeck was equipped with another American tank, the Chaffee, but, on transferring to the 2nd Infantry Division at Iserlohn, these were exchanged for Cromwells. This tank, which came into regular production in January, 1943, was one of the fastest of the Second World War, being capable of 40 mph (although later models were geared down to a maximum of 32 mph to avoid wear and tear on the suspension). It weighed approximately 28 tons and was originally fitted with a 6 pounder gun, which was upgraded to 75mm and 95mm on the later marks, and two Besa machine guns.

The armoured reconnaissance regiments of all the British armoured divisions in the North-West Europe campaign had been equipped with the Cromwell and it was in this capacity that the 10th was to serve in 2nd Infantry Division. However, when in 1950 the Regiment was assigned an anti-tank role as Divisional Regiment RAC, coming directly under the command of the GOC, the Cromwell was exchanged for the Valentine SP, known as the Archer. This was a light, low-profile tank, weighing about 16 tons designed for a purely defensive task and fitted with a 17 pounder facing to the rear, with a limited traverse of 45 degrees on either side of centre. By 1953, in another change of role to armoured regiment in support of an infantry brigade, the 10th had been equipped with the relatively new Centurion tank, which, as we have seen, had already proved itself in the Korean War. A giant compared with its predecessors, this tank was probably the greatest success story in the evolution of British armour. The Mark V, which enjoyed the longest production run, was fitted with a 20 pounder gun and a co-axial machine gun (at first Besa, then Browning). It weighed 50 tons and its 12 cylinder main engine developed 650 bhp at 2,550 revs, giving it a maximum road speed of 21.5 mph and a road range of 60 miles (at 2 gallons to the mile!).

Few 'peacetime' tanks saw as much action as the Centurion, which took part in at least seven wars, starting with Korea in the early 50s. There followed the Suez operation of 1956; the Arab-Israeli War of 1967 (on both sides); Vietnam (with the Australians); the Indo-Pakistan campaigns of 1965 and 1971; and the October War of 1973 (again on both sides). It was highly popular with foreign armies and a great export earner. There were few complaints from its users, most of whom remember the 'Cent' with affection – if such a term may be used relating to a deadly weapon of war.

In 1951 Lieutenant-Colonel M. F. Morley succeeded Lieutenant-Colonel Abel Smith as Commanding Officer and in the next year Brigadier Roscoe Harvey followed Sir Charles Gairdner, who had been appointed Governor of Western Australia, as Colonel of the Regiment, His Royal Highness the Duke of Gloucester remaining as Colonel-in-Chief. Colonel Abel Smith was awarded the OBE for his services.

To the relief of many, the Regiment's long tour of duty in Germany was coming to an end and in the summer of 1953 it returned to England after twelve years' continuous overseas service. Before leaving Germany, the regimental jumping team, consisting of Peter Jackson, Tony Nunn, David Harries and Hugh Dawnay, won the Inter-Regimental event at the Rhine Army Horse Show for the second year in succession. But one sad parting was the handover to a neighbouring Gunner regiment of the pack of foxhounds inherited from the 4th Hussars in 1947.

Chapter 2

TIDWORTH 1953–55

On 26 June, 1953, Major-General B. A. Coad, Commander 2nd Infantry Division, took the salute at a farewell parade at Iserlohn and three weeks later the Regiment departed for England. First stop was a hutted camp at Perham Down, near Andover, but within a few months the 10th Hussars found themselves back at Tidworth whence they, or rather the two officers and seven other ranks who survived from those days, had set out for war in 1939. The old hands found the barracks much changed for the better: centrally heated, and the barrack rooms equipped with bedside lamps and carpets, causing one Old Comrade to remark, 'I'm sorry for you chaps when you go home on leave!'

The Regiment formed part of the 50th Independent Infantry Brigade, with one squadron detached at Warminster as RAC Demonstration Squadron at the School of Infantry. But much of the work was in support of the TA and in training batches of Emergency Reserve men. Far from the comforts of Tidworth, many Shiners spent a cold, bleak six months under canvas at Tilshead tank park equipping and, presumably, un-equipping, TA armoured regiments in fortnightly succession throughout the training season; thus the news of a fairly imminent move to warmer climes must have been welcome when it came.

It will be recalled that in the previous year His Majesty King George VI had died and that the Coronation of Her Majesty Queen Elizabeth II took place on 2 June, 1953, while the Regiment was still in Germany. On that day the Regiment fired the Royal Salute at a parade in Iserlohn whence a contingent

18

had travelled to London for the Coronation itself. This was commanded by Captain J. de B. Carey (adjutant) and included RSM W. Hedley, Sergeant T. Dines, Corporal G. H. Burgwin, L/Corporal K. G. Burton and Troopers L. A. Marston, M. C. Cooney and R. Pennington.

Brigadier A. D. R. Wingfield was appointed a Gold Staff Commander and has described his duties as similar to those of an usher at a wedding. This, of course, provided him with a 'ringside' seat at one of the greatest occasions of state in this century, albeit requiring him to rise at 3.45am to be in position in the Abbey by 5.55am!

On 4 January, 1954, there occurred the unexpected death of Colonel A. S. Turnham, CBE, and a Military Knight of Windsor, at the age of 67. 'Tubby' Turnham had started his military career as a Boy in the 20th Hussars, but was commissioned into the 10th 'in the field' during the First World War. Renowned for his marksmanship and knowledge of small arms and machine guns, he had been a Chief Inspector at the Small Arms School at Hythe. In the Second World War he had served on the staff of the BEF in France and in 1944 was awarded the CBE for his war services. After his retirement he became an active fund-raiser for charity and Honorary Secretary of the 10th Hussars Regimental Association, in which capacity he would address the annual dinner. His funeral took place with full military honours at St George's Chapel, Windsor.

While still at Tidworth, shortly before its departure to the Middle East, the Regiment learnt of the death of another of its distinguished members. Major-General John Vaughan was a cavalry officer of the Old School and the only (future) Shiner to ride with Winston Churchill in the famous charge of the 21st Lancers at Omdurman in 1898. Half-a-dozen or so of the officers who served with the 21st in the Sudan were attached from other regiments and Vaughan was in fact at that time in the 7th, exchanging to the 10th in 1904.

In an immensely active and adventurous career, he served not only in the Sudan campaign but in expeditions to Matabeleland and Mashonaland; the Boer War, where he won the DSO at

Boschmanscop; India, where he achieved a great reputation as a polo player; and in the First World War, in which he commanded a cavalry division. He was not a man who necessarily moved with the times. When asked why the Regiment was having difficulty in recruiting suitable young officers in the late 1930s he expressed the view that the right sort of candidate could not be attracted unless offered two soldier-servants and free fodder for two horses! During the Second World War he commanded the Merionethshire and Montgomeryshire Home Guard and, as his stepson wrote, 'Woe betide the Germans if they had thought of landing on our backdoor by the shores of Harlech!' They would have been confronted with 'every contraption of war, ancient and modern, every booby trap, every menace that had been imagined in the course of military history from Hannibal to Haig!'

He died at the age of 85, perhaps appropriately, following a fall from his horse, and was sung to his rest by a Welsh choir in full voice.

Chapter 3

AQABA 1956–57

The port of Aqaba lies at the extreme north-eastern point of the Red Sea where the frontiers of Egypt, Jordan, Saudi Arabia and Israel meet and is Jordan's only outlet to the sea. In 1956 it was still little more than a fishing village, dominated by the presence of the British garrison which had been there since the end of the Arab-Israeli war of 1948 under the terms of a defence treaty with Jordan.

Although at this time British popularity and prestige in the Arab world, particularly in Nasser's Egypt, was in decline, Great Britain, and especially her army, were still welcome in Jordan, ruled as she was (and still is) by the anglophile King Hussein, Harrow-educated and Sandhurst-trained. However, as we shall see, this state of affairs was to undergo a marked change during the Regiment's tour of duty in Aqaba.

On St Valentine's Day, 1956, at 0700 hours, under the command of Lieutenant-Colonel Alasdair Tuck, who had succeeded Lieutenant-Colonel Morley in 1954, the 10th Hussars paraded in full kit at Bhurtpore Barracks, Tidworth, and embussed for the short journey to Ludgershall Railway Station.

Within a few hours the Regiment had embarked in the troopship *Empire Ken* at Southampton and sailed in mid-afternoon. With stops at Algiers, Malta and Port Said, the ship eventually reached Aqaba to the somewhat disconcerting delight of the out-going regiment, The Queen's Bays.

The age of sea trooping, although it was to continue for a few more years before being entirely replaced by air transport, was

21

drawing to a close and some of the younger officers were struck by the contrast between the quarters provided for them and their men.

'I share a cabin with three other 2/Lts,' wrote Richard Russell, a National Service subaltern, to his mother. 'It is not very substantial but a thousand times better than the troops' accommodation.' Another officer remarked on the 'stiflingly smelly troopdecks' – and it should be recalled that this voyage was taking place in the winter; in the summer in the Red Sea the troopdecks were probably the nearest thing to Dante's Inferno to be endured on this earth with temperatures rising to 150 degrees F.

Russell went ashore at Algiers and found it 'only worth seeing from a distance', but was delighted to win the princely sum of £1.16.0d on the daily mileage sweepstake. At Malta, where no shore leave was permitted, a Gunner battery, also bound for Aqaba, embarked.

On arrival at Aqaba Russell was surprised to find that 'everything out here has impressed me most favourably, and that includes food and bedding. I had painted such a black picture for myself before coming that the reality is a bit of a relief.' Another officer recalls that there were only six European women in the whole of south Jordan; one WVS, three QARANC and two elderly Scottish ladies in Missions to Mediterranean Garrisons, which rather restricted what he describes as 'social life'.

The village of Aqaba boasted one shopping street with ten shops, known imaginatively as Bond Street. The small local population of fishermen and traders was reasonably friendly, of course prospering from the British military presence. Such English as was spoken had been learnt from the garrison and tended to be soldierly in character. One fisherman, trying to extract a crayfish from its rocky hide-out, was heard to exclaim, 'Es gone into 'is f . . . room, but I've got 'im by 'is f . . . fingers!'

There were few concessions to the climate, which grew hotter by the day, and Lieutenant John Friedberger found his new tight overalls, worn four nights a week, 'very prickly'. Another subaltern of the time, Douglas Hill, remembers that 'we had a most unsuitable Service Dress made of calvin cord, with long sleeves, brass buttons and worn with a tie. Myself and two other officers took part in the Queen's Birthday Parade in 120 degrees F wearing this uniform.'

Shortly after the Regiment's arrival the first signs of a deterioration in Jordan's relationship with Britain began to appear, the most startling of these being King Hussein's peremptory dismissal of the long-serving British commander of the Arab Legion (the Jordanian Army), Glubb Pasha.

However, this news, which excited the British Press and no doubt alarmed the Government, was taken calmly by the Aqaba garrison. Richard Russell read in one English newspaper that '500 grim Britons sat tensely at Aqaba, going about their work with semi-expectant cautiousness', or words to that effect, whereas the reality was that 'we were populating the Beach Club and merrily swimming and sunbathing!' Furthermore, a house-warming cocktail party had been held a few days before to which all the 'Big-Wigs' had been invited!

Summer working hours, as recorded by Russell, were: Reveille at 5.30; First Parade at 6; Breakfast 7–7.45; Work until lunch at 12.30; afternoons free for sport, swimming etc. Football, cricket and hockey were all played and a stableful of Arab ponies was kept for polo. These had been purchased in Baghdad and Douglas Hill recalls the circumstances.

'Soon after arriving in Aqaba, Colonel Alasdair Tuck, assisted by the Quartermaster, Major Fred Robson, a former Rough Riding Sergeant in the Skins, went up to Baghdad to buy twelve ponies which were to be trained for polo. The ponies were transported across the desert in regimental 3-tonners as far as Ma'an, where they remained for several months to build up their strength in the relatively cool climate. They were then all taken down to Aqaba where they were ably looked after by Sergeant Monkman and his team of grooms. Not only did they enable the officers to play polo but they were also used for the only meeting of the Aqaba Turf Club on Christmas Day, 1956. Riding School was held near the beach every morning under either the Colonel or Fred Robson.

'When we left Aqaba it was intended to fly them back to England in Valetta aircraft provided by the RAF. Special cages were built by the LAD for the ponies to practice entering an aircraft, but at the last minute the RAF thought better of the venture. Fortunately the Royal Navy came to the rescue and provided a Tank Landing Ship, so the ponies arrived back in Tidworth before the Regiment. Lieutenant Patrick Mesquita was in charge and he managed to deliver the ponies to Tidworth where they gave much further pleasure before being sold.'

Troop leaders were encouraged to take their men into the desert on exercises, both official and unofficial, as frequently as other duties allowed. John Friedberger recalls 'the incomparably beautiful desert area south and east of the Wadi Rhum, now a well-known tourist venue but then visited only by Bedouin', where such exercises took place.

Generally B vehicles (ancient wartime K5s due to be dumped in the Gulf of Aqaba) were used for these expeditions as tank (Centurion) mileage was strictly 'ceilinged'. As a result of the antiquity of the transport these trips were seldom trouble-free. On one of Russell's ventures, two out of three vehicles 'thoroughly misbehaved themselves' and one ended up towing another. Nonetheless, despite a diet of bully-beef and tea, once back in camp his men were clamouring eagerly to be off again.

Douglas Hill remembers that 'until about July, 1956, the Regiment was able to carry out a number of exercises all over the desert and along the old Hejaz Railway. It is reputed that our tank tracks messed up the filming of *Lawrence of Arabia* as the virgin desert was ruined even two or three years later. Exercises with the Arab Legion ceased soon after Glubb Pasha was dismissed but we still continued fairly extensive training ourselves until about July ... On one occasion at Petra I was surrounded by about 80 small boys brandishing sticks and knives and pulled from my pony. They only dispersed when my troop, also mounted on ponies which we had hired for the ride along the Suq into Petra, came charging to the rescue!' Surely the last mounted action of the Shiny Tenth!

The Aqaba garrison, which consisted of an armoured regiment, an AA Battery, an infantry company and supporting troops, was known as O Force. A few months prior to the arrival of the 10th, Captain Robin Wilson had joined O Force HQ as GSO3 Ops/Int. By this appointment it was hoped to ease the relationship between HQ and the armoured regiment which had not been very good in the past. In this role, Wilson was perhaps more conscious than most of his brother officers actually serving with the Regiment of the deteriorating relationship between Britain and Jordan following the nationalization of the Suez Canal by Nasser and the resulting international tension.

With the outbreak of hostilities in the autumn of 1956, when the Israeli army reached the Canal in 100 hours and the Anglo-French landed at Port Said and Port Tewfik, O Force found itself in an invidious and precarious position; was it on the side of the Israelis, with whom Britain and France were in collusion if not alliance, or of Jordan (at least in theory in sympathy with Egypt) with whom Britain had a defence treaty of which O Force was the physical manifestation? A signal was sent to GHQ Cyprus asking this question but no reply was ever received. However, according to Douglas Hill, the Regiment was about to set off for Suez when it was discovered that the Anglo-Jordan Treaty precluded Britain from using Jordan as a starting point for an attack on another Arab country. Doubtless GHQ Cyprus was aware of this but was perhaps keeping its options open.

One Squadron (A at the time of the Suez operation) was permanently detached at Ma'an, some eighty miles inland from Aqaba, and had already loaded its tanks on to transporters in anticipation of a dash to the Canal. The officers debated whether black or white dinner jackets should be included in their baggage for the Cairo night-life they expected soon to be enjoying. However, the only order they received was to remain within the camp perimeter.

Little sympathy was shown for the Aqaba garrison in its isolated predicament by Colonel Wigg MP, whose much vaunted military rank gave him a spurious authority as an Opposition defence spokesman and who blamed O Force HQ for failing to give warning of the Israeli invasion of Sinai. Of course it was suspected then and confirmed later that the invasion plan had been carefully co-ordinated with HMG and the French Government.

Although Anglo-Jordanian relations gradually returned to something like their former warmth with the ending of the Suez crisis, there can be little doubt that this bungled operation marked a watershed in Britain's position in the Middle East and British prestige never recovered from the débâcle. Nonetheless, considerable efforts were made to mend fences and the British Ambassador in Amman, Sir Charles Johnson, was especially successful in regaining the goodwill of King Hussein. Officers of the Regiment and the Band were invited to the capital and cordially received by the Monarch, and a polo match was played against an Arab Legion team. But, despite this, the treaty did not survive and the whole of O Force was withdrawn in the summer of 1957, never to return.

'A succession of LSTs came into Aqaba from early May onwards,' writes Douglas Hill, 'and removed all our vehicles and all decent furniture from our tents. Morale was not too good as the men were used for garrison fatigues from about the end of April onwards. A complete ordnance depot had to be evacuated as well as a mass of RAF equipment.'

In the course of this withdrawal the Regiment suffered its worst post-Second World War tragedy when an RAF Valetta carrying twenty-three 10th Hussars and attached personnel (part of the advance party to Tidworth) and a crew of three crashed shortly after take-off from Aqaba on 17 April, 1957.* The luckiest man that day was Second Lieutenant Christopher Spence who missed the plane. The cause of the accident is uncertain but may have been extreme air turbulence which snapped off a wing tip.

The victims were buried in the British Military Cemetery at Habbaniya (Iraq), the funeral being attanded by the new Commanding Officer, Lieutenant-Colonel Peter Jackson, and several other members of the Regiment. For Peter Jackson, who

---

* See Appendix for list of casualties.

had taken over only days earlier from Alasdair Tuck, this must have been an especially melancholy duty to perform so soon after his arrival.

It should not be forgotten that concurrently with the Suez Crisis an equally momentous event was taking place in Europe, witnessed by a 10th Hussar, Lieutenant-Colonel Noel Cowley, British Military Attaché at Budapest.

The Hungarian Uprising of 1956 was a bright but shattered dream in the long, dark night of Communist domination of eastern Europe and the vivid eye-witness account of the uprising by Lieutenant-Colonel Cowley is to be found in the *Gazette* of June, 1957.

Finally, we cannot leave Jordan without recording an incident which earned a young National Serviceman, L/Corporal Arthur Petford, a Queen's Commendation for Brave Conduct while transporting a Centurion tank from Ma'an to Aqaba on 4 July, 1956. The rear wheels of the tank transporter caught fire, efforts to extinguish the flames were unavailing and it seemed that both trailer and tank would be destroyed. The rear anchor chains securing the tank to the trailer were too hot to remove, nor could the ramps be let down. Despite this, and the fact that the tank was full of 20 pounder and machine-gun ammunition as well as 75 gallons of petrol, Petford unshackled the front anchor chains, got into the driving seat, started the engine and reversed the tank against the rear chains and ramps, managing to break the ramp and drive the tank through the flames to safety. The trailer was completely destroyed, but, thanks to Corporal Petford's courage and quick reactions, a valuable tank was saved and the possibility of a massive explosion which might have caused casualties averted.

Chapter 4

ENGLAND – GERMANY – ENGLAND 1957–64

The Regiment sailed from Aqaba in the troopship *Devonshire* on 6 July, 1957, taking with it the remains of O Force (A Coy 1st Middlesex and 187 Bty RA). As we have seen most of its equipment* had been shipped home earlier, as had the precious polo ponies.

The return journey was lengthy as there was uncertainty whether, in the aftermath of the Suez Crisis, the ship would be allowed to transit the Canal. In the event, after calling at Aden and Mombasa with the prospect of a voyage round the Cape, the *Devonshire* about turned and sailed through the Canal after all, her destination Liverpool via Famagusta.

Robin Wilson and Douglas Hill remember some aspects of the voyage.

'We proceeded south to Aden escorted by one of HM destroyers,' writes Wilson, 'spent the day in Aden and then on to Mombasa, bucking our way into the south-westerly monsoon ... It was so hot that most officers slept on deck. During the day there was compulsory PT and the junior officers took their troops on education, as a result of which we had a 100% pass in ACE 111 [Army Certificate of Education Class Three], quite a feat in the days of National Service.

'We spent three nights in Mombasa. It was wonderful to see

---

* Some of the tanks were sold to the Iraqi Army, and were delivered to Basra in a Tank Landing Ship by a party of 10th Hussars under Captain N. S. M. Delamain.

the lush greenery of Kenya after arid dry deserts. Kenneth Combe, John Willis, Humphrey Wakefield, Peter Jackson, James Ingram, several others and myself left on a two-day safari in the Tsavo National Park and spent the night at a small hotel in the foothills of Mt Kilimanjaro run by two elderly German ladies.

'We were at sea, other than the three days at Mombasa, for a month before we eventually arrived at the southern end of the Canal. We passed a troopship coming from the north and we both stopped and transferred from the other ship a senior officer who briefed us on going through the Canal (as) we were the first troopship from the south since the Canal had been blocked. All our cameras and binoculars were locked in the Purser's Office so that they could not be used to photograph or look at military installations. In fact there was very little to see. After the Canal we went to Cyprus and stopped there for a day and then on to England. There was a Force 8 gale in the Bay of Biscay and no one was allowed on deck. We arrived at Liverpool in the evening and were met by Brigadier Roscoe Harvey and Diana Jackson, wife of the commanding officer.

'The returning troops all went to the port side of the ship to catch a first glimpse of the Liver Birds and friends that may have come to welcome them. In fact we heeled the *Devonshire* so much that we had to order the troops back inboard so that she could be docked.

'The Regiment disembarked next day and went by train to Aliwal Barracks, Tidworth, and from there on disembarkation leave.'

Douglas Hill recalls that on arrival at Aden the Resident Naval Officer had invited him to dinner and sent his barge to collect him from the troopship. 'The Colonel and other senior officers, who were invited to the Governor and C-in-C, shared a "bumboat" to go ashore and were not amused as I cruised past in my smart barge with a sailor standing in the bows!'

It appears that an unpopular figure on the voyage was the Baggage Officer, Second Lieutenant Humphrey Wakefield, 'who,' according to Hill, 'would constantly speak on the ship's tannoy to summon those requiring to visit the "Wanted on Voyage" in a most dictatorial manner. His final comedown was when he went on the safari (in Kenya) taking the key with him!'

On arrival at Tidworth the 10th found themselves part of the 3rd Infantry Division at Aliwal Barracks where they had been billeted in 1936 on returning from India.

As a piece of British social, rather than military, history it may be worth recording one officer's impression of the train journey by which the Regiment was conveyed from Liverpool to Tidworth, a journey which would be impossible in our post-Beeching era.

'We disembarked early one wet August morning straight into a waiting train on Liverpool Dockside,' recollects John Friedberger. 'It chuffed very slowly with frequent stops (never at stations) along single-track lines through deepest Gloucestershire and Wiltshire to Tidworth Military Station (on which now rests the NAAFI). On arrival we formed up by squadrons and marched behind the regimental band to Aliwal Barracks. The advance party greeted us and a log fire was burning in the Officers' Mess before dinner.' Thus might a regiment have returned from overseas duty at any time in the previous hundred years.

In the following year the Regiment was fortunate in escaping the first wave of post-war amalgamations but unfortunate in the retirement of Major Jack Garcia as editor of the *Gazette*, an arduous and somewhat thankless task which he had undertaken with great diligence since 1947.

Of this period at Tidworth there is little to be said and some have seen it as the low point in the Regiment's post-war history. With the retirement of Lieutenant-Colonel Jackson it was found necessary to introduce a new Commanding Officer from outside the Regiment and on 15 June, 1959, Lieutenant-Colonel J. M. D. Ward-Harrison of the 5th Inniskilling Dragoon-Guards took over. At about this time the 10th returned to Germany and were based at Barracks at Munster in the 6th Infantry Brigade Group.

Within days of taking up his appointment Colonel Ward-Harrison made clear his determination to improve standards of efficiency when he called all the officers together and announced that 'the gloves were off'. He knew that the opinion had been expressed in high places that the Regiment was 'unfit for war', an intolerable slur which had to be removed without delay. He set about the task with ruthless gusto and, in due course, in the face of many difficulties and obstacles, brought, in the words of one of his officers, 'the 10th Hussars to a commendable state of efficiency as an armoured regiment, culminating in a successful brigade exercise and a first-rate Guidon Parade'.

One of the Colonel's significant appointments was that of the recently commissioned Lieutenant Dougie Covill, a Shiner with many years service and a Distinguished Conduct Medal, as Technical Quartermaster – a move which transformed the mechanical standards, and thus to a great extent the battle-worthiness of the sabre squadrons.

At the other end of the scale, the *Gazette* of June, 1959, reveals another remarkable tale of single-mindedness and determination. Pakhar Singh was born in Malaya shortly before the war and, having witnessed the liberation of the country from the Japanese by British troops in 1945, set his heart on joining a British armoured regiment. In 1957 he made friends with a National Serviceman in The King's Dragoon Guards, which regiment had replaced the 11th Hussars in south Malaya the previous year. This young man took his release locally and he and Pakhar Singh set out for Calcutta on bicycles on New Year's Day, 1958. On reaching their destination two months later the ex-KDG decided to stay on for a while, but Pakhar Singh pressed on for England and his goal of joining an armoured regiment.

Lack of funds forced him to sell his bicycle in Calcutta so the rest of this remarkable journey was continued on foot and by hitch-hiking. Through Delhi and Lahore, up the Khyber Pass and into Afghanistan trudged the intrepid Sikh, perhaps in the footsteps of his forbears who may have served in the old Indian Army on the North-West Frontier or in one of the Afghan campaigns. Across the wild mountains of Afghanistan, through Iran and into Turkey, over the Bosphorus and into Greece, then Yugoslavia, Italy, Switzerland and France, he marched and 'thumbed' his way, arriving at Dover on 21 November, 1958, nearly eleven months after setting out on his epic journey. We may wonder whether such an enterprise would be possible today, so seriously has the security situation in several of the countries along Singh's route deteriorated.

On arrival in England he went straight to Southampton where his KDG friend lived and found that he had returned by sea. Five days later our traveller reported to the local recruiting office, having taken the wise precaution of removing his beard, and enlisted in the 10th Hussars. A week at Tidworth, where he appeared on television, basic training at Catterick and then to Germany on 4 April, 1959, as a fully-fledged (and re-bearded by special permission of the Colonel-in-Chief) Shiner, probably the first and last Sikh ever to serve in the ranks of the 10th Hussars.

In February, 1960, the Regiment moved to Barker Barracks, Paderborn, to form, with the Scots Greys and 3rd RTR, the 20th Armoured Brigade Group under Brigadier J. A. d'Avig-dor-Goldsmid. The same year saw the retirements of Major (QM) F. Robson and RSM D. A. Whittlestone* who were succeeded by Lieutenant (QM) H. Storer and RSM T. Knight.

The outstanding event of 1961 took place on 30 June and was combined with an Old Comrades weekend. Preparations for this notable occasion started in January and no aspect of these was more vital than foot and arms drill, never a cavalry regiment's strongest points, which, under the supervision of Drill-Sergeant Price of the Grenadiers, were eventually brought, in the words of the Colonel of the Regiment, 'to a standard as near to perfection as humans could produce'.

It is not clear from earlier histories when the last Guidon had been presented, but, according to the preamble to the Guidon Supplement in the *Gazette*, no Guidon had been in the Regiment's possession since 1812. Thus there were no recorded precedents for what was about to take place and there were many questions to be answered. Which uniform was to be worn? What weapons were to be carried? Where were suitably steady horses to be obtained, and, above all, who was to pay for it all? The Supplement does not disclose precisely how

---

* Later commissioned.

these difficulties were resolved but simply ascribes their solution 'to the initiative, ingenuity and powers of improvisation displayed by all departments and, in particular, by the two Quartermasters (Captain Storer and Lieutenant Covill) and their staffs'.

Eventually it was decided that of the four Guards on parade, one would be equipped with swords and the other three with FN rifles (this after experimenting with the Sten-gun which proved to be a 'highly unsuitable ceremonial weapon'). No 1 Dress was to be worn by all and horses were to be borrowed from the German police. These, however, failed to display the sense of discipline required of them and one nearly unseated the Commanding Officer during a rehearsal. Fortunately the Guards Brigade were generous enough to provide replacements which proved to be more amenable.

Friday, 30 June, was a day of sweltering heat but no one on parade fainted or fell out. The Colonel-in-Chief, Field-Marshal HRH the Duke of Gloucester, took the salute and presented the Guidon to SQMS W. Todhunter who was escorted by SQMS R. Churchward and Sergeant C. Wass. No 1 Guard, which trooped the Guidon, was commanded by Major J. B. Willis and the other three Guards by Major B. C. Greenwood, Major J. A. J. Nunn and Captain A. J. W. Gordon. The Parade Adjutant was Captain P. H. G. Bengough. The Drum Horses and Escorts were ridden by Sergeants Monkman, Johnson and McGee, the Drums being draped with the Drum Banners, which, bearing the regimental battle honours and devices, had served in the place of a Guidon since 1812.

The new Guidon was consecrated by the Venerable Archdeacon I. D. Neil, Chaplain General to the Forces, assisted by numerous clergy including the Regimental Chaplain, the Rev A. G. Derbyshire. Among the 3,000 guests were the Commander-in-Chief BAOR, General Sir James Cassels, the Air Officer Commander-in-Chief, Air Marshal Sir John Grandy, and the British Ambassador to the Federal Republic of Germany, Sir Christopher Steele.

Addressing the Regiment, the Colonel-in-Chief drew attention to the strong loyalties and traditions of the 10th Hussars as illustrated by the fact that no fewer than thirty-six serving members were the sons, grandsons or nephews of earlier 10th Hussars, and that the two escorts to the Guidon were both the sons of past RSMs. He looked back on his own happy memories and forward to the prospect that one of his sons* would soon be joining.

After the Parade special celebration lunches were consumed with great appetite by both participants and guests alike and in the evening the Warrant Officers and Sergeants were hosts at a magnificent ball. On the Saturday there were various displays and a polo match, followed by an All Ranks dance in the gymnasium and a smaller one in the Officers' Mess.

On Sunday the Duke and Duchess of Gloucester attended the service of dedication for the new garrison church, St Peter's, and after lunch they left by helicopter. Later the Commanding Officer received a number of messages of appreciation, several of which emphasized the emotion of the occasion, in such terms as 'I for one am quite unashamed to admit that tears rose to my eyes when our old Colours, the Drum Banners, were marched off to Auld Lang Syne.'

The next day, Monday, gunnery training was resumed.

1961 was also the year in which the last National Servicemen left the British Army and from then on every regiment and corps became responsible for its own recruiting arrangements.

In April, 1962, Colonel Ward-Harrison, after a highly successful term as Commanding Officer which earned him the award of an OBE, handed over to another 'import' in the shape of Lieutenant-Colonel W. S. P. Lithgow, formerly of the King's Troop, Royal Horse Artillery. Bill Lithgow was no newcomer to the Regiment, however, as he had spent the previous nine months as a kind of understudy to the outgoing Commanding Officer with the unusual title (according to the Nominal Roll) of Commanding Officer Designate.

His appointment came about in a rather curious and unorthodox way, which he has described in his own words.

---

* In fact HRH Prince William joined the Foreign Office and was later tragically killed in an aircrash.

'Back in the late 1950s I was quietly minding my own business at a Meet of the Heythrop when I became aware of Brigadier Harvey alongside me. "What are you going to do when you leave the King's Troop?" he asked. "I don't know, Brigadier," I replied, wondering for a moment if he was going to offer me a job racing, "they haven't told me yet." "Come and command the 10th Hussars," he said. "What a wonderful offer," I answered, "but I can't, I absolutely can't. The Gunners would murder me for having given up the enormous privilege of commanding the Troop!"

'I remember later that morning meeting my mother who was out in the car and saying I had had an unusual morning, two fairly stiff foxes and an offer to command the 10th Hussars!

'A month or two later, again out hunting, the Brigadier raised it again and this time I said I would go and see the Director Royal Artillery. "Just what I want you to do!" he said. So off I go to General Ted Howard-Vyse, the most charming of men, who so far from murdering me said that amongst others he had suggested me.

'What a wonderful way for the Brigadier to do it! A lesser mortal would have sent for the "boy" to be interviewed with all the attendant formalities.'

Brigadier Harvey himself retired in 1962 and handed over the Colonelcy to Major-General David Dawnay.

On 19 February that year Home Headquarters was established at Winchester, more or less in the centre of the recruiting area, with Major (Retd) R. A. Archer-Shee as Regimental Secretary assisted by Miss Yvonne Allen. In the words of the *Gazette*, 'It (Home Headquarters) exists to serve the interests of the Regiment in every way. It acts as a liaison office in England on behalf of the Commanding Officer. A very full co-operation is made with the Old Comrades Association and the Regimental Association.'

It is interesting to note from the same *Gazette* article that 'work' is in preparation on a Regimental History covering the period 1946–65' and that 'by 21 July, 1965, our 250th Anniversary date, it is intended that a history of the whole 250 years will have been written.' Neither of these projects seems to have come to fruition, although a brief history was published in 1969.

*

In the football season 1962–3, the Shiners, captained by Sergeant B. J. Moriarty, won both the Cavalry Cup and the Army Cup, defeating the Carabiniers in the first final and the Sherwood Foresters in the second. Almost immediately, they also collected the BAOR, 4th Division and 5th Brigade Group Cups. This remarkable winning team included Sergeants Moriarty and Scriven, Corporals Turnbull and Heather, Lance-Corporals Parkes, Curtis, and Ferriday, Troopers Newman, Thompson, Burns, Curtis, Boxall and Hall. The team was managed by Captain A. J. W. Gordon and it was the first time in the histories of the Army and Cavalry Cups that both had been won by the same regiment in the same season.

The 10th Hussars sporting record in the early 1960s was outstanding, with Lieutenant D. C. Edwards winning a Silver Medal for rowing in the 1962 Commonwealth Games; Captain O. N. P. Mylne and Lance-Corporal E. Pomfret representing Great Britain in the Pentathlon and Athletics; Mylne was also Army Epée Fencing Champion in 1963, while Pomfret scored a hat-trick with Inter-Services, Army and BAOR Steeplechase Championships in that year. Victory in the BAOR Squash Team Championship went to Major Uloth, Captains C. Dawnay and P. Mesquita and Lieutenants Dwerryhouse and Malet, who beat the Queen's Own Hussars in the 1963 final.

Early in this triumphant year news reached the Regiment that it was to return to Tidworth in 1964, convert to armoured cars and depart for duty in Aden and Sharjah. This brought to an end a spell with 5th Infantry Brigade during which the respective squadrons had built up a close and efficient relationship with the infantry battalions with whom they had been temporarily affiliated; A with the Royal Highland Fusiliers, B with the King's Own Royal Border Regiment and C with the Royal Welch Fusiliers. 'We would like to thank them all for the fun we have had,' wrote the editor of the *Gazette*, 'and wish them well wherever they may serve. With luck we will meet again soon.'

Chapter 5

THE AIR – A LOST OPPORTUNITY

For most of this chapter and its related Appendix C the author has relied, gratefully, on the invaluable contributions of three intrepid 'Air Cavalrymen', David Edwards, Tony Uloth and Richard (Fred) Perry. Edwards in particular is quoted more or less verbatim although, for the sake of simplicity, inverted commas have been omitted in most places.

However, in order to justify the second half of the chapter heading, it may be appropriate to open with the thoughts of another contributor, Major-General John Friedberger, who writes of the cavalry role in army aviation:

> 'The subject is still pertinent in the 1990s and shows that the 10th Hussars were in the forefront of technical and operational thought in the mid-1960s. Had this line been followed:
> a. The RAC would truly have regained the full and proper operational role of traditional cavalry.
> b. The British Army would have led, not lagged, in the use of helicopters on the battlefield in the 1980s and 90s.
> c. The overheads in forming the Army Air Corps would have been saved.
> d. (Arguably) Inter-service rivalry between Army and RAF would have been pre-empted – the Army would have flown all battlefield helicopters.
> e. (Also arguably) 10th and 11th Hussars might never have been amalgamated!'

In the early 1960s the Army decided upon a major expansion in aviation. Previously it had used mainly fixed wing aircraft for gunnery observation and communications flying. Improvements to helicopters meant that it had become practical to operate small helicopters from forward positions on the battlefield and this offered obvious opportunities for much wider roles in reconnaissance of all types. As Fred Perry puts it, 'the Ministry of Defence decided that Army Aviation should be integrated into the teeth arms. Each Armoured Regiment, Gunner Regiment, Infantry Battalion and Engineer Regiment was to have its own troop of three Sioux helicopters.'

In about 1961 a trial of the concept of integrated flights was carried out using the Queen's Dragoon Guards with the Saunders Roe Skeeter. This was sufficiently successful that in 1962 the 10th Hussars were notified that they would be one of the first regiments to receive an integrated squadron when they converted to the recce role and went to the Middle East in 1964.

The intention was that this squadron of six aircraft would be formed in Aden with the new light helicopter, the Sioux. However, in the event, insufficient aircraft were available and a troop rather than a squadron was formed under Captain Nick Mylne. The other pilots were Captain Andrew Jones RTR and Staff Sergeant Jim Thirst.

Among these pioneers should have been Lieutenant George Duckett, who had been trained at Middle Wallop but whose flying career had been brought to a sad and premature end when he was badly injured in a road accident. George remembers his instructor at Middle Wallop, the late Joe Ruprecht, with admiration.

'Why,' Ruprecht used to ask coolly in moments of sheer terror, 'are we dropping like a brick shit-house?'

The troop's role in Aden and the Radfan will be covered in the next chapter, but the squadron proper was not formed until 1965 at York Barracks, Munster, where, over a period, it was joined by such 'Aces' as Captain Edwards, Perry and Capper-Jackson and Sergeants Goulter and Farmer (11th Hussars).

In Germany the Regiment's principal task was the escort of nuclear ammunition supply convoys and facilities, and the defence of 1st British Corps' rear areas. The role of the Air Squadron included reconnaissance, artillery observation post duties, route and site reconnaissance, Forward Air Controller, casualty evacuation, re-supply of urgently needed spare parts and liaison. In practice the tasks varied enormously. The Air Squadron would carry out unusual requests in order to show that they could be done quicker and better by helicopter. These included the laying of field telephone cables and the insertion of SAS groups at night on an exercise in Denmark, as well as such unofficial duties as conveying the Colonel to polo matches and racing the Adjutant in his Mercedes!

The basic organization of the squadron was laid down, but, like much else in the army, depended to an extent on what men and equipment could be wheedled out of the Commanding Officer and the Quartermasters. The establishment was six pilots, both officers and NCOs; a Troop Sergeant; two corporals and half-a-dozen lance-corporals and troopers. To service the aircraft there was a REME Artificer Staff Sergeant and six corporals or craftsmen as air mechanics. One curiosity was that, owing to the rapid expansion of army aviation, a number of Air Mechanics were seconded from the Navy which was in the process of reducing Carriers. These men are remembered by their Shiner colleagues as 'a splendid bunch'.

The ground equipment included a Saracen armoured command vehicle, two Landrovers, two 3-ton lorries (one for aviation fuel) and a four-wheeled trailer for aircraft spares. The latter was a horrendous impediment to rapid and tactical movement near the battle area and was swopped with the echelon for a Stalwart, which was used to carry fuel, thus freeing a 3-tonner for spares and general equipment.

Although the squadron was a fully integrated part of the Regiment, there were some interesting command ramifications. The 10th Hussars were Corps Troops but came under the administrative command of 4th Division and the technical control of Brigadier Royal Armoured Corps. The Air Squadron, however, came under the technical control of 2nd Division, which was closer and had fewer aircraft than 4th Division. David Edwards recalls that the opportunities for playing the various command agencies off against each other and doing 'one's own thing' were considerable!

The Sioux helicopter was built by Westland under licence from Augusta Aircraft of Italy who, in turn, built under licence from Bell Helicopters of the USA. It was a derivative of the Bell 47, one of the world's first helicopters, and had the characteristic 'goldfish bowl' canopy. It normally seated two but could take three at a pinch and could carry two casualties on panniers of metal webbing mounted on the skids. It could also carry underslung loads of up to half a ton. It had a Lycoming 6-cylinder engine with turbo supercharging, which enabled it to maintain normal performance at height and on hot days when helicopter performance falls off rapidly. One 10th Hussar helicopter reached 19,700 feet over Munster. Illegal but fun, says David Edwards! The Siouxs operated by the Regiment were unarmed.

The intention of the integrated air squadrons was that regiments should provide their own pilots and the 10th were fairly successful in this, although occasionally they had to borrow from elsewhere. In addition to those already mentioned, regimental pilots included Julien Turner, Simon Arthur, Nigel Budd, Tony Uloth, Richard Fearnehough, and Muff Capper-Jackson, although not all these actually served in the Air Squadron.

The selection tests and flying courses were arduous and the success rate only about 30%. These tests were carried out mainly by the RAF at Biggin Hill and were the same for jet aircrew as for army helicopter pilots. Tests included IQ or mental reasoning, mental arithmetic, mechanical understanding and instrument interpretation, all conducted against the clock with barely time to think, let alone write down the answers. There were also physical tests and a demanding medical examination. Candidates then went to Middle Wallop for further tests on military knowledge, tactics and procedures.

The flying courses lasted approximately nine months at Middle Wallop. From time to time there were changes in the format but in general the basic trainer was the Chipmunk, a single-engine, fixed-wing aircraft in which about 30 hours, including 15 solo, were flown. After the Chipmunk, the trainee moved on to Basic Rotary, which entailed another 30 hours on

1. Dedication of the Second World War panels of the 10th Hussars
War Memorial, Lubeck 1947. Lieutenant Colonel A. Abel Smith

2. Drag Hunt meet, Germany, 1947

3. Centurion of C Squadron, 10th Hussars, on winter training in 1953

4. The Duke of Gloucester with Major R.J. Griffith inspecting A Squadron in 1954

5. The Coronation Contingent, 1954 — L to R: Captain J. de B. Carey, Sergeant T. Dines, Corporal G.H. Burgwin, Lance Corporal K.G. Burton, Troopers L.A. Marston, M.C. Cooney, R. Pennington, Regimental Sergeant Major W. Hedley

6. MT Troop exercising on the Guweira Plain, Jordan, 1956 — L to R: 2nd Lieutenant R. Russell, Troopers Walker, Boucher, Court, Lance Corporal Bell and Trooper Durrant. Back row: Lance Corporal Patterson and Trooper Burgess

7. Maintenance halt on the road to Petra, 1956. On the right 2nd Lieutenant J. Sclater

8. Officer's Beach Club — Aqaba

9. 10th Hussars aboard
HMS *Decoy*, a Daring Class
destroyer, visiting Aqaba

10. Centurion with mono-wheel trailer in Aqaba during the evacuation,
1957

11. Guidon Parade, 1961 — Trooper Singh (with beard and turban) travelled at his own expense from Malaya to join the Regiment

12. Guidon Parade, 1961 — Drum horse and escort

13. The Band of the 10th Hussars at Warburg in 1961. Warburg (1760) was the first battle honour to be granted to both the 10th and 11th Hussars.

14. Captain P.C.C. Kaye and Captain R.L. Perry — Dhala, Western Aden Protectorate, 1964

15. The grave of 2nd Lieutenant I.A.G. Scott, who was killed on the Dhala Road. Ian Scott was the only 10th Hussar to be killed in action since the Second World War.

16. A Saladin armoured car of C Squadron in the Western Aden Protectorate, 1964

17. Major-General Sir David Dawnay, Colonel of the 10th Hussars, with his son Capt H. Dawnay and an officer of the Royal Air Force at Salalah, Oman, 1964

18. A Scout Helicopter with a Ferret Scout car of the 10th Hussars — Western Aden Protectorate, 1965

19: 10th Hussar Air Troop — Aden. L to R: Captain O.N.P. Mylne, Staff Sergeant J.V. Thirst, Lieutenant A. Jones RTR, Sergeant Dawson and Corporal James

20. Major Julian Gordon with Scout helicopter (pilot Captain Mylne) in the Radfan, 1964

21. Staff Sergeant Grimble of the LAD schooling a polo pony in Aden

22. Major Piers Bengough exercising "April Rose" on the morning before the Grand National, 1965

23. Air Troop 10th Hussars in Munster 1967. Corporal Gaskin REME refuels a Sioux

24. 10th Hussar Air Squadron 1967 L to R — standing: Cpl Craig REME, Sgt Dawson, Tpr Cockell, Tpr Yeates, S/Sgt Gilchrist REME, S/Sgt Bartlett REME, Tpr Williams, Tpr Crush, L/Cpl Shelton, Sgt Gaskin REME, Cpl Yates, Cpl Curtis. Seated: Sgt Mead RA, WO2 Thirst, Lt Turner, Capt Perry, Capt Edwards, Capt Mylne, Lt Capper-Jackson, Sgt Farmer 11H. Kneeling: L/Cpl Richardson REME, Tpr Burt, Tpr Bettridge, Tpr Hale, Tpr Pennels

the Hiller 12. This was an extremely basic and unstable helicopter, fairly underpowered and with some unpleasant habits, like chopping off its own tail boom if a practice 'engine off' landing was misjudged!

Having survived this stage, the trainee then progressed to Advanced Rotary, was introduced to the Sioux and did some 50 hours including tactical exercises and a certain amount of night flying.

Operationally, the pilot normally flew with an observer. These observers were trained in the Regiment and assisted the pilots by map-reading and recording radio messages. In particular, the observer was charged with the observation of any activity on the ground, helping the pilot to plot the position and warning him of wires and other obstructions and hazards. These men, usually NCOs, acted as observers in addition to their other tasks within the Squadron and received a small pay increment. Some of those who fulfilled this role were Sergeant Nobby Dawson, Corporal Curtis and Lance-Corporals Cockell and Maich.

There were, of course, numerous untoward incidents, humorous or hair-raising or both, recalled by members of the squadron and others.

Commanding officers seem to have been in particular peril while being flown by regimental pilots. On one occasion David Edwards crashed with Colonel John Willis (himself a pilot) on board into a forest in the Moselle Valley. Fortunately they were unhurt and the Colonel went to get help while Edwards remained with the wreckage. The first person to appear was a German policeman who surveyed the scene and then asked, 'Did you not know it is an offence to cut down trees in Germany?'

The command of a previous Colonel, Bill Lithgow, had nearly come to an abrupt end when his pilot, Tony Uloth (not actually a member of the Air Squadron), had difficulty landing a borrowed Auster at Detmold in a severe thunderstorm. But Lithgow, nothing daunted, went up again with the same pilot a few days later!

When an aircraft was involved in an incident, a huge form

"It's lucky yours holds more than mine.. Sir!"

had to be filled in and submitted to the RAF with no less than nine copies. Nick Mylne had a fire in the rotor brake, used to slow and stop the rotor on landing, and when the fire-extinguisher failed to quench the conflagration, his passenger, Colonel John Willis, eventually put it out by relieving himself on it. The incident report went in complete with a cartoon depicting the scene. The RAF were not amused.

At the time the 10th Hussars were so keenly and closely involved in army aviation that an officer referred to them as 'a Recce Regiment in support of an Air Squadron'. But the end came in 1969 when the Regiment left Munster to return to England before amalgamation. The last leader of the squadron was Major Peter Stonor of the Queen's Own Hussars. Upon departure, the aircraft and equipment were handed over to the incoming regiment (the Carabiniers) with the pilots, fitters and some of the ground crews either remaining or being dispersed to other aviation squadrons. 'Thus,' writes David Edwards, 'ended a brief but eventful episode in the Regiment's history, performed with panache and flair in the best traditions of the 10th Hussars and the cavalry.'

Several of those mentioned in this chapter continued their flying careers. Fred Perry flew Whirlwinds with the RAF on exchange and later commanded the last of the cavalry air squadrons, that of the 16th/5th Lancers. Simon Arthur (later Lord Glenarthur) also served with that squadron and, at the time of writing is Chairman of the British Helicopter Advisory Board. Earlier, he spent seven years flying over the North Sea as a pilot with British Airways Helicopters and in the 1980s held several political and industrial appointments.

The concept of the integrated air squadron fizzled out in the course of the 1970s and finally died in 1977 with the closure of the 16th/5th squadron, no doubt through lack of support in high places.* In years to come, when the advance of military technology has rendered the tank obsolete, just as it did the horse, the failure of the Royal Armoured Corps to seize and hold the 'Air Arm' for itself may be recognized as the beginning of the end for that Corps. A lost opportunity indeed, although perhaps not too late to be retrieved.

* Appendix C is relevant and, although we do not have General Holden's response to Brigadier Ward-Harrison, we may be fairly certain that it was negative. See also pps 150–1 in the 11th Hussar section of this book.

Chapter 6

THE ARABIAN PENINSULA 1964–5

To the British Army, which had guarded the Empire from both internal and external threat for two hundred years, was also given the unenviable task of supervising its dissolution.

The principal imperial trouble-spot of the 1960s was the Aden Protectorate, a conglomerate of petty sheikhdoms which had accepted British protection, originally as a safeguard against the Turks who occupied neighbouring Yemen in the 1870s. With the appearance on the Middle Eastern stage of the Egyptian dictator, Gamal Abdel Nasser, in the 1950s and the consequent rise of Arab nationalism, a serious anti-British movement began to develop in Aden Colony itself and the Protectorate, usually against the wills of the sheikhs who had more to fear from Nasser than from their so-called 'colonial oppressors' under whom they had at least survived, even prospered. They were not, however, capable of controlling their subjects, heavily influenced by the propaganda blasts of Cairo Radio.

In the early 60s, in a perhaps counter-productive attempt to bring about a more manageable unity, the British created the Federation of South Arabia, which, for a diversity of reasons, was popular with no one. By the end of 1963 the tribes of the Radfan Mountains, some sixty miles to the north of Aden, had burst into open revolt, armed from across the border by the new Nasserite Republic of Yemen, itself in a state of civil war.

The most intense period of this uprising lasted for about six months and, officially, came to an end on 31 July, 1964, after a campaign involving a British Brigade and several battalions of the Federal Regular (Arab) Army with RAF support. However, dissident activity rumbled on and it is at this point, August, 1964, that the 10th Hussars enter the picture.

From April to July of that year, the Regiment had undergone its conversion from Armoured (tanks) to Armoured Recce (Saladin armoured cars and Ferret scout cars) while based at Lucknow Barracks, Tidworth. Conversion training had taken elements of the Regiment to the extremities of the United Kingdom, A Squadron reaching John O'Groats and B Squadron Land's End. The Saladin, which had come into service in the late 1950s, had replaced the long-serving Daimler with which British armoured car regiments had been equipped since the North African campaign of the Second World War. A six-wheeler with a laden weight of 10.5 tons, the Saladin was powered by a Rolls-Royce 8-cylinder petrol engine giving it a maximum (governed) road speed of 45 mph and a range of 250 miles. It was armed with a turret-mounted 76mm gun, a .30 in Browning co-axial machine gun and another independently mounted .30 for the use of the commander. It had a crew of three.

The Ferret was a development of the vintage Dingo scout car which it replaced. The Mark 1 was open but the Mark II (as used in Aden) was fitted with an armoured machine-gun turret mounting, originally, a .30 in but later a 7.62 LMG Browning. Powered by a 6-cylinder Rolls-Royce engine with a maximum road speed of 58 mph, it had a range of approximately 200 miles. The two-man crew consisted of a Commander/Gunner/Operator and a Driver. In the 1990s the Ferret and the Saladin are both still in service. From November, 1990, to July, 1992, D Squadron, The Royal Hussars, was equipped with these vehicles in Cyprus.

As the 10th Hussars 250th Anniversary was due in 1965, by which time they would be in the Middle East, it was decided to celebrate the event prior to departure in 1964. On 30 May an Old Comrades' Day, attended by the Colonel-in-Chief and Princess Alice, was arranged at Tidworth. Many members of the Regiment, past and present, met the Duke and Duchess and among others who put in an appearance were several former

Commanding Officers including Colonels Morley, Tuck, Jackson and Ward-Harrison.

On 5 June an Officers' Ball was held at St James's Palace. Major James Scott's diary testifies to 'an unforgettable evening', the guests, including many former National Service officers, dancing the night away to the music of Ian Stewart's Orchestra and the Band of Angels.

In order to release the 4th RTR for service in the Far East, the move to the Arabian Peninsula got underway a month earlier than originally planned. The age of 'air trooping' having dawned, a C Squadron Advance Party flew to Sharjah in the Trucial States on 3/4 August, 1964, followed by the rest of the squadron a week later.

Some members of C Squadron chose a less conventional route to their new posting at Sharjah. Captain Friedberger with Lieutenant Landon, Sergeant Fox, Corporals Gidding and Robinson and Trooper Bainbridge set out from Tidworth in two Landrovers. Their journey took them through Belgium, Germany, Austria, Yugoslavia, Greece, Turkey and Iran, finally crossing from Bandar Abbas to Dubai in a dhow. Temporarily abandoning their vehicles at the port and with a certain disregard for their dignity, they eventually arrived at Sharjah by taxi!

By mid-September the whole Regiment was in place, disposed as follows: – RHQ, HQ Squadron and the rear elements of two sabre squadrons at Mareth Lines, Falaise Camp, Little Aden.

One squadron at Thumeir with troops detached at Dhala, Blair's Field, Paddy's Field, Monk's Field and Hayaz.

One squadron at Beihan with troops detached at Mukeiras, Ataq, Wadi Ayn and Manawa.

One squadron at Sharjah with two troops and ½ SHQ detached at RAF Salalah (Muscat and Oman).

The sabre squadrons were periodically rotated and all three served in the various locations at different times. Throughout this year-long tour in the Middle East A Squadron was commanded by Major Robin Wilson, B Squadron by Major Julian Gordon and C Squadron by Major Tim Hope.

Sharjah was the most sedentary of these squadron locations

46

as the Trucial States were peaceful at this time and the role in support of the Trucial Oman Scouts was undemanding. In neighbouring Muscat and Oman the revolt by the Imam of Oman, which had as its high point the Jebel Akhdar campaign of 1959/60, was virtually over but trouble broke out in 1964 in the southern province of Dhofar stirred up by Yemeni, Egyptian and Russian interference. 'This is first-class bandit country,' wrote James Lunt in his book *Imperial Sunset*, 'honeycombed with caves which provided excellent refuges for small guerrilla gangs whose tactics were those of ambush intimidation and the raiding of plains villages . . .'

Soon after arriving in Sharjah, two troops of C Squadron under Captain Friedberger with Lieutenants Turner and Capper-Jackson as troop leaders, were airlifted by Beverley to Salalah, primarily to protect the small RAF staging post, one of whose NCOs had been killed when his truck was blown up and which had been attacked by mortar and machine-gun fire. Major Peter Hamer, 11th Hussars, accompanied the detachment on the initial deployment as he was the staff officer in Bahrain responsible for operations in the area.

However, during the 10th's tour of duty the serious fighting had not begun and the situation, although tense, was not particularly dangerous. Nonetheless, it was here that the Regiment suffered one of its casualties, when, on 22 October 1964, Lance-Corporal Preece and Trooper Finney of 5th Troop C Squadron struck a mine while on night patrol in a Ferret. The mine exploded under the rear wheels, the scout car overturning several times and catching fire. Preece suffered a head wound which kept him out of action for three weeks but Finney was more or less unscathed. As we shall see, mines were the cause of almost all the Regiment's casualties, both to personnel and vehicles, during its tour of duty in the Arabian Peninsula.

The confidence of the insurgents, who styled themselves the Dhofar Liberation Front, backed by the newly independent and Communist-ruled People's Republic of South Yemen, increased with Britain's withdrawal from Aden in 1967. By 1970 it was clear that the main obstacle to the defeat of the rebels was the continued rule of the reactionary Sultan and, on 23 July that year, a palace coup was planned and executed with the aid of a British officer, placing the Sultan's son, Qaboos, on his father's throne. The officer concerned was a former 10th Hussar. From then on the tide turned against the rebels as the new and more enlightened ruler gradually began to win the trust and loyalty of the population. Nevertheless, in the period 1967 to 1976 some 200 Omani, British, Iranian and Jordanian troops were killed in the Dhofar campaign and about 600 wounded.

However, the principal preoccupation of the British authorities in the years immediately preceding the abandonment of Aden was the continuing unrest in the South Arabian Federation, which had been for some time Nasser's main target in his political and propaganda campaign against British interests in the Middle East; a campaign which, in the end, bore little fruit for the Egyptian dictator. While it cannot be denied that his activities helped to influence the British Government in its decision to hand over both the Federation and the Colony in a remarkably short space of time, sadly it was not, in the event, to Nasser or his adherents, the Front for the Liberation of South Yemen (FLOSY), to whom the Colony and its hinterland fell, but to his opponents, the Communist National Liberation Front (NLF). It was fortunate for the 10th Hussars that their tour of duty was over long before the final act in the chaotic handover of Aden to a vicious and tyrannous régime, surely one of the unhappiest and least successful episodes in the history of Britain's withdrawal from empire.

Thus, while all three sabre squadrons served at different times in the various areas mentioned previously, that is to say Aden Colony, the Federation, and Sharjah and Salalah, it was in the Federation that most of the action took place. Indeed, it was there that the 10th Hussars were to suffer their last fatal casualty from hostile activity and experience their last exchange of fire with an enemy.

Former troop leaders like Julien Turner remember this tour as 'a wonderful opportunity for real soldiering, the like of which was not really repeated thereafter'. Troops detached at such curiously named outposts as Paddy's Field or Blair's Field, airstrips in the Radfan mountains, enjoyed an independence seldom experienced by junior officers and men. Although regularly visited by the Commanding Officer and Squadron Leader, the Troop Leader was accountable locally to the resident infantry Company Commander, who often had a troop of Gunners under command as well. 'It was a marvellous opportunity to build a troop,' writes David Edwards, 'which I suspect seldom comes any more in quite the same way in today's army.'

A battalion with whom the Regiment developed something of a special relationship was the 2nd Coldstream – a friendship not necessarily based on a slightly suggestive recruiting slogan then in use to the effect that 'I've got a pal in the Coldstream Guards!', although stickers bearing this confession were sometimes to be seen stuck to 10th Hussar vehicles. Major Andrew Napier of No. 4 Company remembers the troop which was under his command at Thumeir and Monk's Field as 'first rate and most efficient'. This troop was led by Staff Sergeant F. W. Nicholas of C Squadron who was to receive the British Empire Medal. His citation read as follows: –

'Because of a shortage of junior officers, Staff Sergeant Nicholas commanded a troop of armoured cars on active operations from 1st February to 31st July, 1965, with only two short breaks of ten days in Aden.

'During this time he was usually on troop detachments some distance from squadron headquarters. For most of this period he was liable to be attacked by dissidents at any time.

'In all, his troop was engaged six times and on a further occasion two Ferret scout cars were destroyed by mines. Also vehicles in convoys which were being escorted by his troop were mined on several occasions. Twice his troop escorted the night evacuation of casualties where the use of helicopters was not possible.

'Despite rough and ready living conditions and constant hazardous and arduous operation, he maintained the morale and efficiency of his troop at the highest possible level. His personal example was in the highest traditions of the Army.

'He supported 3rd Btn Federal Regular Army on many occasions and earned from them their complete confidence and unqualified praise.

'His coolness and calmness under fire inspired confidence throughout his troop and his steadfastness over a long and difficult period of operation has been an example to the whole squadron.'

Curiously enough it was to be several years before Nicholas, by then an SQMS, was to receive his medal which was eventually presented to him on 11 January, 1968, by the British Ambassador to West Germany, Sir Frank Roberts.

As was emphasized in the citation, contact with the enemy in the Federation was not infrequent, particularly in the Radfan Mountains. On one occasion David Edwards found himself bracketed by a bazooka while on patrol. 'Needless to say,' he recalls, 'the Forward Observation Officer at that moment was unable to observe and I learned very quickly how necessary it was to be able to direct artillery fire.' Two Hunter ground attack aircraft were summoned but 'we were very nervous of the fact that we were well in front of the Bomb Line.'

Nevertheless, the patrol emerged from the episode unscathed, although this was not always the case. On 25 April, 1965, the Regiment suffered its last fatal casualty from enemy action when Second Lieutenant Ian Scott's Ferret was blown up by a mine while escorting a convoy in the Dhala area. Scott was killed and his driver, Trooper Edward Clarke, seriously burnt.

These convoys from Aden into the Federation were an important aspect of the work of an armoured car regiment. A weekly convoy consisting of twenty to thirty 3-tonners and some other vehicles would set out at dawn heading for Brigade HQ at Thumeir. The first part of the route was relatively good but deteriorated as the road, strewn with rocks and interrupted by patches of soft sand, wound into the mountains. Mines were a hazard but punctures caused the greatest problems. These were frequent and seldom came singly. The convoy commander had to decide whether to detach a scout car to guard the punctured vehicle or halt the whole convoy. Usually the former was preferred as the convoy was expected to reach its destination in time to unload and return to Aden the same day. Even so, Thumeir was not necessarily the end of the line for the whole convoy and some vehicles would continue on to Dhala or Paddy's Field.

Arrival at destination had its rewards. David Edwards remembers 'the exquisite pleasure of being able to suck a frozen one pint lozenge of milk when we reached Thumeir, like a large iced lolly!'

By the mid-sixties supply by air was fairly well developed. Beverleys, which could carry an armoured car, Twin Pioneers and Belvederes were regular visitors to Thumeir airstrip carrying urgently needed spares and other stores, and the Regiment's own helicopters, to which the preceding chapter was devoted, were used when available by the Commanding Officer, Bill Lithgow, and his squadron leaders for their visits to detached troops.

The Air Troop had been formed on 1 February, 1965, but the aircraft were not delivered until April. The troop shared an airfield with 653 Squadron, Army Air Corps, from whom it received the fullest co-operation. Unfortunately, however, teething troubles plagued the troop during its brief sojourn in South Arabia and only two or three months in all were spent in operational activity.

On 19 July, 1965, Major Robin Wilson and a Gunner officer were flying in a helicopter in the Dhala area when they came under machine-gun and mortar fire. A nearby troop leader, Lieutenant A. H. Lyall Grant, tells the full story in his report.

'On the morning of 19 July Major Wilson 10H and Major Ohlenschlager RHA were flying in a Scout helicopter reconnoitring a route from Hayaz to Awabil (reference given) when they were fired at by MG and Mortars from the area of Ardah.

'When this had been reported, 5 FRA [5th Bn Federal Regular Army] were ordered to investigate. 5th Tp A Sqn 10H at Hayaz had two cars off the road so at 0945 3rd Tp were ordered to produce two Saladins from Dhala.

'Two cars, commanded by Lt Lyall Grant and Cpl Rowley, arrived at Hayaz at 10.20. They linked up with 2 Coy from 5 FRA and set out at 11.00, one Saladin (Tp Ldr) in front and the other at the rear of the column. Two guns from 28 Bty, 19 Lt Regt, RA, based at Dhala, set off at 1000 and were in position nr

Jalas by 1200. They were escorted by 2 × Saladin from 5th Tp under Lt Round and by two sec[tion]s from 5 FRA.

'The road climbs steeply from GR 815 250 and is narrow and overlooked. Pickets were sent along the north side of the route from this point, the personnel being taken from the Coys making the move.

'The pickets bumped opposition in the area GR 837 257 at 1300. They were fired on with rifles and explosive bullets by about 30 dissidents. One Gundee [Arab soldier] from 5 FRA was hit in the stomach and later died. Fire was returned by the pickets and the dissidents retired into the wadi bed to the NW.

'The leading SAC got into a fire position and engaged targets with HE and .30 MG at ranges between 400 and 800 yards. At first the enemy were not seen by the commander and fire was directed by Qaid [Lt-Colonel] Ali from the back decks. Then the driver, Tpr Walrond, observed several dissidents running for cover behind a tree. He informed the commander and a second round hit was achieved on the tree by Tpr Howell. That evening a body was recovered from the position, having been killed by a very near miss with HE, a certain "kill" for 10H.

'The enemy fired back with rifles and a mortar but achieved no more casualties. Gunfire was brought down on this position from 28 Bty. The enemy retired round a ridge to the north.

'Another 2 secs of 5 FRA, advancing NE to Ardah, reported 30 more dissidents and opened fire. Both Saladins were dispatched to this position (1400), Tp Ldr's car having by now developed a serious hydraulic leak and having no brakes and only manual steering. They took up positions in the high ground to the south of Ardah. The enemy had by now retired to the ridge NW of the village. Both cars engaged a sangar [stone shelter] containing enemy at 400 yds with HESH. Two bodies were recovered from it that evening but were found to be killed by MG fire from the Infantry.

'The enemy continued to retire and the Infantry mounted an attack. The Saladins fired on positions passed to them by the FRA at ranges up to 1500 yds. The dissidents retired to the NW and the pursuit was stopped at 1600. The enemy were seen to be carrying 7 dead or wounded.

'Back at Dhala, Sgt Reid and L/Cpl Roberts arranged replenishment of ammunition, food and water for next morning, and a helicopter lift of bedding and oil for the hydraulic system, which reached the forward troops at 1730. They worked late into the night.

'At dusk, having eaten, the Saladins' crews collected into a close leaguer, still in fire position covering Ardah. The Infantry were brought back into a close defensive position. The AFV crews slept beside their vehicles.

'At 0500, 20 July, the force stood to, no enemy were observed and we prepared to move back. However, the damaged Saladin presented a formidable problem. 2 × SAC from 5th Tp under Lt Round set out for our position and arrived at 0745. The guns, which had withdrawn to Dhala for the night, were again in position at 0715.

'We started back at 0830, first of all trying to drive the SAC in first gear. However, on a steep place, the gear-band slipped and we shot for the precipice.

'Tpr Walrond kept his head admirably, wound on the hand-brake and steered into a large rock, stopping the vehicle yards from the edge. After this mishap the two Saladins were hitched to the back with tow ropes and the party completed the rest of the journey uneventfully, met our 3-tonner and ammunition at Jalas and Sgt Reid's Saladin at Hayaz and 3rd Tp reached Dhala at 1200. Latest intelligence reports suggest 5 dissidents killed and 7 wounded.'

Thus ended what was probably the last action of any significance in which the 10th Hussars were to be involved in their 254-year history, and it is perhaps fitting that it should have take place in a remote, dusty, barren and apparently worthless spot, typical of the terrain over which so much of that history, and indeed the history of the British Army as a whole, has been made.

Lyall Grant concluded his report with some interesting observations.

'In suitable places,' he wrote, 'Saladins are invaluable and can provide fire support much faster and more accurately than the Guns. However, the enemy were very foolish in choosing two of the very few places along the route to make their attack where good fire positions can be obtained. This particular route is very steep and narrow; two Saladins now have gear trouble because of it; recovery is extremely difficult; we nearly lost one vehicle. This route should not be used again by armoured cars, but they are ideal vehicles for close support in less strenuous terrain.

'British commanders find it very difficult to see men-targets at ranges over 400 yards in this country. Once a target was observed, the standard of Gunnery was good.'

In June, 1965, Captain John Friedberger and a small party were sent to Saudi Arabia to demonstrate the qualities of the Ferret scout car. The team, which included Sergeant Mapplebeck, Corporals James and Lowther, Lance Corporals Tanner (fitter) and Mansbridge (cook), Troopers Presswell and Smith (222), flew by Beverley with two Ferrets to Riyadh via Bahrain. The demonstration was connected with a major defence contract which was in the process of negotiation with the Saudi Air Force. The main contract was eventually concluded but it is unclear if any Ferrets were purchased, although their performance had been satisfactorily demonstrated.

It is unlikely that the members of the team enjoyed themselves very much. 'Dry' Saudi Arabia was an even drearier place in the 1960s than it is at the time of writing and, although the party was accommodated in one of the two so-called luxury hotels in Riyadh (the services of Corporal Mansbridge were not required), few of the entertainments appreciated by the British soldier were available and even non-alcholic beer cost the shocking sum of three shillings a bottle!

In July, Lieutenant-Colonel Bill Lithgow handed over command to Lieutenant-Colonel John Willis. Colonel Lithgow was the last Commanding Officer of the 10th Hussars to have seen active service in the Second World War during which he had served in the Western Desert, Sicily, Italy and the Far East.

During 1965 three junior NCOs, Corporals Johnston, Hunt and Doyle RAMC, received Commander-in-Chief's Commendations.

Johnston had been the medical orderly at Manawa Camp near

the Yemeni border when the Royalists launched a major attack against the Republicans in the course of the civil war in the Yemen. A large number of refugees, including many women and children, crossed the border seeking medical assistance. Johnston treated more than fifty cases, working continuously for forty-eight hours, until a doctor with a medical team was flown in.

Corporal Hunt had been in command of two Ferrets escorting a Federal National Guard convoy to Wa'alah Fort, about twelve miles west of Dhala, when the convoy commander's Landrover was blown up, presumably on a mine. The Arab officer and his driver were wounded, the driver losing a foot. Hunt immediately called for a 'casevac' helicopter to stand by. Then he organized local defence and gave first aid to the driver who was bleeding to death. Having stopped the bleeding he dressed the wound and administered morphia. Finding a suitable area for a helicopter to land, he passed the information by radio and guided the helicopter in. The medical officer who accompanied it considered that no further first aid was required to supplement that already given by Hunt.

Hunt then reorganized the convoy which completed its journey. Throughout this emergency Corporal Hunt had displayed exemplary leadership and his first aid undoubtedly saved the life of the Arab driver.

The last to receive the C-in-C's Commendation was Corporal Doyle RAMC, attached to C Squadron at Manawa between May and June, 1965. During this period he extended his work well beyond the military camp into the local villages, gaining the respect and confidence of the Arabs by his skill and devotion to their needs.

On 29 June two Arab women were brought to him, having been badly wounded by a Yemeni or Egyptian MIG fighter. One of the women had a shattered leg and arm, while the other had been severely wounded in both legs, with one foot partially severed. Doyle amputated the second woman's foot with a razor blade in the absence of proper surgical instruments and stopped the arterial bleeding. He dressed and applied splints to both women's injuries and administered morphia. He worked with great speed and coolness throughout, thus saving the life of the more seriously wounded woman.

In the course of their 14-month tour in the Arabian Peninsula many members of the Regiment had come under fire at one time or another, losing one officer killed and several other ranks wounded. A total of seven Ferrets, two Saladins and a Scammell were mined.

This had been the Regiment's most exhilarating and memorable period of service in the post-Second World War era and was to be its last in an Active Service role.

Chapter 7

GERMANY AND AMALGAMATION 1965–69

At the conclusion of its Middle East tour the Regiment returned to England by air in September, 1965, was granted six weeks' 'block' leave, and reassembled at York Barracks, Munster, in early November. Its new role was that of Armoured Reconnaissance Regiment, 1st British Corps.

As we have seen, 1965 was the 10th Hussars' 250th birthday and few, if any, could have foreseen then that its life as an individual entity was drawing to a close. Proud and confident messages received from the Colonel-in-Chief and the Colonel of the Regiment contained no hint of what might lie ahead.

Field-Marshal HRH the Duke of Gloucester wrote:

'I am delighted to send through the *Gazette* my best wishes to all Past and Present Members of the Regiment on the occasion of the 250th Anniversary of our formation.

'I am sure all 10th Hussars are as proud as I am of our history, and, with me, confident that the present serving members and their successors will guard the Regiment's high reputation and traditions.'

Major-General David Dawnay sent the following message:

'In this historic year, during which the 250th Anniversary of the raising of the Regiment is recorded, I have been very lucky to have had the opportunity of visiting the Regiment in Arabia.

'I know all Old Comrades would have been proud to see the way in which All Ranks were carrying out an unspectacular but important task in the field. The Spirit, for which we are justly famed, was everywhere in evidence and for good measure we succeeded in winning the Middle East Athletic Championship, being the first Armoured Regiment to do so.

'Today the reputation of the Regiment stands very high and will I am certain, be jealously safeguarded by all, past and present alike, over the years to come.'

A notable event of this Anniversary Year was Major Piers Bengough's performance in the Grand National when he managed to stay on board his horse April Rose and finish eleventh in spite of a couple of nasty moments. At Beecher's he had been squeezed between two fallers and towards the end of the first circuit a loose horse ran across in front of a fence, nearly causing a pile-up. Friends listening on the BBC Overseas Service at Salalah were enraged when transmission of the race commentary failed temporarily but fortunately resumed in time for the finish.

For a serving officer, Bengough's steeplechasing career was remarkable. Over a period of some twenty years, he rode four times in the Grand National and no less than thirteen times in the Grand Military, in addition to many other races, both in England and Germany. In the 1957 National he had fallen on the perhaps inaptly named Go Well, but, as we have seen, in 1965 he came in eleventh on April Rose and completed the course on the same horse in the following year. Unfortunately, in 1967 he and April Rose came a cropper.

He won the Grand Military for the first time in 1960 on Joan's Rival and followed this with three successive wins in 1970, '71 and '72 on his horse Charles Dickens, and was placed on five other occasions. Charles Dickens then crowned it all by running third in the 1974 Grand National with Andy Turnell up.

In April, 1965, there occurred the death of another celebrated horseman, Colonel Paul Rodzianko, once described by a leading authority as 'probably the greatest instructor of this century'. A former officer of the Imperial Russian Cavalry, he had captained his country's show-jumping team from 1910 to 1914 with resounding success. Forced into exile after the Revolution, he took refuge in England where he soon established himself as a leading horse trainer and riding-master.

In 1922 King George V, then Colonel-in-Chief of the 10th

Hussars, let it be known that he wished Rodzianko to be considered as an officer of the Regiment and as such he was recognized for the rest of his life. After the Second World War he was persuaded by General Dick McCreery to come out to Germany as Chief Instructor at the BAOR School of Equitation established at Herford. In charge of the six-week equitation course, Rodzianko was described by one of his pupils as 'a thick-set moustached figure in a 10th Hussar cap, a battledress blouse adorned with five rows of medal ribbons and the rhinoceros flash of the long extinct 1st Armoured Division, white breeches and near-white Newmarket boots.'

A member of the Regimental Old Comrades Association of longstanding, a letter enclosing his subscription and a request for a new regimental tie was received on the day of his death.

The Regiment was represented at his funeral by Lieutenant-Colonel Peter Jackson, himself a considerable horseman, and Captain George Hartigan.

The final years of the Regiment's existence were uneventful – routine exercises and training in Germany in its role as Corps Armoured Recce Regiment, but with special emphasis on the convoying of nuclear ammunition. Then in 1967 came the devastating news of amalgamation.

In a Foreword to the following year's *Gazette*, the Colonel of the Regiment, Major-General David Dawnay, did his best to put a brave face on it when he wrote:

'The 18th July, 1967, saw the official announcement of the forthcoming amalgamation of the 10th Royal Hussars (Prince of Wales's Own) with the 11th Hussars (Prince Albert's Own) to form a new regiment. Thus after 252 years of service to Crown and Country both regiments, which had been formed on the same day – 23rd July 1715 – learnt of their impending demise as separate entities.

'I wish to state clearly two facts. Firstly, sad as this decision is, in the light of the conditions which have prevailed since 1918, the Regiment has been most fortunate to escape amalgamation for so long. Secondly, we ourselves, had we been asked to do so, could not have chosen a nicer or better regiment with which to

be joined. We must therefore count our blessings which have
been and are many.

'The aims of us all now, whether we be Old Comrades or in
the Serving Regiment, should surely be to combine to form a
new regiment, which will prove itself to be of superlative quality,
to remember with great pride the traditions and glories of both
regiments and to resolve to build the future inspired by our joint
past histories. Meanwhile we must maintain the great reputation
of the 10th Royal Hussars (Prince of Wales's Own) both
militarily and in the field of sport.

'From what I have seen and heard of the Regiment in recent
years, and above all stimulated by the supreme spirit which has
pervaded all ranks for so long, I have every confidence that these
aims will be achieved.'

It is, of course, the uneviable duty of a Colonel of a Regiment
on such an occasion to express this kind of anodyne sentiment,
but privately, and in some cases publicly, there was much
bitterness and ill-feeling directed at politicians and the hierarchy
of the Army. One former officer of another regiment wrote at
the time, 'Having already done its best to destroy the Territorial
Army, it [the Government] is equally unscrupulous about
abolishing or amalgamating famous regiments that have as much
to offer in peacetime as in war. It is a great pity that those in
political authority find it necessary to destroy something which
they can see to be functioning perfectly.'

But however bitter the pill, the *Gazette*'s editor, Major James
Courtney-Clarke (now Scott), swallowed it as bravely as his
Colonel, pointing out that since 1949 no less than five pairs of
brothers had served or were serving in the two regiments.

Perhaps the closest links between the two regiments had been
forged over the years by General Lord Norrie, a Cherrypicker
turned Shiner, who was equally devoted to both and whose
sons made up one of the pairs of brothers mentioned by
Courtney-Clarke. In a speech to the Old Comrades Dinner,
Lord Norrie remarked upon the extraordinary contrast between
the Regiment he had joined as Commanding Officer in India
forty years earlier when the establishment had been 568 horses,
as compared with the 80 assorted armoured cars and six

helicopters of 1968. On amalgamation, he noted, the new regiment would revert to tanks, with which the 11th were already equipped.

In his speech at the same dinner, the Colonel of the Regiment set out the programme for the build-up to amalgamation. In the course of 1969 both regiments would return to England from Germany and would be accommodated at Perham Down in Wiltshire. The actual amalgamation Parade would take place on 25 October, 1969, at which a Guidon would be presented to the new Regiment. The date was particularly appropriate as it would be the 115th anniversary of the Battle of Balaclava (the 11th Hussars Regimental Day) and within two days of the 27th anniversary of the opening of the Battle of El Alamein, celebrated by the 10th.

In these years several changes took place within the regiment. In 1968 Colonel John Willis handed over command to Lieutenant-Colonel Bernard Greenwood, a third generation 10th Hussar and destined to be its last Commanding Officer.

In the previous year Major Dougie Covill had taken over as Quartermaster from Major Bob Storer. To add to his Distinguished Conduct Medal, in the 1968 New Year's Honours List, Covill was made a Member of the Order of the British Empire in recognition of his untiring work and loyalty to the Regiment and the army. The last adjutant of the 10th Hussars was Captain the Hon G. B. Norrie and the last Regimental Sergeant-Major, WO1 G. R. Reddish. Prior to amalgamation several officers and other ranks transferred to other regiments. These included Captain Alan Lyall-Grant to the 16th/5th Lancers and Lieutenant Richard Morrisey-Paine to the Life Guards.

The final issue of the *Gazette* (Vol XXII No 8) appeared in the spring of 1969 with another Foreword by the Colonel of the Regiment, who had been appointed KCVO in the previous year.

'The 10th Royal Hussars *Gazette*,' wrote Sir David, 'was first published in 1908 and was brought out regularly until 1914. After the First World War publication was not resumed until

1928, when the Regiment left the shores of England for Egypt; it ceased again in 1939. The final years of the issue have been from 1947 to date.

'I would like sincerely to thank all members of the editorial staff, both past and present, for the hard work they have put into and the trouble they have taken over the production of our *Gazette* during the three periods of its life. I would like also to thank the many contributors who over the years by article or photograph have helped to maintain interest and to add to the enjoyment of readers.

'After amalgamation it is planned to continue a similar publication, and I am confident that this will provide as much pleasure and interest as in the past.'

One of the last official duties the 10th Hussars were required to perform was the provision of a contingent for the investiture of the Prince of Wales at Caernarvon on 1 July, 1969. The Commander of the contingent was Captain Julien Turner who has described the event and the build-up to it.

'The party left Munster on 16 June and arrived at Perham Down to spend the next ten days with the 11th Hussars. During this time we continued practising our drill procedures for lining the processional route which was to be our task. This was done under the expert guidance of CSM Elliott of the 1st Coldstream.

'On 26 June, after a lot of hard work, we left for Caernarvon (by train from Euston via Waterloo) where we were met by the RCT who took us the last ten miles in 3-tonners and so it was that after ten hours' travelling we arrived at what was to be our home for the next six days, Llandrog Camp.

'We knew that we were to be accommodated in a tented camp on a disused airfield but the sight that greeted us was unexpected. As we climbed out of the vehicles we could see nothing but row upon row of brown tents of varying shapes and sizes. Somewhat reminiscent of a Boy Scouts Jamboree Camp!

'In the reception office the location of our tent was pointed out to us on a large model and, having been handed out a mass of literature on the facilities available, we were despatched to settle ourselves in.

'The next day we were able to take a good note of our

surroundings. The camp had been built especially to accommodate some 3,500 troops who were taking part in the Investiture. The squadron of Engineers and Regiment of Artillery which formed the permanent staff and administrative element had arrived only some six weeks earlier. When they had come there had been nothing at all, except three tarmac runways and flocks of sheep grazing on the grass beside them. It was much to their credit that there was now this vast complex – accommodation, electricity, water tanks and pipelines, wash-houses, cinema and, lastly, in the largest marquee, a NAAFI. The sheep continued to wander in and out at will, obviously highly offended by this intrusion of their once peaceful home.

'There were to be two rehearsals prior to 1st July. To move 3,000 men in road transport in a short time is no simple task. On Friday evening the whole camp practised the procedure for embussing and debussing. The transport was numerous and varied, 3-tonners, coaches, Minibuses, landrovers and even buses from Aldershot. Each vehicle was to leave camp at a specific time and it was essential that the correct people should be on it, so that on arrival at the other end the troops could march on to the processional route in the correct order.

'On Saturday 28 June at 0300 hrs we got up and again converged on our own vehicle. With some 100 vehicles all with headlights on and hundreds of squads of men marching in the dark it was rather like a "General Mobilization". We set off, speeded on our way by Military Policemen who were stationed at every key junction to ensure that no other traffic interfered with the smooth flow of this vast column.

'By 0500 hrs we were stationed on the route in our places and there we waited for a minor procession to come down the route to enable us to practise the compliments we would have to carry out.

'On this occasion the procession consisted of the GOC Wales and the Duke of Norfolk in a staff car (it will be remembered that the Duke was responsible for the running of the Investiture).

'By 0700 hrs we were back in camp with the day's work done. There was the Test Match and Wimbledon to watch on the television. On Sunday a trip was arranged to Pwehelli, which everyone enjoyed and gave an opportunity to get out of the camp.

'On Monday 30 June we had a similar dawn rehearsal to that

of Saturday. The object of having to do these so early was, of course, to ensure that the normal traffic and daily routine of Caernarvon was not disrupted any more than was absolutely necessary. It was, however, amusing to see that even at such an early hour many people turned out to review these rehearsals and on the Monday the stands in the town square were as full of people as they were on 1st July.

'1st July. The Great Day had arrived. We left camp at a rather more amenable time of 1100 hrs and drove out to the Ferodo factory where the Royal Family were to get out of the train. Here we ate our lunches and at 13.15 marched on to the route. The 10th Hussars detachment were No 9 Half-Company and were thus only 500 yards from the point at which the procession commenced. This in turn meant that we were a good mile and a half from the town centre and the Castle in which the ceremony took place. Nevertheless, our view of the procession was, of course, perfect.

'There were three parts to the procession – firstly members of the Royal Family in cars, followed by HRH Prince Charles in an open carriage and lastly the Queen and the Duke of Edinburgh in another open carriage (the last two being escorted by the Household Cavalry). When they had passed we had a one and a half hour wait, during which we were able to go off to a specially prepared point for a drink and to stretch our legs. Back on the route for the returning procession and then it was all over.

'Before we were able to march off parade we had to wait for the remainder of the half-companies to march through our own position and so one was able at least to see all the others who had taken part. The qualification for taking part was a connection with Wales itself or the Prince of Wales. In the Regular Army this meant all the Welsh regiments, the 3rd Carabiniers (POWDG), the 9th/12th Lancers (POW), the 10th Royal Hussars (PWO), the Lancashire Regiment, the Cheshires and the Staffords. There were also contingents from the Royal Navy, the Royal Air Force, the Royal Marines and the majority of the remainder consisted of Welsh cadets, ACF and CCF.

'On 2 July we arrived back at Perham Down and next day everyone went off for a well-deserved leave.

'To line a processional route and to have to stand for some hours is not what one would call enjoyable, especially if it is warm, which it was. But it would not be unfair to say that those who had the opportunity to represent the Regiment on this great occasion are probably now very glad that they did so. It is unlikely that such an opportunity will occur again for quite some time.'

The 10th Hussar detachment consisted of the following:

Captain Turner (commanding)
RQMS Kolaczkowski
Sergeant Riley
Corporals Ninnim, Aitkenhead, Brightman and Barter
Lance-Corporals Hutchinson, Suggit, Paine, Clark and
    Cronshaw
Troopers Stinger, Pullen, Hawkins, Elsey, Curd, Franklin,
    Thurlow, Cush and Frier.

The senior Non-Commissioned Officer of the detachment, WOII Joseph Kolaczkowski, who, as his name implies, was Polish, had been with the Regiment since the end of the Second World War. In 1943 he had managed to join the 7th Lubelski Lancers of the Polish Free Army at Taranto in Italy, having marched and fought his way through 700 miles of German-held territory, in the course of which journey six of his eleven companions had been killed and two too seriously wounded to continue. He fought in the Italian campaign, winning two Polish medals for gallantry, and transferred, as did many of his compatriots, to the British Army at the end of the war rather than return to communist-occupied Poland. In 1965 he had been awarded the Long Service and Good Conduct Medal and retired from The Royal Hussars in 1970.

In the summer of 1969, an 'Amalgamation Office' under Major Piers Bengough, assisted by Captain Greville Malet, was set up at Perham Down to carry out the detailed work of planning the 'nuts and bolts' of the forthcoming marriage. In liaison with his opposite number in the 11th Hussars, Captain Christopher Thompson, Bengough's task fell into two categories, namely the implementation of decisions reached by the Colonels of the two 'old' regiments on all aspects of the amalgamation, especially manning, and the planning of the ceremonial and administrative details of the parade to be held on 25 October.

On that parade, which will be described at the beginning of The Royal Hussar section of this book, a great regiment passed into history on the 94th day of the 255th year of its existence.

TREU UND FEST

The Eleventh Hussars

(Prince Albert's Own)

Chapter 8

GERMANY 1945–53

The Eleventh Hussars fired their last shots of the Second World War, mostly in celebration, on the outskirts of Hamburg at about 8 a.m. on 5 May, 1945, just under five years after 4th Troop A Squadron under Troop Sergeant Major E. S. N. (Nobby) Clark had 'opened the bowling' on the Egyptian/Libyan frontier.

They were to spend the next eight years in Germany, the conquest of which had cost them so much in blood, sweat and tears. Few regiments of the British Army had spent as much of the war in contact with the enemy as had the Cherrypickers and there were men among them on that spring day in north Germany, including their Commanding Officer, the legendary Bill Wainman, who had missed hardly an hour of the action. The chapter headings of Dudley Clarke's *The Eleventh at War* tell the story in essence: The Western Desert, Cyrenaica, Tripolitania, Tunisia, Southern Italy, Normandy, The Seine, The Scheldt, Holland, Western Germany, Bremen and Hamburg and it is fitting that the last momentous event of the war in Europe in which the Regiment was involved should be recalled in the words of one who had followed that long, hard road from Egypt.

'Commanding a squadron (D) of armoured cars,' [wrote Major Toby Horsford forty years later] 'on 3 May, 1945, I was ordered to enter Hamburg ahead of 7th Armoured Division (The Desert Rats). A strict curfew had been imposed by General von Wolff.

With no opposition we motored on north-west until reaching the small village of Quickborn. Many miles ahead of the rest of the Army we were ordered to stop and await the arrival of "Super Enemy Sunray (Commander)". This was a disappointment as, with tails up, we were looking forward to liberating Denmark. Opposition had virtually ceased. Unarmed German soldiers and Displaced Persons were streaming south.

'Next morning, after a comparatively uneventful night, I went two miles north of the village to visit my forward patrol who were enjoying ham and eggs cooked for them by the willing locals.

'Suddenly my attention was drawn to something moving towards us on the road ahead. It was two elderly Mercedes with a large white flag on either side of the bonnets. Excitement was intense. We knew that this could mean only one thing, the end of that long devious journey that had begun on 10 June, 1940, in the Western Desert.

'The Mercedes contained three officers and the drivers who quickly opened the back doors and stood smartly to attention. The senior officer was in naval uniform and on his neck the "Ritterkreis and Diamonds", one of Germany's highest honours. The wearer was General Admiral von Friedeburg, C-in-C of the German Navy. Obviously embarrassed, he saluted and handed me a paper signed by Doenitz, Hitler's successor, asking that he should be escorted to Field-Marshal Montgomery's headquarters to sign the surrender of all German troops on the Western Front.'

The scene was sketched for posterity by one of Horsford's men, Trooper Grice, and photographed by Willy Cracco, the Belgian interpreter.

Friedeburg was soon whisked away to 21st Army Group HQ and the Field-Marshal but D Squadron's role in the surrender process was not quite over. 'The next day,' continues Horsford, 'Admiral Hoffman tried to hand me the German High Seas Fleet, but I settled for a small corvette with which we went fishing off Heligoland!'

The Regiment's first post-war task was the military government of an area of Schleswig-Holstein on the banks of the Kiel Canal. Its attitude to this role was straightforward and practical. 'We knew nothing whatever about military government', wrote

Richard Brett-Smith, 'and relied, therefore, upon rule of thumb and common sense, and left the Germans, who knew their business, to get on with it.'

Very junior officers found themselves in positions of absolute power. For example the Town Major of Brunsbüttel on the Elbe was a subaltern in the 5th Dragoon Guards. At this early stage the whole of Germany was in turmoil and the Western Allies – British, American and French – were faced not only with the administration of their own zones but with vast hordes of refugees, both military and civilian, from the east, desperate to escape the horrors of Russian occupation.

One of the major problems facing the military government were the Displaced Persons, former slave-labourers who had been imported into Germany from all over occupied Europe and who now sought to wreak vengeance upon their erstwhile masters. A former officer of the Regiment recalls how one of the duties he was called upon to perform was to command a firing-squad which summarily executed a DP for murder and rape!*

Ironically the British, stretched to the limit, often had to use armed German troops to guard and control these liberated slaves and to patrol the streets of the towns and villages to maintain some semblance of law and order. Somewhat desultory searches were made for fugitive SS men and other war criminals and the life of a town would be brought to a standstill when numbers of public employees, policemen and tradesmen would be mistakenly arrested in dawn raids.

However, by June more professional (but not necessarily more effective) military administrators from the Control Commission had begun to take over from the front-line troops and the Regiment moved to Berlin on 4 July, 1945. Here it was accommodated in Von Seekt Barracks, Spandau, the troops losing no time in adapting the name to a description of the condition in which they found it. Previously it had been occupied by the Russians and a small army of German women was conscripted into the task of making the place habitable for

* The condemned man's victims were reputed to have numbered 67.

relatively civilized human beings, which included the removal of a dead German and a dead horse, the latter from outside the cookhouse.

The victorious Allies found Germany a country of strong contrasts. 'The standard of living in the Third Reich had been amazingly high,' wrote the first post-war editor of the *Journal*, Richard Brett-Smith; 'plenty of luxuries unobtainable in England, much of it looted from France, Belgium, Denmark, Norway and Holland. On the small farms there was an abundance of food, many head of cattle, plenty of grain, indeed plenty of everything.' Brett-Smith was referring to the situation in the Schleswig-Holstein countryside, but in the larger towns and cities the picture was starkly different and in those early days life for most urban dwellers was a grim struggle for existence.

On arrival in Berlin, Brett-Smith goes on to note the contrast between a graceful yacht sailing on the Wannsee, giving every impression of peacetime normality and the

'dirty, half-human Panzer Grenadier from behind the Urals who staggers in to Hakenfelde Camp; a living death after scores of train journeys under conditions worse than cattle, or months of trudging through the plains and villages of the Ukraine and Poland. No one can help noticing the contrast – the false gaiety of the Femina or the Rio Raita [night clubs] and the ragged hopeless refugees grubbing for cigarette ends in the Potsdammer Bahnhof.'

The first major event in the Regiment's Berlin calendar was a victory parade when 7th Armoured Division, of which the Regiment had been part for most of the war, and the rest of the Berlin garrison, was inspected by Winston Churchill on 21 July. Accompanying the Great Man was as glittering an array of British War Leaders as has ever been gathered in one place; Attlee (soon to become Prime Minister himself), Eden, Field-Marshals Montgomery, Brooke, Wilson and Alexander, Admiral of the Fleet Sir Andrew Cunningham and Air Chief Marshal Sir Charles Portal. The United States was represented by General George Marshall (of Marshall Plan fame) and Fleet Admiral King. The Russians and the French also sent senior representatives. 'It was a moving spectacle,' recalls George Hodgkinson, then a subaltern in A Squadron, 'as we drove six armoured cars abreast along the Charlottenburg Chaussee.'

Afterwards Churchill opened a soldiers' club, named after him, in the Kurfürstendamm and addressed his audience thus:

'Soldiers of the 7th Armoured Division, I am delighted to be able to open this club and I shall always consider it a great honour that it should have been named after me.

'I have, not for the first time, had the pleasure of seeing your troops march past, and this brings back to my mind a great many moving incidents in these last, long, fierce years.

'Now, here in Berlin, I find you all established in this great centre, from which, as from a volcano, fire and smoke and poison fumes have erupted all over Europe twice in a generation. And in bygone times also German fury has been let loose on her neighbours, and now it is we who have our place in the occupation of this country . . .

'Now I have only a word more to say about the Desert Rats! Dear Desert Rats!! May your glory every shine! May your laurels never fade! May the memory of this glorious pilgrimage of war which you have made from Alamein, via the Baltic to Berlin, never die! It is a march unsurpassed through all the story of war so far as my reading of history leads me to believe. May the fathers long tell the children about this tale. May you all feel that in following your great ancestors you have accomplished something which has done good to the whole world, which has raised the honour of your country and which every man has a right to be proud of.'

To everyone's surprise, not least his own, as he left the Winston Club he was cheered and clapped by a crowd of Germans. It seems that for once he was at a loss for a suitable response and only half-raised his arm in acknowledgement.

That evening the 11th Hussars held their Victory Dinner in the Officers' Mess at Von Seekt Barracks. Among the guests were Anthony Eden, Field Marshals Alexander and Maitland

Wilson and the commander of 22nd Armoured Brigade, Brigadier 'Looney' Hinde.

It will be recalled that until the recent collapse of East Germany and its reunification with the West, Berlin, like Germany as a whole, had been divided into British, French, American and Russian sectors. However, before the construction of the infamous Berlin Wall there were few physical barriers and both civilians and Allied soldiers could move more or less unimpeded from one sector to another. This sometimes led to incidents, even confrontation, between troops of the various nationalities; principally, needless to say, between the Russians and the Western Allies. One officer of the Regiment was fired on by a Russian, who fortunately missed, and at least one British soldier was killed by Soviet troops.

Black-marketeering was widespread among officers and men of all nationalities and once a Russian general was arrested by the British Military Police in the course of a raid on a 'thieves' kitchen'. Black-market prices were astronomical and the potential profit huge. A loaf of *Brotbaum* (illegal) bread could cost the equivalent of £2 10s and coffee £10–£12 a pound. It was said, only half in jest, that the cheapest commodity was a girl, at about half a crown! Cigarettes were regarded as currency and had often nearly disintegrated before being smoked.

Basic rations for the German population were barely sufficient to support life, so anyone with any money spent it on the black market. The main suppliers were, of course, the Allied Occupation Forces themselves. Here was a never-to-be-repeated chance to turn a dishonest penny and few resisted the temptation. Anyway, in most cases the degree of dishonesty was marginal and may even have served to keep alive some people who could otherwise have died. Even real estate was traded for food and fuel and one (probably mythical) lance-corporal was rumoured to have acquired several blocks of flats in this way. An unlikely story as few were still standing!

Many varied and strange duties fell to members of the Regiment. Lieutenant (now Doctor) Anthony Flood found himself, perhaps appropriately, in charge of a trainload of mutilated German POWs, who had been dumped in the British sector by the Russians. There being no accommodation for these poor wretches in Berlin, Flood was ordered to take them to Munsterlager, normally about twenty-four hours' distance by rail, in cattle-trucks. To look after 1,000 seriously wounded men he was provided with four or five German nurses. Constantly obstructed *en route* through the Russian zone, the journey took seven days and nights in the course of which, at various stages, the Soviets removed the engine; arrested Flood himself (and released him); tried to abduct and rape the nurses and lost one of their own men, shot by the guards on the train. To cap it all, Dr Flood discovered that the rations with which he had been provided to feed his prisoners had been looted and the tins of bully-beef replaced with lumps of coal, itself a valuable commodity which, he reminded himself later, could have been 'flogged on the black market for a good few marks'!

Miraculously, he seems to have delivered his pathetic cargo, mostly still alive, to Munsterlager and returned to Berlin more or less unscathed.

Lieutenant (now Sir Charles) Markham recalls being given the task of equipping the Officers' Mess with cutlery and other furnishings. Aided by a sinister Communist burgomaster, Markham was able to 'borrow' many of these items from various householders who, according to the burgomaster, were Nazis and whose names and addresses he had listed in a large book.

Cutlery and other silverware in adequate quantities and of high quality was also discovered in the Imperial Japanese Embassy in the course of a search spearheaded by a trooper who had graduated into the Regiment from Borstal.

However, the *pièce de résistance* of the Mess was a vast blue carpet liberated from Hitler's Chancellery. Originally forty yards long and twenty wide, it took an entire troop to load it on to a lorry. Sadly it has not survived the many subsequent moves.

In September the new Colonel of the Regiment, Major-General John Combe, who had recently taken over from Brigadier-General Sir Archibald Home, visited Berlin and three months later Lieutenant-Colonel Bill Wainman, whose service with the Regiment had been unbroken since the outbreak of war, handed over to Lieutenant-Colonel Peter Payne-Gallwey. Wainman's health had been deteriorating since before the end of the war, a fact which he had managed to conceal with his usual undaunted courage, but which was to lead to his tragically premature death some five years later.

The first year of peace saw the return to the Regiment of the 'Stonebreakers', those who had been unfortunate enough to be taken prisoner during the war, including Majors Pitman and Halliday, Sergeant-Major Howarth and Trooper Nightingale.

There were also some losses, in particular the death in a car accident of Sergeant D. J. Fitzpatrick, MM, a man who, in the words of his obituary, 'had spent the whole war surviving a succession of unpleasant incidents'. By a strange quirk of fate his troop leader, Lieutenant (later Lieutenant-Colonel) Dick Sutton, with whom Fitzpatrick had been taken prisoner in Belgium in 1944, was to die in the same tragic way many years later.

By the spring of 1946 the Regiment was on the move again, first to Wolfenbüttel, a few miles south of Brunswick and then to Jever near Wilhelmshaven. In the course of these moves there were many goodbyes, including the departure of Willy Cracco, the Belgian interpreter, who had witnessed and photographed the historic appearance of Admiral von Friedeburg on 4 May, 1945. There was much satisfaction when, in due course, he was appointed MBE.

While at Jever the Regiment was called upon to send a demonstration team to Denmark and a party under Major John Turnbull with Lieutenants George Hodgkinson, Dick Sutton and SQMS Cameron left for the town of Randers where it was accommodated and entertained by the Jydske Dragoons. SQMS Cameron, demonstrating the 75mm gun on the Staghound heavy armoured car, demolished not only all the wooden targets but the butts as well!

Another departure was that of RSM Jimmy Moore, a recipient of the French *Croix de Guerre*. His replacement was RSM 'Soapy' Hudson. This was Hudson's second appointment as

RSM, a position he had held in 1941/42 before being posted to the RAC Depot at Catterick.

The war over, the British Army was able to return, in the immortal words of a Guards Sergeant-Major, to 'real soldiering', a way of life in which sports of all kind loomed large. In Berlin the 1936 Olympic Stadium was used for cricket, soccer, rugby and athletics: the local Siemens factory provided squash-courts and the former German Officers' Club boasted no fewer than nineteen hard tennis-courts which doubled as ice-rinks when they froze in winter. A 'pack' was formed and Lieutenant 'Squire' Jaffray appointed Master of Hounds, a motley collection consisting of a Newfoundland, a Pointer, two Alsatians and two Spaniels. The pack's most productive country was a sewage farm, but it will come as little surprise to the reader that no kills were reported and the hunt does not seem to have survived the move to Wolfenbüttel.

Shooting in Germany in the mid and late 1940s was something of a free-for-all. German civilians, generally speaking, were forbidden sporting guns and the Allied Occupation Forces, so long as they did not encroach upon each other's territory, had more or less the run of the countryside. In the late 1946/47 season the following remarkable total bag was recorded: 556 pheasants, 466 partridges, 325 hares, 46 teal, 20 widgeon, 9 shoveller, 3 gadwall, 2 shelduck, one tufted, 21 pinkfoot, 6 whitefront, 11 barnacle, 29 snipe, 5 woodcock, 40 pigeon, 21 various.

The next move, in April, 1947, was to Delmenhorst near Bremen, described as 'a pleasant town with a noisy main street which never seems to be empty or free from road repairs'. But this was, once again, little more than a transit stop and in February of the following year, the Regiment was on the road again, this time to Osnabrück. Prior to that, however, in January, C Squadron under Major Tommy Pitman was dispatched to Berlin again where trouble with the Russians was brewing. The Cold War had begun.

Perhaps, with the collapse of the Soviet Union, the Kremlin archives may soon reveal more of the origins of the Berlin

Blockade than we know at the time of writing. However, there is little doubt that the plan, dreamed up in the recesses of Stalin's evil mind, was to drive the Allies out of Berlin. The Western presence was becoming an increasingly grave embarrassment to the Russians. As recovery and prosperity burgeoned under capitalism so, in stark contrast, did the Communist system in East Berlin (and in East Germany as a whole) stagnate and fester.

The Marshall Plan for the reconstruction of Europe was already showing signs of success and standards of living were beginning to rise everywhere except in those areas under the heel of the Soviets. However, in Germany inflation was rife and the Reichsmark virtually worthless. This was in part due to excessive printing of paper money by the Russians. The Western Powers were determined to rectify this potentially disastrous situation (memories of the fall of the Mark in the 1920s were still quite fresh) and secretly planned a currency reform without the knowledge of the Russians. This was announced on 20 June, 1948, to come into effect next day. At first Berlin was excluded from the use of this new currency, the Deutschmark, but, after failing to agree its implementation with the Russians, the Allies introduced it unilaterally on 25 June.

The Soviets had been impeding and harassing traffic between Berlin and the Allied zones of West Germany since March but the crunch came on 24 June when they halted all passenger, goods and water traffic to and from Berlin. On the following day they announced the prohibition of all food supplies to the Western sectors of Berlin and the largest and longest air supply operation in history, known as the Berlin Airlift, began.

The Allied garrison consisted of about 6,500 men of whom some 2,000 were British, including C Squadron, 11th Hussars, the Norfolks, the Worcesters and the Queens. In any armed conflict they would probably have been quickly overwhelmed by the 18,000-strong Russian garrison, reinforced from the 30,000 men of the Soviet Occupation Army in East Germany which, unlike the Allies in West Germany, would have had unopposed access to the city.

The officers who moved to Berlin with C Squadron under

Tommy Pitman were Major E. W. (Gus) Penny, Captain E. S. N. (Nobby) Clarke – he of the 'first shot of the war' – and 2nd Lieutenants Harding, Gosling and Hall. The SSM and SQMS were WO2s Howarth and H. Smith. However, in order to give as many members of the Regiment as possible experience 'at the sharp end', personnel, particularly officers, were rotated every few months. Tommy Pitman himself remained in command throughout the Squadron's fifteen-month tour in Berlin and got married in the process.

The blockade and airlift lasted for nearly a year during which potential flash-points were numerous. Although with the wisdom of hindsight it seems unlikely that the Russians had any intention of starting a war (they did not yet have an operationally effective atomic bomb), at the time it was felt that the most insignificant incident – say, a confrontation between an Allied sentry and a drunken Russian (by no means a rare species) – might precipitate the Third World War.

A particularly serious incident occurred on the very first night of the blockade. News reached the Worcesters at Montgomery Barracks, Kladow, that Russian troops were loading scrap metal on to railway trucks at Lehrter Railway Depot in the British sector. Elements of the Worcesters, Norfolks and a troop of C Squadron under Captain de Quincy of the Worcesters managed to bluff the Russian colonel in charge into believing that the British were in far greater strength and prepared to use force to prevent the removal of the scrap. In fact there was no such determination on the part of the British Headquarters in Berlin and reference was made to Downing Street for instructions. Mr Attlee and, above all, his Foreign Secretary, Ernest Bevin, men of strong nerves and firm resolution, ordered the British garrison commander to hold firm for at least twenty-four hours. The ploy worked and by midmorning the next day the Russians had unloaded the scrap and departed. Whether this was a test of Allied resolve or simply an attempt by a local Russian commander to steal some scrap metal will never be known, but at least it had the effect at an early stage of establishing that the Allies were (apparently) prepared to risk armed conflict in defence of their rights.

But there was also a lighter side to the Blockade and Ian Bruce, one of the 'rotated' C Squadron officers, tells the story of Dusty and his escape from Berlin:

'The Blockade trapped Dusty, Tommy Pitman's Grade A Hanoverian show jumper, in Berlin, along with some less distinguished German horses adopted by C Squadron. We rode them in the Grünewald, fed them *Havel* grass [chopped reeds from the lake's edge] despite the vets' warning that it took more energy for a horse to digest it than it replaced, and fantasized, some of us, that when the Squadron's job of defending Gatow Airport was done, we stood a better chance of escape on a horse than in a Daimler Armoured Car!

'We planned to save Dusty, at least, for a more glorious and better-nourished future back with the Regiment in the British zone, a hundred Russian-patrolled miles west.

'Hans Kuhse, recently a German gunner officer and later the Regiment's stable manager at Osnabruck and Wesendorf (later still Charles and Molly Sivewright's in Gloucestershire), volunteered to drive Dusty to freedom, if he would be driven. A suitable cart was found and bought for coffee beans. Screened from public curiosity, in the vast ruins of the Olympic Stadium, disenchanted Dusty was persuaded with whip and rationed carrots to pull the cart round and round Hitler's arena in endless laps of dishonour.

'Kuhse, meanwhile, was equipped with a wide range of polyglot papers of doubtful value, rations and blankets for himself and Dusty and the address of a friendly farmer on the Helmstedt border where he would, God and the Russians permitting, rendezvous with an officer of the Royal Dragoons, whose patch of Germany it was, at 0300 hrs six nights and two frontiers later.

'The exodus went miraculously well, Kuhse reported after their escape, until, safely back in the West, Dusty celebrated his release from the shafts by kicking bits off the Royals' three-tonner and cutting his leg to the bone. He was "off games" for months, but recovered to win prizes when Tommy rejoined him from Berlin, by air!'

In due course the Blockade ended with a whimper rather than a bang. By January, 1949, it was becoming obvious to Stalin that he was losing the first major battle of the Cold War. It seemed to him that the Allies had both the capacity and the will to maintain the airlift almost indefinitely. Furthermore, Allied counter-restrictions on the shipment of coal, steel and other commodities from West to East Germany were biting.

Negotiations between the US and USSR delegates at the United Nations began in February and on 12 May the Blockade was lifted. A formula had been found to save Stalin's face but he had achieved nothing. By then C Squadron had already rejoined the Regiment at Osnabrück in time to take part, on 6 May, in a parade to dedicate the Memorial to the one hundred and fifty officers and men of the Regiment who fell in the Second World War. The Memorial, which may now be seen in the Regimental Museum, was unveiled by the Commander-in-Chief BAOR, General Sir Brian Robertson, in the presence of Major-General John Combe, representing the Colonel-in-Chief, His Majesty King George the Sixth; the Army Commander, General Sir Charles Keightley, and Brigadier R. P. (Perry) Harding, commanding 7th Armoured Brigade.

Draped with Union flags, the oak-panelled Memorial was guarded by Sergeants Christie and Cowley, who had known many of the fallen personally, in full-dress uniform. After an address by the Commander-in-Chief, the laying of wreaths and a Service of Dedication, the Regiment marched past in slow time.

Among those on parade were SQMS (later RSM) Leslie Greensides whose brother, Lance-Corporal S. J. Greensides, had been killed in action in 1945 and whose name appears on the Memorial.

Of the many veterans of the war serving with the Regiment were five Polish soldiers, all of whom had enlisted in the 11th Hussars after the most amazing adventures. Corporal Joseph Modelski, a farmer's son, had, from the age of fifteen, been a slave-labourer for the Germans and an underground fighter against them. Later he was arrested by the Russians, but escaped to the Polish forces in Italy with whom he served as a wireless operator and storeman. After the war, via the Polish Resettlement Corps, he joined the 11th Hussars in Germany and served much of his career in the Quartermaster's department under the formidable Major Reg Chadwick. In Malaya he took part in a notable anti-terrorist operation – but that story comes later.

Lance-Corporal Rudolph Skrabania had been taken to Germany as a slave-labourer while still a schoolboy. Later transferred to France, he was liberated by the Americans and joined the Polish Army in 1944. In 1948 he enlisted in the 11th Hussars and, as a German speaker, became a clerk in the Intelligence Office.

The experiences of Lance-Corporals Murias and Morzajew and Trooper Jan Cichocki were even more remarkable. All three eventually found their way into the Regiment via Stalin's Siberian labour camps, 'the Gulag Archipelago', escaping to Tashkent, travelling through Iran and Iraq to Palestine and finally joining the Regiment together from the Polish Resettlement Corps. From the age of fifteen Cichocki had carried his young sister, sharing the burden with his mother, some 250 kilometres from the labour camp to Uzbekistan, finally reaching Palestine in 1942. Murias, taking more or less the same route, had to wear the boots of a man who had frozen to death next to him in the night as his own had been stolen. These men survived under conditions in which millions had died and, if they were lucky to be alive, the Regiment was fortunate to have them in its ranks.

But life for the British Army in Germany was (and still is) a good deal less exciting; indeed perhaps the greatest hardship the average soldier had to endure was boredom. 'Ceiling' mileages and strictly rationed ammunition kept training to a minimum. The soldiers, many of them National Servicemen, spent most of their working hours tinkering with already over-maintained vehicles and weapons. Until well into the 1950s the re-equipment of the army was low on the list of Government priorities. It seemed that all available resources were to be given to the new-born Welfare State. As far as the reconnaissance regiments were concerned their principal fighting vehicle, the Daimler Armoured Car, remained in service until the late 1950s, over fifteen years after it had been introduced in the North

African campaign. The Dingo, Humber and White scout-cars, as well as the 'soft-skinned' vehicles, were equally ancient and dilapidated, constantly in and out of workshops, having covered tens of thousands of miles across deserts and over mountains and forest tracks. Small arms such as the Lee-Enfield .303 rifle and the Bren and Sten guns were still standard and communications equipment, principally the 19 Set, had all seen much rough wartime service.

Wireless communication was, by today's standards, primitive and the 'wireless procedure' of some of the older members of the Regiment left something to be desired. One pre-war veteran, summoned to the set to speak to his squadron leader in his troop leader's absence, was heard bellowing into the microphone, "Ullo, Sir, I'm 'ere!' – no doubt to the mystification of the Russian listeners monitoring the exercise.

Regular interruptions to the even tenor of life in Germany were the Great Autumn Exercises when one or more divisions of BAOR, sometimes with Allied reinforcements, would be pitted against each other across huge tracts of heath, forest and farmland. These were the nearest most soldiers, particularly National Servicemen, came to the 'real thing'. For an armoured car regiment they were principally wireless exercises.

The actual distances driven were small as the AFVs were transported by rail from barracks to exercise area and back, and few, if any, weapons were fired. Those who took part will have vivid memories of loading and unloading vehicles on and off railway flat-beds in pitch darkness and driving rain. Thanks chiefly to the guiding skill of the troop sergeants and corporals few ended up sideways or upside-down on the railway track! Most would agree that the best part of these manoeuvres was getting back to a hot bath and a square meal after days of compo rations and wet bivvies.

Sometimes these departures and returns to and from exercise had unfortunate, even dramatic, consequences. On one occasion an officer left his dog, a large Boxer, with a subaltern who was to stay behind as duty officer during the exercise. Unfortunately the subaltern was a man who, perhaps unconsciously, had a strangely hypnotic effect upon animals (he was also a mighty hunter). On returning from the exercise and going to the subaltern's room to collect his dog, the owner found that it had no intention of going with him; indeed when force was exerted the animal flew at its master, savaging him about the arms and face. Rabies being endemic in Germany, drastic measures had to be taken and, as even the subaltern could do nothing with the enraged beast, it had to be shot through the glass top of the bedroom door. However, when the brain was analysed no disease was found.

Apart from these exercises perhaps the most taxing and stressful event in a trooper's routine was Guard Parade. Although at this time the only uniform in use by other ranks was khaki battle-dress, the standard of turnout was extremely high. Best boots of dazzling brightness were the oustanding feature of the parade and various closely-kept cleaning techniques and magical formulas were used to achieve the most blindingly brilliant effect upon the inspecting Orderly Officer, in whose gift was the award of the cherished Stick. This meant that the man appointed Stick Orderly (the real meaning of the term is lost in the mists of tradition) was excused further guard duty for a considerable time.

Sometimes the Orderly Officer's duties were not so purely formal. One former National Service subaltern recalls an urgent summons from the Café Wilkens, the only pub in the village of Wesendorf (whither the Regiment moved after Osnabrück), which a number of the rougher elements were in the process of reducing to rubble. On arrival in the village, accompanied by the Orderly Sergeant-Major and several members of the guard armed with pick-helves, concealing his funk the young officer made to advance boldly through the door of the café, but the politely restraining hand of the Sergeant-Major touched his shoulder. 'Best you stay out here, Sir; if one of our blokes thumps you he's in real trouble!' The advice was taken, without too much reluctance, and the dull thud of hickory on flesh soon brought the rumpus to an end. Shouting, swearing and singing raucously, in some cases bleeding and vomiting, these fine representatives of the Regiment were loaded on to a three-tonner while the Orderly Officer began damage assessment with the irate proprietor. While this was in progress a young German civilian confronted the officer and bawled in English: 'You keep your British soldiers out of here; this place is for German people!' Feeling at something of a disadvantage the subaltern held his peace, but afterwards reflected upon what might have been the reaction of his equivalent in the German Army of Occupation in the United Kingdom had the fortunes of war taken a different turn.

1949 saw the retirement of many regimental stalwarts includng Lieutenant-Colonel Payne-Gallwey, the holder of no less than three DSOs, who handed over command to Lieutenant-Colonel Tony Robarts; Majors David Lloyd and Toby Horsford, Captain Tony Hunter and RSM Hudson, who was replaced by RSM E. G. Scrivener, also departed for civilian life, but A Squadron was resuscitated under Major Tony Crankshaw after nearly two years in suspended animation.

In the *Journal* of that year the death of Mr David Chapman, at the age of 87, was reported. Mr Chapman, who had joined the Regiment in 1879, was probably the last survivor of the two officers and forty-three men who had formed the 11th Hussar detachment in General Wolseley's Light Camel Regiment which took part in the Gordon Relief Expedition of 1884/85. He had retired as a Squadron Sergeant-Major in 1901 but was commissioned in an infantry regiment in the First World War.

Early in 1950 rumours started to circulate of the Regiment's imminent return to the United Kingdom, where it had not been seen, apart from a brief sojourn in preparation for the Normandy landings, since 1934. First it was to be Barnard Castle, then Trowbridge; Linneyhead in Wales, Hereford, Tidworth and Omagh in Northern Ireland followed in quick succession. Eventually, in July, an Advance Party under Captain I. M. Davies was dispatched to Carlisle. Among those who accompanied him were Corporals Barker and Gregory, Lance-Corporal Elkington and Bandsman Raper, the latter three arriving in time to sound the trumpets for the opening of the Carlisle Assizes. However, for reasons probably known only to some obscure clerk in the War Office, the main move never took place and Captain Davies – something of a specialist in commanding Advance Parties, for he led a more successful one to Malaya a few years later – and his men returned to Germany in October in time to move from Osnabrück to Wesendorf with the rest of the Regiment.

Wesendorf, the nearest British garrison to the East German fronter, was a somewhat bleak former *Luftwaffe* barracks and airfield within easy striking distance of the pleasant towns of Celle and Brunswick and the Harz Mountains. It was to be the Regiment's last 'home' in Germany for many years and in some respects its stay there was marked with sadness.

Shortly before the move Lieutenant-Colonel W. Wainman DSO MC died in London after a long illness at the tragically early age of forty-two. Bill Wainman was born in London in 1908 but when his father was killed in action in 1916, his mother took him and his two brothers to Canada where he spent an unconventional and adventurous youth working as a drummer in a dance band, a taxi-driver and a lumberjack. Eventually returning to England he was commissioned in the Regiment in 1929. A fine horseman and polo player, life in Egypt in the 1930s suited him well. Adjutant at the outbreak of war, he progressed to commanding a squadron in the desert, where he was awarded the Military Cross, and the Regiment itself from Normandy to Berlin, thus serving with the 11th Hussars without a break from the beginning to the end of the war. His period of wartime command was rewarded with the DSO but the strain of five years of unbroken front-line service had taken its toll upon his health. After the war, ably assisted by another PAO of renown, RSM Jimmy Moore, he commanded the 59th Training Regiment RAC and is still remembered with affection and respect by those whose first taste of Army life was experienced in the austere surroundings of Catterick in the 1940s. Returning briefly to the 11th Hussars in 1948, his health soon deteriorated further (he was suffering from Hodgkin's Disease) to the extent that he was forced to retire to Ireland. Early in 1950 he returned to England where he died on 28 September. Bill Wainman was perhaps the most universally popular Colonel the 11th Hussars ever had, of whom one of his subalterns wrote, 'I do not think any Commanding Officer could have been better loved, more admired and more readily obeyed. Under such a man it was hard *not* to be a good soldier.' Two crowded memorial services were held in his memory, one in London and one in Germany.

A few months later another Regimental hero, this time of the First World War, died. Lieutenant-Colonel T. G. (Tom) Upton OBE DCM had started life as an ironmonger's apprentice in Eastbourne but in 1904 he 'went for a soldier' against his family's wishes and joined first the 13th and then the 11th Hussars. Rising through the ranks with great rapidity, by 1915 he was RSM of the Regiment in France where he was awarded the DCM and commissioned in the field. From 1919 to 1932 he was Quartermaster. A great rifle shot and football coach, he won many prizes and cups in these sports, both for the Regiment and as an individual. After a period as Quartermaster at Sandhurst he retired to become Lord Leigh's agent at Stoneleigh Abbey where he died in harness at the age of sixty-seven on 21 March, 1951. His son, Lieutenant-Colonel Peter Upton, served with the Regiment for many years and was Regimental Secretary to The Royal Hussars until his retirement in 1984.

A shock to the Regiment, and to the nation, was the early death in 1952 of its Colonel-in Chief, King George the Sixth, on which occasion Major-General John Combe as Colonel of the Regiment sent the following telegram to Her Majesty the Queen: 'With humble duty all ranks 11th Hussars past and present send their most sincere and heartfelt sympathy on the death of their Colonel-in-Chief and assure Your Majesty of their extreme loyalty.' Later General Combe marched in His Majesty's funeral procession together with the Colonels of the Royals, the Scots Greys and the Royal Tank Regiment.

These years saw the retirement of the Regiment's oldest serving soldier, Sergeant P. W. Knight MSM who had joined the 11th Hussars in 1914 and left for the last time in 1950. Of these thirty-six years 'Algy' Knight had spent all but half-a-dozen serving with the Regiment, including four years in the trenches in the First World War. His last job was that of Provost Sergeant in charge of the dreaded Regimental Police, a turn-up for the prisoners for, in the words of the *Journal*'s editor, Algy 'was an old and true friend who has set us all an example in loyalty and kindness which we shall seldom see equalled.'

Another Old Warrior who soon followed him into retirement was Corporal Nightingale, one of the former 'Stonebreakers' (POWs). After twenty-five years' service with the Regiment he finally accepted promotion, got married and departed for the unfamiliar hazards of civilian life. Marriage was something of an epidemic at Wesendorf where no less than fifty-eight 11th Hussars took unto themselves wives, nineteen of them German ladies. There must have been something in the tea!

But it was something in the ground which made a former 11th Hussar who had emigrated to Canada at the turn of the century probably the richest-ever Cherrypicker. A butcher's boy from Lincolnshire, William Henry Wright enlisted in the Regiment in about 1895. Sent on draft to the Boer War he served at Ladysmith. The war over, he left the Army and sailed, penniless, for Canada where, after many adventures and incredible hardships, he and his partner struck gold. By the outbreak of the First World War he was earning the equivalent of £600,000 a year – many millions in today's terms – but this did not prevent him from enlisting in the Canadian Army as a private and serving in France. Later he owned several newspapers and, true to his origins as a cavalryman, retained an interest in horseflesh until his death in 1951.

This interest in horseflesh has, of course, been shared by many 11th Hussars over the years. In the post-Second World War era several former members of the Regiment have distinguished themselves in the racing world. These have included Peter Payne-Gallwey who trained for the flat and National Hunt, Peter Hamer who served the Jockey Club as an administrator, Miles Gosling a steward of both the Jockey Club and the National Hunt Committee, Tim Forster who trained no less than three Grand National winners and Ivan Straker who, as Chairman of Seagrams, rescued that great race with sponsorship.

In 1952 Lieutenant-Colonel Tony Robarts handed over command to Lieutenant-Colonel Peter Arkwright and RSM Scrivener to RSM C. P. Lamb, whose record of war service with the Regiment was second to none, earning him both the DCM and MM in the desert. Soon rumours began to circulate that the Regiment would be on the move again before long and by the end of the year the word Malaya began to be murmured. (One former officer claims that he first heard the news from a German civilian petrol-pump attendant at Gifhorn, just down the road from Wesendorf!)

Once confirmed, frenzied activity began. This was to be a three-year tour so there were many arrangements to be made, both Regimental and personal. Officers and men with less than a year to serve would be posted elsewhere to complete their service, but at least one of these signed a Type C engagement extending his service for a further year in order not to miss the adventure. As this particular form of contract with Her Majesty has never been heard of before or since, there are those who are convinced that it was the resourceful invention of the then Adjutant, Captain David Sivewright. In the event, some 162 men were lost on posting or release, while 184 joined the Regiment before departure.

In March, 1953, the exceptionally diligent Major Davies, the Advance Party specialist, left Wesendorf for Aldershot on the first leg of the 8,000-mile haul to Malaya. On this occasion he was accompanied by Captain Jim Benson, who had been with the 8th Hussars in Korea, representing B Squadron; Lieutenants Eddie Farquhar (C) and John Trotter (A); 2nd Lieutenants Patrick Langrishe (C), Henry Keown-Boyd (A) and Ian Haig (B), with thirty-four Other Ranks.

On arrival at Waterloo Barracks, Aldershot, the Advance Party was struck by what today would be described as a 'culture shock'. Accustomed to nice, clean, well-appointed German barracks, officers and men found themselves in a squalid, dilapidated dump. It was said that the place had been condemned as unfit for human habitation over half a century earlier but no one had told the War Office. As an example of its structural condition, the floor of one of the barrack rooms had a wide wall-to-wall gap in it through which could be seen the (uninhabited) stables below, a hazard which had to be traversed in order to reach the insanitary washroom at one end. However, with embarkation leave and other duties and preparations, little time was spent in the barracks and on 9 April the Advance Party sailed from Liverpool in the SS *Empire Pride*. The main body of the Regiment reached Aldershot on 31 March and sailed for Singapore in the SS *Empire Clyde* on 28 May, 66% of its strength being Regulars and the remainder National Servicemen.

Before reaching Malaya perhaps we should return momentarily to Wesendorf. On leaving 7th Armoured Division after fourteen years and perhaps for ever, the Regiment paraded before the Divisional Commander, Major-General 'Splosh' Jones who, in an address after taking the salute, thanked the Regiment for its services to the Division and wished it Godspeed. He did not, however, confirm a request, believed to have been made privately, that the 11th Hussars should be permitted to wear a Desert Rat on their cuffs in perpetuity, had been granted as, indeed, it had not. Presumably it was felt that such a request, if allowed, might set an awkward precedent.

A few days after the Regiment sailed Her Majesty Queen Elizabeth the Second was crowned at Westminster. The 11th Hussars contingent which took part was commanded by Captain John Woodhouse MC and consisted of SSM L. Greensides, Sergeant Jack Christie, Corporal F. D. Haith, Lance-Corporal (later Major) J. M. Lemon, Troopers E. Gathercole and J. Nelson. Although drenching rain ruined hours of 'bulling', pressing and blancoing, it was an unforgettable experience for the participants. The New Elizabethan Age had dawned.

Chapter 9

MALAYA 1953–56

At half-past eight on the morning of 16 June, 1948, a British rubber planter called Walker was murdered by terrorists on his estate near Ipoh in the State of Perak. Half an hour later and ten miles away two other planters suffered the same fate. These outrages marked the beginning of what soon became known as the Malayan Emergency, a political euphemism for a full-scale terrorist campaign which, over the next dozen years, was to involve tens of thousands of men from many nations of the Commonwealth and Empire. Before it was over, at least 11,000 people had been killed in action or murdered, including 7,000 Communist terrorists (officially CTs; unofficially 'bandits'), and 2,000 members of the security forces.

Despite the length of time taken to destroy a guerrilla force which probably never exceeded a strength of 5,000 men and women at any one time, the Malayan campaign was the most completely successful fought by British-led forces throughout the era of our retreat from empire. At the end of it, Malaya (now Malaysia) emerged independent, prosperous, secure and on reasonably good terms with the former colonial power. Above all, the native Malay people had been rescued from the potential tyranny of an alien philosophy, which a small section of an immigrant race, the Chinese, had attempted to impose upon them.

Briefly, the origins of the Emergency lay in the Japanese conquest of Malaya and Singapore in 1941, when British Imperial forces, greatly superior in numbers to their Asiatic conquerors, were seen by the populations of those countries to be ignominiously defeated after a far from heroic defence. As was also the case in many of the European countries occupied by the Germans at that time, the main resistance to the new masters came from the Communists. Backed by the famous Force 136 under Colonel Spencer Chapman, the Malayan Peoples' Anti-Japanese Army, consisting largely of Chinese Communists, harassed the Japanese throughout the four years of their occupation and emerged from the war admired, respected and, above all, armed.

Inspired by incipient signs of the decline of the British Empire and by Mao Tse Tung's successes against the Chinese Nationalists, it was no great step for these former resistance fighters to change their name and objective from anti-Japanese to anti-British. But the movement was in practice as much anti-Malay as anti-British. If Malaya was to be granted independence, and the British made it clear at an early stage after the war that this was their policy, then the Chinese, especially the Communists, could see no advantage to them in the country being handed back to the Malays. The Malays themselves, on the whole a passive people not given to great exertions of any kind, had played no significant role in resisting the Japanese who, generally speaking, had left them to their own devices. Much of the commerce of the country was already in Chinese hands and many of the skilled artisans were Chinese, as indeed was a large minority of the population as a whole. Therefore it did not seem illogical (or unattainable) to the Communist leader, Chin Peng, and his followers that the government of Malaya should be handed over to them rather than to the Malay majority as represented by the Malay politicians and the Sultans of the various States of the Federation, whom they regarded as reactionary anachronisms.

At first the methods used by the Communists, who were already dominant in the trade unions, to oust the British prematurely and to seize power for themselves, were principally industrial and economic; strikes, the intimidation of workers, especially on the rubber estates, and sabotage. But it soon became clear that these methods by themselves would be at best too slow and at worst futile, so, at a jungle conference of leading Communists in early June, 1948, a military strategy was devised. Rubber being Malaya's most important product and largely British-owned, the main human targets were to be the British plantation managers, their families and employees.

A force of some 5,000 trained personnel of the former Anti-Japanese Army was available, as were jungle camps and caches of food, weapons and ammunition provided by the British during the war but hidden in secret locations. Additionally the Communists controlled a network of spies and informers, many in the Civil Service or on the staffs of British officials, planters and businessmen.

The first reactions of the British administration under the Governor, Sir Edward Gent, were slow. Gent refused to recognize the terrorists as a serious threat and, on paper at least, his military position was fairly strong. Against Chin Peng's apparently puny force he had at his disposal over 10,000 policemen and eleven battalions of British, Gurkha and Malay infantry. But, as ever in such circumstances, the terrorists held the initiative. Moreover, despite the lessons which should have been learned from the Japanese invasion, the security forces were largely untrained in jungle warfare.

Shortly after declaring the Emergency in June, 1948, Gent, who had been summoned to London for 'consultations' – in other words, to be sacked – was killed in an air crash. He was replaced by the more robust Sir Henry Gurney, who, careless of his own security, was to die in an ambush in October, 1951. However, by that time the tide had already begun slowly to turn against the terrorists. Their main source of supplies, information and recruits were the Chinese villagers, known as 'squatters', who inhabited the fringes of the jungle and rubber estates. Under the Briggs Plan, a scheme devised by the Director of Operations, General Sir Harold Briggs and his chief security adviser, Sir Robert Thompson, these people were re-settled in protected areas known as New Villages. This made it much more difficult for them to provide help and succour to the terrorists in the jungle. Also by then the security forces had improved their efficiency and training and their numbers had been increased. For a few months after Gurney's murder the situation stagnated. Then, at the insistence of Winston Churchill, who had been returned to power as Prime Minister in the 1951 General Election, a combined civil and military supremo was appointed for Malaya.

A slight, wiry infantryman, General (later Field-Marshal) Sir Gerald Templer was perhaps the most able and dynamic soldier-administrator of the latter years of the British Empire, comparing favourably in stature and achievement with such giants of the past as Kitchener and Allenby. It would be unfair to all the others who played their parts, great and small, to say that it was Templer who destroyed the Malayan People's Liberation Army, but it was under his inspired leadership that the circumstances which made this possible were brought about.

Although, during his tenure of office, which lasted a little over two years, Templer was involved as much in civil affairs as military, here we are really only concerned with the latter. The Malayan campaign was primarily an infantryman's war. Working usually on information but sometimes 'on spec', the infantry – British, Gurkha, Malay, Australian, New Zealand, Rhodesian, Fijian and West African – would sweat and hack their way through the steaming twilight of the jungle in pursuit of the bandits, covering scores of miles for every kill or capture. Most of the information with which they were provided was obtained by the police Special Branch through the interrogation (sometimes none too gentle) of captured CTs or from informers and turncoats who received substantial bounties in return for the deaths, capture or surrender of their former comrades. But such intelligence was not always readily passed on to the Army by the police who preferred to set their own ambushes and traps for the enemy. In fact the police, through the activities not only of their own infantry, known as Jungle Companies, but also the covert operations of their Special Branch detectives (themselves mostly Chinese), accounted for over 50% of terrorist 'kills' during the Emergency. At the same time they suffered 70% of security force casualties.

The role of the armoured-car regiments (no tanks were used) in Malaya was regarded, understandably, as 'cushy' by the infantry. Nonetheless, responsible for keeping roads and plantation tracks open, convoying food and escorting VIPs, the cavalry played an important role in containing the terrorist threat, though opportunities for 'jungle bashing', to the relief of many, were limited and therefore the number of kills and captures achieved were small.

In mid-1953 the 11th Hussars arrived in Malaya to take over from the 13th/18th Hussars in the States of Selangor, Negri Sembilan and Johore, thus embarking upon their last 'shooting' war, a curious kind of war with an enemy seldom encountered or even seen. Perhaps less than 10% of the Regiment ever saw a bandit, at any rate a live and active one. It has been suggested that the presence of the cavalry regiments in Malaya by about 1952 was largely 'decorative', in the words of the famous phrase, 'lending tone to a vulgar brawl'. This is unfair and there can be little doubt that the constant patrolling of the arteries of commerce and the convoying of all food distribution did much to deter terrorist activity and to deny them vital supplies.

To arrive in Singapore is to enter a large open-air sauna. Although the climate has not changed, in most other respects this, the second (after Hong Kong) greatest Far Eastern seaport, has altered beyond recognition since the 1950s. Today an oriental version of Monte Carlo, little remains of the exotic romanticism which the reader may associate with Stamford Raffles or Joseph Conrad. But traces of that past still lingered when Ieuan Davies's Advance Party drove through its sweltering streets and spicy odours from the harbour to the infamous Selarang Barracks at Changi, now demolished but where so many British and Empire POWs had suffered and died after the fall of Singapore. However, little time was spent there and within a few days the Advance Party broke up into its squadron constituents and moved over the Causeway into Malaya itself.

The B Squadron party had the shortest journey; just across the Causeway which links Singapore to the Malaysian mainland, to Johore Bahru, while those of A Squadron and RHQ took the overnight sleeper to Seremban, the capital of Negri Sembilan, and C Squadron continued north to the Federal capital,

Kuala Lumpur in Selangor. At these destinations all three parties were received and accommodated by the outgoing Regiment, the 13th/18th Hussars.

In the case of A Squadron and RHQ the first omens were inauspicious. For some reason part of the Officers' Mess silver had been shipped with the Advance Party rather than the main body. Within hours, or at the most days, of its arrival at Paroi Camp, Seremban, and before being unpacked, the silver disappeared. Consternation and the heated apportionment of blame ensued, not least upon the head of the unfortunate subaltern under whose signature this priceless treasure had travelled from England. Soon it was discovered that two troopers of the 13th/18th were also missing and shortly thereafter were apprehended by the police when attempting to stow away on a ship in Singapore Harbour. These men had conceived and in part carried out a plan of almost unbelievable idiocy.

They had stolen the silver and buried it in the scrub just outside the perimeter of the camp. Then, notwithstanding that they, with their Regiment, were about to embark for England, deserted, made their way to Singapore and sought to stow away on a ship bound for the same destination! The next step in their plan was, apparently, to return to Malaya as merchant seamen (this may have been their civilian profession) when the heat had died down, disinter the loot, sell it and live happily on the proceeds ever after. Unfortunately for them, who they were and what they had done soon became apparent to the Military Police who had been informed of the theft. The problem was to discover where these two master criminals had stashed their booty as they denied all knowledge of the deed and were so far charged only with desertion, a serious enough offence itself while on active service. In due course the detectives of the Special Investigation Branch came up with a cunning scheme. A certain Highlander, arrested on a serious charge and seeking to mitigate his crime and sentence, agreed to act as a 'grass'. Placed in the same cell as one of the thieves, he quickly gained the confidence of his fellow prisoner and soon the two were chatting away happily about their respective crimes, while the Holmeses and Watsons of the SIB glued their ears to the wall of the adjoining cell. It was all over bar the shouting. Confronted with the evidence of this Scots Judas, the resistance of the two troopers collapsed. They were returned under escort to Seremban where they pointed out the temporary grave from which the silver was recovered, none the worse for its ordeal, some of it, no doubt, to this day an adornment to the Officers' Mess of The King's Royal Hussars.

By this time the main body of the Regiment, which had sailed from Liverpool in the SS *Empire Clyde* (by strange coincidence the same vessel under another name which had transported the Regiment from Italy to the United Kingdom ten years before) on 28 May, had arrived in Singapore on 22 June. Early the following month the take-over from the 13th/18th had been completed and troops from all three sabre squadrons were installed in their respective detachments throughout the States of Selangor (C), Negri Sembilan (A) and Johore (B).

From a troop leader's point of view the system of troop detachments, by which the roads and plantation tracks of Malaya were policed and kept clear of terrorist activity, was undoubtedly the most attractive aspect of the Malayan tour. For the men too, although the bright lights of a town were lacking, detachment life had much to recommend it. Absent were the eagle eyes of the RSM, SSM and other guardians of orthodox dress and deportment. Troop leaders, and even troop sergeants, tended to take a relaxed view of such matters, while a *dhobi*-cum-*char wallah*, usually Indian or Pakistani, for a small fee took care of laundry, what little 'bulling' there was to be done and produced char and wads on demand.

Apart from occasional visits by the squadron leader or his second-in-command, sometimes accompanying a Brass Hat, the troop leader was left much to his own devices. Generally speaking his duty was to liaise and co-odinate his patrols with the local police lieutenant and/or the neighbouring infantry company commander. Sometimes a troop would come under command of an infantry battalion or even brigade, usually 99, 63 or 26 Gurkha Brigade (the Regiment as a whole was under command 17 Gurkha Division), for a special operation

---

A L I F   G U L

("Nick" to his friends)

By appointment to many chota and burrah sahibs

PUKKA BLIGHTY CHARWALLAH.

PAROI CAMP, SEREMBAN

Early Morning Tea a speciality

Our Slogan:—

"This is no 'played-out' tea"

---

such as a village search, an ambush or the grisly business of transporting to the local police station the corpses of terrorists killed by the infantry in the jungle several days before.

Those troops not on detachment were usually occupied with food convoying (no food was allowed to be transported anywhere in Malaya without an Army or police escort) and VIP escorts. However, when from time to time a shortage of infantry arose in the Regimental area, the local squadron (and, on one notable occasion, RHQ) would be required to produce an infantry patrol, usually in about platoon strength. One of the first of these operations took place in September, 1953, when Woodforce One from A Squadron was lifted by helicopter into a remote area of swamp on the Negri Sembilan-Pahang border, later to be known as Fort Iskander.

The principal task of this patrol under Captain Paddy Wood (now Major Haselden-Wood) with Lieutenant The Hon Michael Allenby, SQMS 'Nobby' Hall, twenty-five NCOs and men and a Junior Civil Liaison Officer (JCLO) was to kill or capture any terrorists encountered in the area and, in the words of Paddy Wood's report, 'to spread confidence among the Sakai [aboriginals] and concentrate them into one area, therefore giving them protection from the CTs and stop the handing over of food'. The Sakai or Semeli, a shy and unwarlike people, were much exploited by the CTs of whose aims they had no comprehension. Armed with nothing but bows and arrows they would understandably side with whoever was nearest and in the greater strength, in other words the British when they were at hand and the terrorists when they were not.

By the end of the second day camp had been established with a strong perimeter and Sergeant Maloney of the Royal Signals, wrestling manfully with an ancient 19 set, had made contact with RHQ 100 miles away. Daily patrols covered the area within a radius of four miles of the camp, sometimes travelling by Sakai canoe. No terrorists were encountered but three Sakai 'collaborators' (it is unclear how they were identified as such) surrendered and fifty other tribesmen and their families were collected together and settled round the camp.

Once a landing zone had been constructed Woodforce was visited by the Brigade Commander (Brigadier 'Honker' Henniker), Colonel Arkwright and the A Squadron Leader, Major Gus Penny, the latter thoughtfully bringing with him a bottle of beer each for Paddy Wood and Michael Allenby but inadvertently drinking them both himself. Only ten days' rations had been provided but on the tenth day 1911 Flight RAF made an airdrop which saw the patrol through for the next three days when they were 'lifted out'.

In his memoirs of the Malayan Emergency Brigadier Henniker, a most popular commander, wrote of this operation: 'The reasons for sending 11th Hussars to a place they could only get to by leaving their armoured cars a hundred miles away were the worst possible ones from a military point of view. But in aid to the Civil Power you have to compromise over military principles occasionally.' The next time, nearly two years later, that these military principles were compromised and 11th Hussars, again under Paddy Wood, returned to this remote and dangerous area, the results were rather more spectacular. But we shall come to that later.

Although, as we mentioned before, direct contact with the enemy was relatively infrequent, at least four members of the

Regiment in two separate incidents on the same stretch of road were extremely lucky to escape with their lives.

At this distance in time and with sparse records it is difficult to be precise about dates, but the first of these incidents took place in January or February, 1954, when Lieutenant David Laidlaw, detached from the Regiment as Intelligence Officer to the Negri Sembilan Operations Room, and his driver, Trooper E. W. Morgan of RHQ Squadron, were bowling along the road between Tampin and Gemas. Laidlaw was on his way to visit a company of the 1st Gordons at Gemas and in his mind were thoughts of lunch and the beauty of the countryside. The manner in which these pleasant musings were interrupted is best described by David himself:

'All along this road the jungle had been cut back say fifty yards on both sides, the intervening space being covered with a low scrub. As the jeep [jeeps were rare in Malaya, the Landrover having taken over as the Army's riding-horse by then] approached a cutting I recollect that I had a vague thought that this would be an ideal ambush position; this may have made me rather more alert. The jeep entered the cutting, the driver slowing down because of the bends. At that moment a machine gun (I believe it was a captured Bren gun) opened fire on the jeep from the top of the bank at the left side of the cutting. The machine gun was firing obliquely downwards at a range of fifteen feet, which may be excusably described as point-blank. However, its field of fire was extremely limited. The instant effect upon its target was a series of astonishingly loud bangs, provoking in my case a flash of surprise, aggravation, excitement and apprehension. As is frequently described in bad novels, time stood still. Whatever my driver thought, he acted with exemplary coolness.

'Although entirely unable to aim at any target because of the windscreen and the canopy [of the jeep] above us, I nonetheless returned the fire, firing short bursts from my Sten, which happily did not jam, into the air. I like to think that this instantaneous response, however blind, had an important deterrent effect.

'Fortunately the jeep and its occupants emerged safely the other side of the cutting completely unscathed. As the jeep emerged into more open country it began to swerve violently from side to side and the engine began to falter. We discovered subsequently that two bullets had struck the vehicle. One had hit one of the front tyres and the other had smashed the distributor head. Everything now depended on Trooper Morgan. With highly commendable skill and great coolness he managed to keep the jeep on the road, his passenger urging him: "Keep going! Keep going!"'

And keep going they did, passing an abandoned Landrover which had also been ambushed without injury to its occupants. The jeep's engine finally conked out about half a mile from the scene of the attack. The appearance of a police APC which, presumably, had been alerted by the occupants of the abandoned Landrover, enabled Laidlaw to return to the cutting with the police, but there was no sign of the ambushers, who had slipped back into the jungle.

These terrorists were, it seems, members of the self-styled 6th Independent Platoon and, however bad shots they may have been – and it must be said that Laidlaw's escape had been little short of miraculous – they were not deterred by failure, for, on the very next day, they ambushed the Gordons' padre in more or less the same vicinity. Once again, however, the attempt failed and, despite his scout-car crashing into a log felled across the road, the intrepid cleric scattered his attackers with steady bursts from his Bren.

One of the reasons for this sudden upsurge of terrorist activity in the area was the temporary abandonment, owing to a shortage of troops, of the Sungei Dua detachment post about half-way between Tampin and Gemas. Usually occupied by either an armoured-car troop or an infantry platoon, this lonely outpost was vital for the security of road users between these two important towns, Gemas being the Crewe of the Malayan railway system. The principal role of this detachment was the manning of a roadblock, constant patrolling and 'prophylactic' firing by night, a most enjoyable task which involved blazing away with the Besa machine guns mounted on the Daimlers at all potential ambush sites (such as that where Laidlaw and Morgan had been ambushed).

As a result of these ambushes Sungei Dua was quickly re-occupied by 2nd Troop A Squadron under Lieutenant John Trotter. There was no drinking water in the camp and for the purpose of transporting it from Gemas, a fifteen-hundredweight water-cart driven by Lance-Corporal C. J. Parkes was attached to the troop. 6th Independent Platoon, nothing daunted by its earlier failures, decided that the water-cart was a soft target, manned as it was only by the driver and a co-driver armed with a Sten gun. Although the cart's journeys were irregular the bandits, after observation, were able to make an educated guess at roughly when a fresh supply of water would be required.

Again history denies us a precise date but in the course of one of its journeys the water-cart was ambushed and Lance-Corporal G. A. Symes, riding 'shot-gun', was wounded in the neck and shoulder. Fortunately, although the windscreen was punctured with bullet holes, the engine was undamaged and Parkes, driving with skill and panache, managed to reach the safety of Gemas. As a result of this incident Symes, who was the troop leader's gunner-operator, has the distinction of being the only 11th Hussar of the post-war era to be wounded by enemy action while serving with the Regiment. Fortunately, he recovered from his wounds and returned to duty.

But there were other hazards on the Tampin-Gemas road besides terrorist ambushes. A mile or two down the road from Sungei Dua was a large Chinese-owned sawmill which, under the Emergency Regulations, was obliged to employ a European security officer. This gentleman was a retired Major of a long-defunct Irish regiment who drove about at great speed and to the danger of the other road users in an ancient Marmon-Harrington armoured car which may well have seen service with the 11th in the early days of the desert campaign.

One National Service subaltern who served with A Squadron at that time and was for a while on detachment at Sungei Dua was Second-Lieutenant Ted Dexter, later Captain of the England Cricket Team on numerous occasions and more recently Chairman of the Selectors. While serving with the Regiment, Dexter scored 183 for Negri Sembilan against Johore and played in the Regimental Rugby XV which was thrashed 61–3 by the Fijian

Regiment. He also captained the A Squadron athletics team to victory in the Regimental Sports. Intellectually, however, his military service does not seem to have been so rewarding. In his *Memoirs* he recalls writing home:

> '. . . it would have been nice to have a serious conversation with an intelligent man or woman on some subject other than the food, the weather or sex, which is the sum total of all conversation here.'

This may explain why it was not unknown for the Great Sportsman to fall into a deep sleep during dinner!

During 1954 in the A Squadron area two other terrorist contacts were made. Near Bahau four CTs approached Lance-Corporal Earp as he lay in an ambush position but fled when he opened fire, and Corporal Bigglestone, who was at that time Troop Corporal of 3rd Troop, spotted a CT while on foot patrol but was unable to get a shot at him.

Arthur Bigglestone, who had an unusual and varied military career, is one of the select few to have served in both the 10th and 11th Hussars. In 1953 he transferred from the 10th to the 11th as one of the 184 NCOs and men who joined the Regiment at Wesendorf prior to departure for Malaya. On completion of his engagement in 1956 he returned to England and left the Army, only to be recalled from the Reserve later that year with the outbreak of the Suez crisis. Posted to The Queen's Bays in Tripoli he was disappointed not to reach Egypt and, the crisis over, returned to civilian life. However, he was soon back in the Army, this time with the KDGs who by then had replaced the 11th in Malaya, so Bigglestone found himself once again at Paroi Camp! A parachute course in Singapore led to his selection for the SAS with whom he served in a number of operational theatres including Oman, Aden and Borneo. He retired as a Staff Sergeant in 1974.

Meanwhile down in Johore B Squadron was involved in a couple of brisk skirmishes. 5th Troop (Second-Lieutenant Bathurst), carrying out dismounted searches of possible ambush positions ahead of a food convoy, flushed four or five bandits with whom there was an exchange of fire, but there were no casualties on either side and the convoy passed through in safety.

The second incident occurred on the eve of Balaklava Day, 1954, involving – perhaps for the first time in action – the newly-issued Saracen APC which had recently replaced the old GMC. A half troop (Daimler and Saracen) under Second-Lieutenant Michael Cooper-Evans on routine patrol between the B Squadron detachment at Jemaluang and Mersing was ambushed in a cutting three-and-a-half miles from camp. Cooper-Evans describes the action:

'The leading Saracen APC was fired on from the jungle to the west of the road at a range of twenty-five to thirty yards. The Saracen accelerated out of the ambush whereupon fire was concentrated on the DAC. Both vehicles were hit by bursts of automatic fire, rounds striking the turret roof of the Daimler and severing the radio aerial of the Saracen.

'As commander of the DAC I immediately returned fire with my Sten gun. A moment later the Browning machine gun on the Saracen opened fire, followed almost at once by the 2 pdr and Besa of the Daimler together with the small arms of the now dismounted assault troopers. After a few moments hostile fire ceased but friendly fire continued for some ninety seconds until the dismounted troops had circled to within twenty yards of the ambush position and were ready for the final assault. Alas, by this time the enemy had fled. In all 6th Troop fired fourteen rounds of 2 pdr HE and almost 1,500 from its Browning, Besa and Bren guns during this brief argument. The Troop suffered no casualties.'

A follow-up party arriving a few minutes later found blood-stains in the ambush position which led into the jungle before disappearing in a stream. The Regiment's elusive 'first kill' was still nearly a year away, but there is little doubt that on this occasion a terrorist had been severely wounded.

Those involved in this spirited action were the following:

DAC crew: Patrol and car commander: 2/Lt Cooper-Evans; gunner-operator: Lance-Corporal Gracie; driver: Trooper Cartwright.

25. Entry into Berlin, 1945. Leading Daimler armoured car Lt J. Gale,
L/Cpl D. J. Hale. Scout Car: Cpl Jones, Second Daimler: Sgt Davies MM

26. Berlin, 1949. C Squadron L to R — Sgt Adams, Tpr Farrell, L/Cpl
Shaddick and Field Marshal Montgomery.

27. The Band of the 11th Hussars (PAO), 1949

28. Berlin — The Prime Minister, Mr Clement Attlee, with Major General Geoffrey Bourne and SSM Scrivener, inspects C Squadron, 29 March 1949

29. Tpr Jack Christie, later Sergeant, one of the leading lights of the Regimental Athletics Team

30. Major R. Chadwick MBE, Quartermaster and anchorman for the Regimental Tug-of-War Team, 1949

31. The Officers of RHQ and A Squadron 11th Hussars, Paroi Camp, Seremban, 1954

32. Food convoy escort, Negri Sembilan

33. Saracen Armoured Personnel Carrier, introduced into service in Malaya, 1954

34. RN Helicopter resupplying Woodforce I near Tasek Bera, Malaya,
September 1953

35. Woodforce II. Back row L to R — Sgt R. Stones, Capt P.H.
Wood, L/Cpl Redman with three other members of the patrol. This
operation accounted for three CT's

36. A Squadron bringing out a dead terrorist

37. 5 Tp A Squadron Patrol Simpang Pertang, Negri Sembilan 15 Nov, 1955. This ambush party killed one ranking CT and captured another. L to R — Tpr G.S. Wall, L/Cpl D.A. Scott, Tpr K. Gould and Cpl E.C. Robinson

38. Her Majesty the Queen dancing with Major-General John Combe at the Balaclava Centenary Ball, 26 November 1954. General Combe is wearing the uniform worn by Lord Cardigan

39. General Sir Gerald Templer with l to r: Captain C.H. Robertson, Captain P.H. Wood, Captain H. King, Major G. Penney, and Lieutenant Colonel P. Arkwright, Seremban

40. Queen's Birthday Parade, Aden, 1961

41. Major Gen Geofrey Baker, Major G.H. Hodgkinson, Sgt J. Lemon,
Captain T.G.C. Holcroft and Gen Sir Richard Goodbody, Sharjah, 1960

42. Loading vehicles for the move to Kuwait, 1961

43. L to R: Major R. Sutton, Mr A. Rothnie, British Consul General Kuwait, Major G.H. Hodgkinson, Capt F.H.D.H. Wills, Brigadier D. Horsford, Capt N.C.P. Winter — Kuwait, 1961

44. "Chieftain" by David Shepherd. Presented to The 11th Hussars by Lieutenant-Colonel P.M. Hamer on giving up command, September, 1968

45. Presentation of the Guidon by HM The Queen Mother, 1965

46. "No 1 Guard Left form." Guidon Parade, 1965

47. Regimental Langlauf Team, 1968

APC crew: Commander: Corporal Martin; operator: Trooper
Phillips; driver: Trooper Shires; assault troopers:
Lalkham (Bren), Rutherford (Bren), Barrass,
Duncan and Robinson.

The follow-up party under Sergeant Woolrage consisted of
Lance-Corporal Betts and Blacklock, Troopers Gathercole,
McLeod, Bowring, Stainsby and Gillott, the last-named being
better known to some readers as Lieutenant-Colonel Peter
Gillott, who retired from The Royal Hussars as recently as 1986.

Perhaps at this point, the eve of the centenary of the Charge of
the Light Brigade, we should interrupt our narration of the
Regiment's deeds in Malaya and travel the 8,000 miles back to
England, where two glittering events were held to celebrate that
heroic occasion.

On 20 November, 1954, a Balaklava Centenary dinner was
held at Deene Park, Northamptonshire, the family seat of that
most famous (or infamous) 11th Hussar, Lord Cardigan, who
led the epic but disastrous charge. The two hundred guests
included the Dukes of Edinburgh and Gloucester; the former,
after pointing out that his only connection with the Charge was
the possibility that a distant relation may have fought on the
other side, proposed a toast to the memory of those who took
part. Also present were descendants of Lords Raglan, Lucan,
Cardigan (Mr George Brudenell, the host), Tennyson and
General Scarlett. The 11th Hussars were represented by their
Colonel, Major-General John Combe, Commanding Officer,
Lieutenant-Colonel Peter Arkwright and Commanding Officer
'designate', Lieutenant-Colonel Martin Grant-Thorold.

A few days later, on 26 November, a magnificent ball was
held at the Hyde Park Hotel attended by Her Majesty the
Queen, the Duke of Edinburgh, The Queen Mother and nearly
650 other guests. Past and serving members of the Regiment
and their wives who were present are too numerous to list in
full but included General Combe (wearing the actual tunic worn
by Cardigan during the Charge), General Sir Louis Spears,
Colonel Peter Payne-Gallwey and Major Bobby Hartman.

Numbered among those serving officers sweating it out on the dance-floor rather than in the jungles of Malaya were Tony Crankshaw, John Woodhouse, Ieuan Davies, Jimmy Troughton, Eddie Farquhar, Ivan Straker and Willie Trotter. The Royal Gloucestershire Hussars provided a Guard of Honour under RSM (later Captain) Jim Richmond.

In Malaya the usual Balaklava celebrations were held at Squadron level but routine operational duty continued. Fortunately or unfortunately, depending upon individual points of view, by no means all armoured-car work in Malaya was as exciting as the episode recounted above. Indeed much was dreary and repetitive, particularly food-convoying which sometimes involved an early-morning start and a late-night return. One of the longest of these, an A Squadron responsibility, left Seremban twice a week and wound its way at an average of no more than twenty miles per hour via either Kuala Pilah or Kuala Klawang through the exotically named but somewhat malodorous villages of Simpang Pertang and Durian Tipus,* terminating at Menchis in Pahang, a round trip of about 150 miles.

Before starting, the cargoes of the overloaded lorries, mostly under-powered Austins and Bedfords, had to be checked against the Bills of Lading in case additional food had been added, either for dropping off *en route* or handing over to the terrorists at destination. Depending on the number of lorries in the convoy, from two to three escort vehicles (DACs and APCs) might be required – one in front, one in rear and the rest in the middle.

Cargoes checked, the convoy would get under way, soon slowing to a snail's pace at the first gradient. Engines screaming at peak revs, the weaker brethren, with clouds of steam belching from their tortured radiators, sometimes fell by the wayside. This would bring the entire convoy to a dangerous standstill, as no food-carrying vehicle could be left to fend for itself. Assault troopers would burst from APCs and take up defensive position while the irate escort commander would remonstrate with the offending driver in terms which left him in no doubt that he

---

* The Durian, after which the village is named, is a fruit which smells like a corpse but is much favoured by both Malays and Chinese.

was required to 'get his f...... lorry f...... moving as f...... quickly as possible' – these exhortations sometimes being reinforced with a swift kick in the backside which protruded from under the bonnet of the white-hot engine.

Occasionally tempers rose to even greater heights of indiscretion and efforts to speed up convoys had unfortunate consequences. The story, with many variations, is told of one young officer in charge of a particularly slow and recalcitrant convoy who so far forgot himself and military discipline as to fire a burst of Besa over the driver's cab of the leading lorry to encourage the man to increase his speed. Unfortunately his gunner had forgotten to fit the Besa-bag and the red-hot empties showered down upon his driver's hands, causing him to lose control and drive the Daimler straight into a paddy-field.

The VIP escort was another important duty fulfilled by the cavalry regiments in the Malayan campaign. Ever since the ambushing and murder of the High Commissioner, Sir Henry Gurney, in 1951, all senior officials and high-ranking officers were provided with an Army or police escort, the helicopter having not yet come into its own as the principal means of transport for such personages.

In the case of Gerald Templer and his successors as High Commissioner, an entire troop, usually of C Squadron as they were based near the Federal capital, Kuala Lumpur, would be provided for his security. Although of uncertain temper, Sir Gerald was very much a soldier's general who never failed to address a friendly word to the men on arrival and departure. He had a good memory for faces and years later recognised one of his former 11th Hussar escort commanders, Joe Harris, at a reception in a TA mess.

On one occasion, shortly after the Regiment's arrival in Malaya, the Press latched on to a story that the Great Man had been unceremonially dumped in a ditch whilst travelling in an 11th Hussar armoured car. Typically he took the trouble to reply to Peter Arkwright's apology in the following terms:

Dear Arkwright,
    Thanks awfully for your letter of 18 July. Of course I was in

no way hurt or even bumped. The Press out here are quite disgusting over this sort of thing, and will invent anything to make a headline. I have told the *Straits Times* what I think of them, not for the first time.

As you know, all that happened was that the armoured car in which I was travelling went on to the grass verge in order to avoid a bad pot-hole and, as usual, the verge collapsed and the two offwheels slid into the ditch. It could happen to anyone, particularly when the drivers don't know how treacherous the verges are in this country. I am so sorry about the whole stupid incident.

I very much hope to be seeing you one of these days. Don't fail to let me know when you come to Kuala Lumpur. Needless to say, we are delighted to have your Regiment with us, and I hope you will all enjoy yourselves in this country.

Yours sincerely
Gerald Templer

By the end of 1954, about half-way through the Regiment's tour of duty, only eighteen officers and 250 other ranks of those who had sailed from England in the *Empires Pride* and *Clyde* were still serving with the Regiment. Thus only the more important departures and arrivals can be recorded here.

Perhaps the most notable departure was that of the redoubtable Major Reg Chadwick, Quartermaster, former RSM and the last of the Regiment's 'horse soldiers'. Short, square and rough of speech, Reg was a cavalryman of the Old School, who did not suffer fools (or a great many other people) gladly. Since he joined in 1925 he had never served a day away from the Regiment. So well known was he to all ranks that one recruit, when asked who had led the Charge of the Light Brigade, replied, 'Major Chadwick, sergeant'! The list of campaigns in which he served reads like the battle honours of a regiment and he probably deserved more than the MBE with which he was rewarded at the end of the war. The Regiment was his life and all that followed was anti-climax. He tried Rhodesia and Australia but neither really suited him. Returning to England from Australia in 1968 he died at sea and was committed to the Deep.

As Quartermaster, Reg Chadwick was replaced by Captain H. J. King and RSM Greensides succeeded RSM Lamb who was invalided home.

Major Ieuan Davies, posted to Lulworth, was Mentioned in Despatches as were the departing Adjutant, Captain David Sivewright (succeeded by Captain Clive Robertson), the Training Officer, Captain Jimmy Finch, RSM Greensides, SSM Hall and Sergeants Lemon, Hodges, Day and Monk (REME).

The next year, 1955, proved to be one of both triumph and tragedy. Tragic were the deaths of three sergeants, Slack, McGhie and Priddice, valuable men with many years of service between them. Eddie Slack and Jock McGhie had both been invalided home but died later, Slack of heart disease and McGhie of TB. Dick Priddice was killed by a grenade which exploded accidentally on the ranges, also wounding Captain Paddy Wood and Trooper Pollard, both of whom recovered.

The Training Wing, where this accident occurred, had originally been established at Paroi Camp, Seremban, under Captain George Hodgkinson, but later moved to Singapore. Its task was to re-train armoured car troops in the light of operational experiences and keep them up to scratch with drill, weapon training etc. These troops, one from each sabre squadron, trained together competitively for five weeks, culminating in anti-ambush exercises in a jungle area using live ammunition. During the Regiment's three-year tour, three other officers, Captains Finch, Wood and Hamer, commanded the Wing, ably assisted by, amongst others, SSM Scott and SQMS Frost.

The triumphs came in the shape of four kills, a capture and a surrender. To deal with the last first, a bandit surrendered to Corporal Clark of 3rd Troop C Squadron and gave information which led to a number of kills by a neighbouring infantry battalion. But the greatest success came in July when the intrepid Paddy Wood, now commanding RHQ Squadron, led a scratch patrol consisting largely of 'back-room boys', on his second expedition into the Fort Iskander area, an operation known as Woodforce Two. In view of the importance of this event, the *Journal* report is quoted here in full, if not quite verbatim.

Woodforce Two consisted of the following:

Captain P. H. Wood	RHQ Squadron Leader
Sergeant R. J. Stones	Escort Troop Sergeant
Corporal J. A. Modelski	QM Storeman
Lance-Corporal H. S. Mitchell	Servicing Trailer
Lance-Corporal R. Redman	Transport Driver
Trooper Clements	Squadron Office Clerk
Trooper D. Wilkes	Officers' Mess Barman
Trooper G. C. Bird	Orderly Room Clerk
Trooper W. Clubb	Escort Troop Driver
Trooper B. M. Evans	Escort Troop Driver
Private Sneddon ACC	Cook
Signalman C. F. Ashley, Royal Signals	Wireless Operator

On Saturday, 16 July, the RHQ Squadron patrol was flown into Fort Iskander from Bahau by Pioneer aircraft. The first two days were spent learning jungle-craft as nobody, except Captain Wood, had ever been in the jungle before.

The Police Lieutenant in charge of the fort had received information that a CT camp, about a day's march from the fort, had two dead CTs in it. On this information the Fort Commander, the twelve 11th Hussars and six Semeli (aborigine) guides went in search of the camp. Each man had to carry four days' rations, one pair of socks, one toothbrush and a poncho (waterproof cape) on his back; not very much for four days but quite heavy enough.

The first day was the hardest, having to carry a full load of rations and not being used to jungle conditions. Nevertheless, 5,000 yards were covered in six hours and camp was made at 1600 hours. This allowed plenty of time to cook and prepare for the night. Most of the camps were made near streams, which were usually cool and clear, the sun never reaching them.

At first light the patrol stood to and had breakfast. Everyone agreed that the worst part was getting up in the morning and putting on dirty, wet, smelly, cold 'jungle green'. For the next four days of the patrol the country varied from thick jungle swamp, river-bed, *lalang* (high grass) and steep hills covered in primary (virgin) jungle. Unfortunately the reported camp was never found, but some new camps (unoccupied), resting places and fresh bandit tracks were, so the search was not in vain.

The patrol returned to Fort Iskander on the fourth day, very tired, bedraggled and leech-bitten, having covered approximately 20,000 yards. But after a day's rest the patrol set off again on Saturday, 23 July, inspired by the Fort Commander's comment that he had known many infantrymen who would not have been able to stick the pace of the four-day deep jungle patrol.

The object was to clear old Semeli cultivation where two bandits had been collecting food. These cultivations were on the edge of the Tasek Berah swamp, about two hours' paddling from Iskander. With the exception of one Semeli guide, this was going to be a completely PAO show.

The journey started badly. The patrol had to travel by aborigine canoes, which are not built for Hussars or compo rations, so before long most of the canoes had submerged and all the compo and personal kit was floating away. This scene was witnessed by some Semeli who soon vanished when they heard the Squadron Leader swearing and shouting, 'Don't panic!' The compo and kit were eventually rescued and the journey resumed.

The patrol arrived at its destination, a disused Semeli *kampong* (village), and made camp there at about 1500 hours. A torrential downpour ensued which lasted three hours and soaked everything including morale. Even the Semeli guide looked miserable, and a jolly Saturday night was spent by all.

Eventually Sunday morning dawned, cold and damp with a thick mist on the Tasek River. At 0800 hours Captain Wood, Sergeant Stones, Lance-Corporal Redman, Troopers Clements and Bird and Signalman Ashley left camp to inspect a cultivation on the other side of the river. On reaching it, fresh footprints and cuttings could be seen and were followed into the jungle for about five minutes. Suddenly voices and the sound of chopping were heard to the front. There was no time to waste. Wood, Stones and Redman went in firing. Four CTs escaped to the left, firing as they went, and three others were fatally wounded or killed in the charge. Stones was lucky not to be wounded when a round from one of the CTs' carbines hit a Sten magazine in the pouch covering his leg.

Clements, Bird and Ashley then came through. The three dead bodies were quickly examined for documents and their weapons removed. The patrol then returned to base camp by canoe where the remainder were waiting anxiously, having heard the firing. The contact was signalled to the Regiment via Iskander and the 25-pdr at the fort shelled the area for an hour to deter any CTs from returning. After the shelling, a stronger patrol collected the bodies and examined the camp throughly for further information. At 1600 hours the patrol paddled back to Fort Iskander with the three bodies. One of the dead turned out to be a terrorist of some importance and very useful information was gained from the documents. Woodforce Two returned to Paroi Camp exhausted but elated and proud, not only for themselves but for the Regiment.

Telegrams of congratulation poured in. John Combe cabled from his home in Hampshire: 'Captain Cardigan Wood – what blood lust Heartiest congratulations you Stones and all mixed grill Hope Sutton* not dying indigestion.'

From the GOC Malaya, General Bourne, came the message: 'Well done indeed your HQ Squadron under Captain Wood. Killing three Communist terrorists in deep jungle and many miles from any armoured car is a startling example of cavalry versatility. Best of luck to the whole Regiment and repeat if you get the opportunity.' Such fulsome praise was remarkable in the light of this general officer's subsequent attitude.

The same observation may be made in reference to the signal from General Anderson, GOC 17 Gurkha Division: 'Well done. A splendid effort. I am delighted.'

Similar messages were received from the Chief of Police and the Chairman of the Negri Sembilan War Executive Committee, but perhaps the most sincerely appreciated signal came from the 'rival' cavalry regiment responsible for the northern half of Malaya, the 15th/19th Hussars: 'Heartiest congratulations. We are very envious. Good shooting.'

In due course, the Commanding Officer, Peter Arkwright,

---

* This probably refers to the fact that Dick Sutton had recently handed over command of RHQ Squadron to Paddy Wood.

recommended Wood for the Military Cross and Stones and Modelski to be Mentioned in Despatches. The response in all cases was negative. Later the recommendation was repeated by Arkwright's successor, Martin Grant-Thorold, with the same result.

Now, nearly forty years on, we can only guess at the reasons for the failure of these recommendations. At that fairly late stage of the Emergency kills of more than one or two bandits in a single action, even by trained and experienced infantry, were rare. That a patrol consisting largely of administrative personnel from the Headquarters of a cavalry regiment, only one of whom had been into the jungle before, should have killed three out of seven terrorists, whom they did not even expect to find and whose numbers were unknown to them, is quite remarkable.

Anyone who has experience of the Malayan jungle will know that visibility, owing to the density of the vegetation and the gloom cast by the thick canopy of leaves overhead, is usually only a few yards. Therefore Wood and his men had no means of knowing by how many armed terrorists they were likely to be confronted. Thus the attack, carried out with much speed, ferocity and accuracy, was an act of considerable courage in itself, enhanced by the discovery a few days after the departure of Woodforce Two of a camp large enough to house twenty CTs within one thousand yards of the PAO's action.

The wording of General Bourne's – and to a lesser extent General Anderson's – congratulations could well have been interpreted as an encouragement to the recommendations which were made. Either no such encouragement was ever intended or they changed their minds. Perhaps in the light of the many unrecognized deeds of derring-do performed by the security forces in Malaya the refusal to award the Military Cross may be understandable, if less than generous, but the decision not to Mention in Despatches any member of the patrol, especially its leader, was, to say the least, niggardly.

But this was not to be the Regiment's only lethal success in an infantry role. In November, 1955, in the course of an operation in the Simpang Pertang area, elements of 2nd and 5th Troops

A Squadron set an ambush near the village of Kampong Ulu Sertang on the night of 14th/15th. One of those involved, Second-Lieutenant Fred Pearson, recalls the discomfort of the occasion:

> 'I remember night ambushes as one of the less attractive aspects of my Malayan campaign. The experience of lying on ever-cooling ground from 1800 hours with remorseless attacks by insects and other night creatures while not moving at all until first light will remain with me always.
>
> 'On this particular evening my feelings were further compounded because I had been badly bitten a few nights before and had developed cellulitis in one foot. I was thus wearing a regulation jungle boot on my left foot and Slazenger's tennis best on my right. As a result I placed myself very much at the back of the action.'

Shortly after two in the morning, Corporal E. O. Robinson of 5th Troop was in the process of handing out tots of rum to his men, Lance-Corporal D. A. Scott and Troopers Gould and Wall, when voices were heard and a torch was seen approaching. Two CTs stopped almost close enough to be touched (which says much for the silence of the 5th Troop men), while consulting a map. As the terrorists moved on, the ambush party dropped the rum, picked up their weapons and opened fire, killing one and badly wounding the other. The weapons used were two Brens (Wall and Gould), a Sten (Scott) and a .303 rifle (Robinson).

The wounded man screamed and whimpered for the rest of the night,* but it was too dangerous to attempt to find him in the darkness. With the dawn, Fred Pearson with Sergeant Maurice Goodby and several of his troops (2nd) cautiously set out to recover the bodies. Pearson continues the story:

> 'At first light the source of the whimpering became apparent. It came from the base of a tree around which was a camouflage of tall grass, hiding the wounded man. I approached the tree warily.

---

* In fact, he survived.

"Watch out for a trap, Sir," came Goodby's level, cautioning voice. At my continuous shout of "Gun into Air" a very ancient rifle suddenly flew out of a bush and crashed on to the ground. A very miserable young CT was revealed, holding a severed foot to his leg as if hoping the two would somehow miraculously join together again. The other terrorist's spirit had long since departed and his corpse was just starting to give off that semi-sickly scent.

'We got the live one on his feet [*sic*] and he hobbled towards the Saracen, carrying his dismembered foot in his hand. I hobbled after him thinking how very young they both were. We must have presented a strange sight, captive and captor both hobbling for different reasons.

'Instructions for travelling with fast-decomposing corpses inside closed armoured vehicles in the tropics had not been included in any of our training courses. This did not deter volunteers Lance-Corporal Allen or Troopers Tucker and Oxtoby, who kept control inside while Sergeant Goodby and I led our by now jubilant troop very fast, first to the Police Post at Kuala Pilah and then back to Rompin.'

There is a rather poignant postscript to the story. In 1989 Pearson returned to Malaya on holiday:

'I had been allowed by the police to keep a souvenir of the ambush,' he writes, 'and had the map the terrorists had carried that fateful night. As a result I was able to find myself back at the precise spot some thirty-four years later. Extraordinarily nothing had changed. The same path down which the two young Chinese boys had walked from the hills to their deaths those many years ago was still there. Even the tree from which the terrorist's rifle had been thrown had not been touched. It was eerie to stand there with all the memories flooding back.'

And one final footnote. In September, 1956, ten months after the action in question and two months after the Regiment had left Malaya, as an example of the speed and efficiency with which staff officers of the British Army carry out their duties, Lieutenant-Colonel Martin Grant-Thorold at Carlisle received the following notification from General Headquarters Far East Land Forces, Singapore: 'You will be interested to hear that

11th Hussars have been credited with a back claim of one male Chinese CT killed and one male CT wounded/captured, since reclassified as SEP [Surrendered Enemy Personnel) – November, 1955. This refers to a patrol in ambush positions (WQ 3760) in Negri Sembilan, Kuala Pilah area who fired on two CTs at 0215 hours on 15 November.'

There were to be no more 'offensive' successes of this nature and the Regiment's tour of duty in Malaya was drawing to a close. Earlier in 1955 there had been some excitement when labour troubles and political agitation, probably unconnected with the Emergency, led to rioting in Singapore. In May pressure on the police increased to the extent that it was decided to move British troops, including an armoured car squadron, from the Federation to Singapore. B Squadron in Johore was alerted and on 13 May three troops arrived in Singapore to be followed by a fourth from Jemaluang (B Squadron's main troop detachment). In the event the Squadron was never called out in aid of the police but remained at fifteen minutes' notice to move for several days and on one occasion a 'Flag March' was carried out through the city, mainly for the reassurance of the European population.

Since it was necessary to continue routine operations in Johore, one troop each from C and A Squadrons drove south and, together with the remaining two troops of B Squadron, were formed into D Squadron (for the first and last time since the war) under Captain Jimmy Finch. Before long, however, the disturbances fizzled out and the situation in Singapore returned to normal.

In August there was a curious incident in the B Squadron area when an ice-cream vendor was shot by terrorists and left dead on the road. By the time 5th Troop had arrived at the scene the bandits had fled, scattering propaganda leaflets in their wake.

By April, 1956, the Advance Party of The King's Dragoon Guards had arrived to start the hand-over process and in early June the Regiment left Malaya and took up residence at Nee Soon Barracks in Singapore.

Only one officer, Lieutenant Ian Haig,* claims to have completed the full three-year tour of duty – in fact he had exceeded it by arriving with the Advance Party in May, 1953 – but unfortunately it has proved impossible to establish how many Other Ranks achieved this same distinction. It was estimated at the time that the 'A' vehicles of the Regiment had driven approximately 4,250,000 miles. Add 'B' vehicle mileage to this figure and the total would almost certainly exceed five million miles, perhaps as great a distance as the Regiment had motored in the Second World War.

A good part of this mileage had been covered by the Saracen APC which had been introduced in the course of 1954 as a replacement for the old General Motors APC (GMC for short), two to each sabre troop. The Saracen was the first new APC to be introduced into the armoured-car regiments of the British Army since the war. A far more sophisticated vehicle than its predecessor in Malaya, which had no roof to its passenger compartment and only lightly armoured sides, its unladen weight was 8¾ tons powered by a 5,670cc engine. A six-wheeler, its principal role was to provide protected transport for the Assault Troopers, who travelled in greater security than before but not always in greater comfort, as the enclosed passenger area was stiflingly hot in the tropics.

Unlike the GMC (or Daimler) the steering was power-assisted but a curious feature was the steering-wheel which slanted backwards towards the driver's chest. The pre-selector gearbox and fluid flywheel worked exactly as on the Daimler, so AFV drivers had few problems adapting themselves to the new vehicle. One operational disadvantage, however, was that its fluid flywheel denied it the ability to drag other vehicles out of ditches, a task for which the tough old GMC was admirably suited and was frequently required to perform!

Its single armament was a Browning .30 machine gun mounted in the commander's turret. This vehicle, with its more heavily armed 'cousin', the Saladin (which eventually replaced

---

* Information received from Ian Haig. No doubt the claim will be challenged!

the Daimler), was to remain in service with the British Army for many years.

For reasons perhaps connected with the festering Suez crisis, the Regiment lingered at Nee Soon for over a month. Although rather dull, this enforced rest was not without its amusements and diversions. These, regrettably, included an incidence of 'flashing' at the garrison swimming-pool. An officer's wife (not in the Regiment) complained that an 11th Hussar trooper had exposed himself in front of her. When called upon to give his name, he replied with that of the Garrison Commander, a Welch Fusilier of great charm and courtesy. An identity parade was ordered, but when the offended lady was unable to identify the perpetrator, the Adjutant suggested that the parade should be held again, this time in the nude. It is hardly necessary to add that the second parade did not take place and thus the rascally fellow escaped unpunished.

At last, on 19 July, the time came to board the troopship *Empire Fowey*, a 26,000-ton former German passenger liner. Lieutenant-Colonel Martin Grant-Thorold and his second-in-command, Major Tommy Pitman, had flown home and command of the Regiment for the return journey devolved upon Major Tony Crankshaw, Squadron Leader of C Squadron. Before departure, Crankshaw received a letter of appreciation from Dato Abdul Aziz, *Mentri Besar* (Prime Minister) of the State of Selangor, which read:

'My committee and I wish to express our appreciation of your services to the State of Selangor both operationally and as escorts during your tour of duty now coming to an end. On behalf of my colleagues and myself I wish you, your officers and troopers *bon voyage* and good hunting at your next station.'

There were few women aboard the *Fowey* so the opportunities for shipboard romance were limited. However, one tantalizing teenager, later to become one of London's leading fashion models, caused much excitement and over-heating among the younger officers. The appointment of a subaltern, reputed to be 'going steady' with a young lady at home, as a minder for the little temptress appears to have kept the wolves at bay, although it is by no means certain how much thought the lucky fellow gave to 'the girl he left behind him' while carrying out his duties.

Owing to the antics of Egypt's President Nasser the return journey took considerably longer than expected. At Aden word reached the ship that the Suez Canal was closed to military traffic and a diversion round the Cape was ordered. One soldier (of another regiment) was so eager to get home that he invaded the bridge, demanding to be sent home some other way. He had to be physically restrained and confined to a cell, no pleasant experience in the climate of the Indian Ocean in midsummer.

There was a brief stop at Zanzibar, remembered principally for the scent of cloves, and at Cape Town the ship was greeted by many residents in their cars, eager to show the travellers the sights of their city and to entertain them in their homes and clubs. One of the officers, John Woodhouse, remembers it as 'a truly remarkable welcome'.

The next and last stop before Southampton was Dakar, the steamy French West African naval base and then, 'On 27 August, 1956', writes Woodhouse, 'we glided slowly past the Needles of the Isle of Wight and into Southampton Water.' One officer, it seems, spotted amongst the crowd assembled on the quay not one but several young ladies he had known three years before. Although none was actually clutching the tiny hand of a toddler, he decided that discretion was the better part of valour and remained on board until the disappointed beauties had dispersed.

The Cherrypickers were home. For their services in Malaya, Colonel Peter Arkwright was awarded the OBE and, in addition to those already listed, Captains T. A. Hall, G. H. Hodgkinson, C. H. Robertson (twice) and WO II H. Addis were Mentioned in Despatches.

Chapter *10*

CARLISLE AND NORTHERN IRELAND 1956–60

It would be impossible to find more sharply contrasting environments than those of the English/Scottish border and the Malay Peninsula. Nor would it be easy to imagine more sharply contrasting roles from active service in suppression of a terrorist movement thousands of miles from home to the training of recruits in the depths and the peace of the Cumbrian countryside.

The Regiment's role at Hadrian's Camp, Carlisle, resulted from the abolition of the RAC Training Regiments (in this case the 67th) which had been formed during the war to provide trained personnel for the armoured and armoured car regiments. It is with some distaste that the author is obliged to record that this splendid and dashing cavalry regiment was, temporarily, to be designated an Armoured Basic Training Unit. Lord Cardigan must have turned in his grave!

'Every other Thursday,' wrote the *Journal*'s editor, Lieutenant A. A. Farrant, 'there arrive at Hadrian's Camp, in natty civilian clothes, about fifty-nine young men. This is the National Service intake and in a year there are twenty-three such intakes. The Regulars, who number anything between five and twenty per fortnight, arrive independently [but] do their training with the National Servicemen. What we do is teach them General Military Training and "one leg" of their trade.'

In order to achieve this, Basic Training and the teaching of specific trades were allocated to each sabre squadron: C –

General Military Training; A – Wireless, Dismounted (Assault Troopers), Potential Officers; B – Gunnery, Driving and Maintenance. The GMT course lasted five weeks after which recruits were expected to turn out smartly and drill efficiently on the square, handle various small arms and classify on the range with a rifle. With the exception of the Potential Officers, the duration of the trade courses was eight weeks, thus the average recruit was ready for posting to a service regiment within thirteen weeks of joining. In the case of Potential Officers, a two-week course was a preparation for the testing by the War Office Selection Board (WOSB) and, if successful, further training at and commissioning from the Officer Cadet School (OCS) at Aldershot.

The reorganization of the Regiment for the training role meant that, to their disgust, many 11th Hussars had to be posted to other regiments as there were very few jobs for troopers in a training regiment.

During the 1956 Suez operation Hadrian's Camp became a mobilization centre for reservists, but none of the Regiment's own personnel took part in the landings.

1957 saw the retirement of the Colonel of the Regiment, Major-General John Combe, who paid his farewell visit to Carlisle on 6 July. He was succeeded by Colonel Trevor Smail.

So long as any who knew him survive, John Combe will be remembered as one of the great PAOs. His most significant service to the Regiment in peacetime was also one of his last, namely to save the Regiment from amalgamation in the year of his retirement, albeit a temporary reprieve. No doubt his efforts had been aided not only by *jeux d'influence* in high places but also by the belief that, as a *Times* leader-writer put it, 'every cavalryman, after placing his own regiment first, would have listed the Eleventh second in excellence.'

John Combe's service with the Regiment began with B Squadron in France in 1914. Over fifty years later his old school friend and brother officer, Bobby Hartman, was to write:

'It is amazing that John Combe emerged from the First World War without a decoration of any sort . . . his lion-hearted courage went unrewarded; perhaps after the brass-hats had helped themselves there were no more decorations left.'

A keen sportsman and racing enthusiast, Combe was also a highly professional soldier who was largely responsible for the Regiment's state of readiness at the outbreak of the Second World War. He had been given command in Egypt in 1939 and led it through the months of desert fighting until early in 1941, earning two DSOs in the process. As a brigadier he was taken prisoner but managed to escape in 1944. His active career ended as a divisional commander in 1947 when he retired to a stud farm in Hampshire. In the same year he married Helen Gosling (irreverently but affectionately known to the Regiment as Auntie Hell), the widow of a 10th Hussar. From 1956 to '58 he served as a Steward of the National Hunt Committee. His death from a sudden heart attack at the age of seventy-two on 12 July, 1967, however sad, was perhaps timely as he did not live to see his beloved Regiment amalgamated two years later. His ashes were buried at Stratchconan, the remote and beautiful Scottish glen where he had spent much of his youth. A trumpeter of the Regiment sounded the Last Post over his grave.

Also in 1957 another Regimental stalwart, Tommy Pitman, retired after twenty years' service with the Regiment. Tommy, who had won an MC in Palestine before the war, was also taken prisoner in the desert and, although he escaped once, was recaptured and remained 'in the bag' for the rest of the war. At the time of his retirement he was second-in-command of the Regiment. Tony Crankshaw was appointed in his place.

On 15 May of that year Lieutenant-Colonel F. H. (Squeak) Sutton died. He had been the Regiment's last 'mounted' Commanding Officer and to whom it had fallen on 10 April, 1928, to give for the last time to the Eleventh Hussars the famous cavalry order, 'Make much of your horses!'*

During its tour of duty at Carlisle the Regiment lost many of its wartime veterans. Martin Grant-Thorold was succeeded as

---

* Over forty years later a similar duty fell to Major Willie Trotter who, as 2i/c, gave the final command to the Regiment before Amalgamation: '11th Hussars! For the very last time to your duties dismiss!'

Commanding Officer by Tony Crankshaw and among others to leave were Major Harry Petch, Captain Oliver Wentworth-Stanley, RQMS Sherwood, SSM Hale and Sergeant Bainbridge. RSM Jim Richmond, who had been for some years with the Gloucestershire Hussars, was commissioned into the Royal Pioneer Corps and SSM Hall promoted in his place. RSM Leslie Greensides retired and was succeeded by RSM Smith.

Leslie Greensides is one of a select few who has been both a Cherrypicker and a Shiner. Joining the 11th in 1931 at Tidworth he was trained as an armoured-car driver (in those days on Lanchesters) and two years later posted with a draft of seventy-five other 11th Hussars to the 12th Lancers in Egypt. When the Regiment arrived at Helmieh to relieve the 12th he returned to the fold. After driving Rolls-Royce and Crossley armoured cars, he went on the staff of the Officers' Mess for two years, including service in Palestine. In 1937 he returned briefly to civilian life but just before the outbreak of war he was recalled to the Colours and posted to the 10th, with whom he went to France as a tank driver.

After the fall of France he was promoted to lance-corporal and returned to the 11th in Cairo in March, 1941, serving first as troop corporal and then troop sergeant of 4th Troop B Squadron under Lieutenant Cape (who was killed) and Toby Horsford. When the Regiment returned to England from Italy Greensides was one of those selected to form D Squadron, with which he served throughout the campaigns in Normandy and Belgium (where his brother was killed). In 1945 he was promoted to SQMS and in the following year took charge of the Officers' Mess. In 1950 he took over as SSM of B Squadron and in 1954 as RSM of the Regiment in Malaya.

In 1959 the Regiment was posted to Northern Ireland, having handed over Hadrian's Camp and its role as an Armoured Basic Training Unit to the 15th/19th Hussars who had been neighbours in Malaya. Although far from exciting, the Regiment's stay at Carlisle had not been without its compensations for all ranks. England in the late 'fifties was an agreeable place to soldier. Wartime and post-war restrictions were a fading memory and the roaring inflation and social upheavals of the late Twentieth Century were phenomena yet to come. It was a pleasant tranquil pool of time between two cataracts in the nation's history. But probably no such philosophical thoughts entered the minds of officers and men, particularly the Regular soldiers, whose homes were simply more accessible than usual and for whom leave and sporting pursuits were more readily available than they had been for some years. For shooting men in particular there was much to be said for Cumberland and the Scottish Borders and, shooting rents being relatively low in those days, various officers were able to acquire some 6,000 acres of rough shooting. The proximity of the Solway made wildfowling an especially attractive proposition and in the course of two seasons the officers had accounted for over 5,000 head of game.

Many other sports also flourished. The Regimental boxing team was particularly strong, reaching the UK Championship Finals, while Lance-Corporal O'Brien won the Army Lightweight title. In athletics, Sergeant Jack Christie, the Regimental mainstay in field events since before the war, achieved third place in javelin in the 1959 Inter-Unit Championships, while the Regimental team came second overall.

Before leaving for Northern Ireland on 1 August, 1959, the Eleventh Hussars were adopted by the Borough of Slough, the adoption ceremony and parade taking place on Agar's Plough at Eton College. According to the local Press (and this may come as a surprise to many former Cherrypickers), 'officers and men marched past with immaculate precision', the salute being taken by the Mayor of Slough, Councillor Doris Smallbone, attended by the High Sheriff of Buckinghamshire, the Vice-Provost of Eton and the Colonel of the Regiment. Perhaps of greater interest to Old Soldiers was the opening, two years later, of a pub in Slough called 'The Cherrypicker' which stands to this day with the original sign painted by Captain Ian Bruce, no doubt freshened up from time to time, still dangling outside.

Northern Ireland in 1959 was not in the state of turmoil that it is today. Nonetheless, the IRA was not entirely inactive and the Regiment's role was an operational one in aid of the Royal

Ulster Constabulary in the counties of Tyrone and Fermanagh. The Regiment, less C Squadron, was based at Omagh, while C was detached at Castle Archdale on the shores of Lough Erne. Castle Archdale, described at the time as 'somewhat like a concentration camp', was little but a collection of Nissen huts, the remains of the wartime flying-boat base from which the *Bismarck* had been located in 1941.

The Regiment found itself equipped once again with ancient Daimlers and Dingoes which, owing to their advanced age and years of gruelling service, kept the LAD busy. Despite this, a considerable mileage was covered in these faithful old friends.

Few incidents were reported during this tour and the only occasion on which anyone came under fire was when a Saracen of 3rd Troop C Squadron (Lieutenant J. Daly) was shot at by the defenders of the Rosslea police station which had been under attack by the IRA until a few minutes before the arrival of the relieving cavalry.

Warned that its next posting would be to the very different climate, meteorologically and politically, of Aden, the Regiment underwent a number of training exercises to prepare for this move. Several transfers to and from the Regiment took place prior to departure, perhaps the most notable of these being that of Lieutenant Lakin's Irish Wolfhound, Sean, to the Irish Guards, Sean thus becoming the only 11th Hussar ever to have transferred voluntarily to the Brigade of Guards!

Chapter 11

THE ARABIAN PENINSULA 1960–61

At the risk of some repetition of what has already been said in the 10th Hussar section of this book, a brief outline of the Middle East situation in the late 1950s and early 'sixties may assist the reader to understand the roles undertaken by the 11th Hussars during their tour of duty in the Arabian Peninsula.

British power and prestige in the Middle East had been in decline since the end of the Second World War and the political failure of the Anglo-French Suez operation of 1956 changed the Arab attitude towards Britain from one of grudging respect to outright contempt.

Despite the defeat of the ramshackle and ill-led Egyptian Army at Port Said and Port Tewfik, Nasser's powerful propaganda machine, aided by the withdrawal forced upon the Anglo-French forces by American diplomatic and economic pressure, succeeded in representing the affair as not only a political but, more importantly, a military victory for Egypt. In the Arab world only strength is respected and Britain was seen as weak, vacillating and lacking in self-confidence (a remarkably accurate assessment). Thus it was inevitable that demands for independence and closer ties with the 'victorious' Nasser would grow ever more strident in Britain's only Arab colony, Aden, and the neighbouring Protectorate.

Far to the north, across the vast deserts of Saudi Arabia, lay Iraq and her tiny but oil-rich neighbour, Kuwait. In July, 1958, King Faisal of Iraq and his veteran pro-British Prime Minister, Nuri es-Said, were murdered in a bloody coup staged by an army officer called Kassem. Kassem was the first in a succession of brutal ruffians who have ruled Iraq to this day, of whom Saddam Hussein is the latest, the longest surviving and probably the nastiest example.

Until the coup, Iraq had been a member of the Baghdad Pact, an alliance brokered by British diplomacy and encouraged by the United States, which also included Turkey, Iran and Pakistan. However, many Iraqi army officers were violently anti-British (Imperial troops had had to crush a pro-German *putsch* by elements of the Iraqi Army in 1941) and thus were opposed to the Pact. Britain's failure at Suez gave them the courage and the opportunity to rise up and smite King Faisal and Nuri es-Said who, in their eyes, were reactionaries clinging to a past 'imperialist' association and impeding the much vaunted but ever elusive dream of Arab unity.

Iraq's claims to sovereignty over Kuwait, of which we have had a recent spectacular reminder, are not new, dating back to the collapse of the Ottoman Empire after Turkey's defeat in the First World War; thus it should have come as no surprise when, following the abrogation by mutual consent of Britain's *de facto* protectorate over Kuwait in June, 1961, Kassem immediately laid claim to the territory, accompanying his demands with troop movements and sabre rattling. But we shall come to that.

The other area of the Middle East with which we are concerned here, the Arab states of the Persian (or Arabian, according to taste) Gulf, has already been dealt with in some detail in the 10th Hussar section of this history.

Although in 1960 the situation in Aden itself was still relatively stable and a far cry from the chaotic and humiliating shambles from which British forces were to withdraw seven years later, this then was the tense and uncertain atmosphere into which the Regiment sailed aboard the troopship *Nevasa* on 17 November, 1960.

The first contingent to leave the British Isles had sailed over two months earlier on the TT *Oxfordshire* bound for Sharjah (via Aden) in the Persian Gulf. This was the A Squadron Advance Party under Captain I. C. de Sales la Terrière (twice

Army Squash Champion) and including Lieutenant Bingley, SQMS Frost, Staff Sergeant Izzard (REME), Sergeants Lemon, Warren and Evans, Corporals Charlton, Christmas, Brady, Pratt, Mander, Anderson (Royal Signals), Ranger (RAPC) and, appropriately, Cook (ACC), Lance-Corporal Brierley, Troopers Connor, Hawkshaw, O'Malley, Wilkinson, Balmanno, Doward, McCone and Gardner, Craftsmen Timms and Jackson (REME). Transiting in Aden they arrived at Sharjah by air on 28 September. A Squadron's role was to be in support of the Trucial Oman Scouts and it was accommodated by the Royal Air Force on Sharjah airfield; but troops were also detached at Nizwa, Muscat and Buraimi, the last being a particularly sensitive area, having for many years been the object of a territorial dispute between Saudi Arabia on the one hand and the Gulf States of Abu Dhabi and Muscat and Oman on the other.

'I suppose I must have been briefed on the Squadron's role,' writes Ian La Terrière, 'but I have no recollection of it; we were an advance post of the British forces in Aden, supporting the Trucial Oman Scouts and overseeing stability in the Trucial States and Persian Gulf area generally.

'I was only in Sharjah for three months and have few memories beyond heat and sand. There was no military activity that I can recall. My most vivid memory is of riding the Trucial Oman Scouts' Arab mares and stallions at dawn most days and often in the evening too. We had a go at teaching the horses a bit of dressage and introduced some of them to a polo ball, but the best fun was dawn on a Sunday morning when we rode them bareback a mile or two down to wash them in the sea. What chaos there was when one of the mares was on heat!'

In neighbouring Muscat there was a British Army detachment in support of the Sultan's armed forces (SAF) and La Terrière recalls being woken at 7 a.m. on New Year's Day, 1961 – 'not funny for a Scotsman!' – by his Squadron Leader, George Hodgkinson, to say that the British Administrative Officer there had been blown up on a mine and that he, La Terrière, was to replace him immediately.

'I discovered that British Administrative Officer was a grand name for a postman. My job was to see that mail and other supplies got to the British Army officers and NCOs seconded to the SAF. I had Sergeant Dan Strike as my Number Two and a detachment of about six 11th Hussars and REME. We also administered a detachment of eight RAF signallers who kept the communications going between Aden, Salalah, Muscat, Sharjah and Bahrain.

'We unloaded transport aircraft about once a week and ran a convoy up-country to detachments at Nizwa, a lovely four-hour drive past the forbidding cliffs of the Jebel Akhdar mountains. At one point the route passed a pit, a circular hole in the desert about thirty feet across with smooth ten-foot sides. Wrongdoers, stripped and thrown into this prison, seldom survived more than eight days without going mad from cold at night and baking sun by day, even if they had a family who could bring them food and water. Penalties were severe: 400 lashes with a camel-cane took some surviving; for theft, amputation of right hand (sealed by plunging in boiling pitch); for adultery, buried to the neck and stoned to death. I was taken round the dreaded Jalali gaol in Muscat once, and in the dim light skeletal forms chained by hands and feet on foul straw were evidence of a régime still to emerge from the Dark Ages. Muscat was indeed a feudal city, attractively quaint, with rigorous rules. After dark carrying a light was compulsory or you were liable to be shot at.

'I handed over the detachment to Steve Bolton but not long after that, [command] having gone from Lieutenant to Captain to Major in the space of six months, the Command Secretary obviously reckoned the job had priced itself out of the market and closed it down!'

Before leaving the United Kingdom, the announcement that the Regiment would convert to tanks on its return from Aden had been made. Ironically, for the last year of its thirty-four years as an armoured-car regiment it enjoyed the rare luxury of new – or newish – equipment; the Saladin (a Saracen plus a 75mm gun) replacing the Daimler and the Ferret Scout-car, the Dingo.

RHQ was based at Balaclava Barracks, Little Aden, but the sabre squadrons (less one at Sharjah) were largely occupied in the hinterland of the Aden Protectorate where disaffection among the tribes was simmering. A visiting journalist, Douglas Kelly, recounted his experiences with C Squadron on convoy duty from Little Aden to Dhala in the Western Protectorate.

'Led by Sergeant Shaddick, a veteran of this fortnightly supply convoy, we journeyed from Aden and through the Colony/Protectorate Frontier Post at Sheikh Othman and on through the incredible fertility of Lahej. Leaving civilization, marked in this case by a passable gravel track, odd tractors and a few motorbikes carrying as many as three pillion passengers, we joined the old camel track to Taiz, in Yemen, which passes by the edge of a wind-blown sand-sea.

'Past Nobat Dakain and into the undulating rock plateau which still bore traces of recent monsoon rains, I began to realize why Kipling once described it as "a barrack stove no one's lit for years".

'This was unfriendly country and our stopping place for a quick gulp of water from canvas bags slung from the vehicles and a briefing from our Squadron Leader.

'As sweating, dust-caked drivers heaved themselves through the hatches of their Ferrets, Browning machine guns were loaded, cocked, and the Sergeant ordered: "If we come to a roadblock, keep in cover, keep your heads down, return fire if necessary."

'We were later to see a jeep which had been fired on while travelling the same route in convoy two weeks earlier. It had six holes torn in the metal. A corporal had been killed and a visiting brigadier severely injured. Passing Fort Thumier, an echo of *Beau Geste*, one hour and twenty bruises later we lurched from deep-cut *wadis* and boulder-strewn tracks and faced the immensity of Kariba Pass, set between two sheer rock faces soaring on each side to 3,000 feet. The unexpected monsoon downpour crystallized my relief that dissident tribesmen had chosen not to waste their bullets on us and my firm conviction that any Hussar who drove this route deserved a medal for endurance.*

'I prefer to forget about the Pass; it comes back now in my worst nightmares. After waiting for a camel train to come down we somehow negotiated the hairpin bends and some kind soul told me to open my eyes when we had reached the top.

---

* Neither the General Service Medal nor the clasp Arabian Peninsula were awarded for the Regiment's tour in Aden and Kuwait.

'Among other mixed-up memories of my night's stay with the Cherrypickers C Squadron, 3 Troop would include the sight of 25-pounder guns facing Mount Jebel* [*sic*] which marks the Yemen frontier garrison; hearing gunfire after dinner and seeing anxious looks exchanged as three officers left hurriedly to check the barbed-wire-and-sandbagged camp perimeter; visiting Dhala's old Turkish fort where prisoners are still kept manacled in the dungeons; and the good laugh we all had to see Sergeant Strefford sharing a hubble-bubble pipe with one of his Arab NCO colleagues.'

In April B Squadron flew to Sharjah to relieve A and in the same month Lieutenant-Colonel Philip Lauder took over from Lieutenant-Colonel Tony Crankshaw as commanding officer of the Regiment. Lauder was soon to be faced with a sharp test of the Regiment's efficiency and fitness for active service. As already explained, Iraq, now under the dictator Kassem, had long lusted after the oil wealth of Kuwait and with the abrogation of Britain's treaty with that country Kassem saw his opportunity to grab this rich prize. Iraqi troop movements towards the Kuwait border rang alarm bells in Whitehall. One day towards the end of June, 1961, the GSO1 Middle East Command telephoned Philip Lauder with instructions to open an envelope marked TOP SECRET TO BE OPENED BY THE COMMANDING OFFICER ONLY. Successive adjutants, first John Trotter and now Michael Allenby, had been aware of this mysterious document but, of course, unaware of the details of its contents. When opened, however, it was found to be empty. Consternation! Apparently what it should have contained were complete movement orders to Kuwait in the event of the eruption of this (not unexpected) crisis. The absence of these orders was unfortunate as Lauder now admits he did not even know where Kuwait was, let alone how to get there. However, in due course, this was explained by a harassed GSO1.

Lauder, Allenby and a small TAC HQ set off immediately for Kuwait, followed in quick succession by A (Major Dick

---

* Jebel means Mount in Arabic.

Sutton who had replaced Major Hodgkinson) and B (Major Tom Hall) Squadrons. C (Major Paddy Wood) did not arrive until August.

'It was a case of the blind leading the blind,' writes Lauder; 'I received very sketchy orders from the BGS at GHQ that we should all go by air, land at Kuwait, draw up vehicles which were stock-piled there [in fact B Squadron took its own vehicles by landing-craft from Sharjah and some of A's arrived by air] and get further orders from 24 Brigade Commander, Brigadier Horsford, arriving from Kenya. Eventually we sorted ourselves out and I attended an O Group and further briefing from the Brigadier. My orders were to make contact with the Kuwaiti Armoured Car Squadron (Sheikh Saleh Mohamed el Sabah, a member of the Royal Family), and, before moving up, to make a recce of the frontier area by helicopter, which I would find at the airport. Michael Allenby and I went to the airport, saw a helicopter, got on board and took off. To my dismay I was told we were going to HMS *Hermes*, not the frontier, so we landed on *Hermes*, were greeted in true RN fashion by a cool, calm, collected Captain, made welcome and after a short time ferried back in another helicopter to the airport.

'I felt rather foolish; eventually we found the right helicopter (luxury civilian machine), did our recce and returned to Kuwait. We set off to meet Sheikh Saleh with Dick Sutton's Squadron (A) and arrived at Saleh's headquarters in a violent sandstorm to be greeted by a tall, hook-nosed Arab who spoke perfect English. He looked worn out and said he had had no sleep for four nights. I explained to him that he must sleep and that I would be responsible for the frontier until he had slept.'

In due course it was arranged that responsibility for frontier patrolling would be divided on a two-thirds 11th Hussar and one-third Kuwaiti Armoured Car Squadron basis. This arrangement worked well and a rapport was soon reached between the British and Kuwaiti soldiers, confirmed in a friendly exchange of letters between Saleh and Lauder a couple of years later.

Dear Colonel Lauder,
    When I remember the serious days we spent at the borders in

the desert ready to defend our country, Kuwait, against aggression I found your picture alive in my mind. It is not easy to forget those gentlemen who came from abroad to stand with us in our crisis.

Now how are you? Are you still remembering Kuwait? The weather is good nowadays and we expect a moderate summer this year.

I do regret for not sending you a letter before this date and that is due to the absence of your address which I couldn't get before yesterday.

Before I close this letter I would like to thank you for the good comradeship you showed here, wishing you good luck and happy days always.

Please give my regards and best compliments to Major T. A. Hall and to all your fellow officers whom we met there. Thank you.

[*Signed*] Colonel Saleh Moh'd Al-Sabah

Philip Lauder replied:

Dear Sheikh Saleh,

It was with great pleasure that I received your letter dated 18 May, 1963. We too remember those dark days of 1961 when we came to stand by your country in her hour of need.

I myself shall never forget our first meeting in a sandstorm and how the bond of friendship and mutual respect was forged between your soldiers and ours in the heat of the desert.

All of us have happy memories of Kuwait and many members of the Regiment have said how much they would like to serve in your country again. As you probably know, the desert has always held a fascination for Englishmen. One of our NCOs, Staff Sergeant Stones, is indeed serving now with our Liaison Team in Kuwait.

Major T. A. Hall returns to the Regiment next year. Major R. D. Sutton, who commanded the right-hand squadron (and grew the large moustache!) takes over command of the Regiment from me this autumn. Major G. H. Hodgkinson and all my officers join me in sending our very best wishes to you and the officers and men with whom we served.

[*Signed*] Lieutenant-Colonel P. D. S. Lauder

Fortunately, the Kuwait operation never developed into a shooting war (at least not for another thirty years), but other hazards faced the troops, principally the tremendous heat which reached shade temperatures of up to 130°F and there was no shade. For medical purposes, experiments were carried out in closed-down armoured cars, Sergeant Piorkowski sticking it out for one-and-a-half hours in a temperature of 152°F. However, an air-conditioned rest-house was provided by British Petroleum at Ahmadi where all ranks were able to spend the occasional cool night. Also Tom Hall requisitioned a cold-store from an oil company across the border which provided a welcome change to compo rations. Later, back in Germany, Philip Lauder received a large bill for this but a polite reply, thanking the company for its generosity, seemed to satisfy the directors and the claim was not pressed.

The War Office, with its usual insouciance, was apparently unaware of the climatic conditions in Kuwait, reinforcements from England or Germany arriving in battle-dress. As a result several men died of heat exhaustion. However, apart from Corporal Taylor-Stokes, REME, attached to B Squadron, who was accidentally killed during the move from Sharjah to Kuwait, the 11th suffered no casualties. This was, at least in part, due to the rule that every man must drink a minimum of twelve pints of water per day.

Once in position on the frontier, B Squadron was responsible for the west side of the main Kuwait-Basra road (a route familiar to television viewers in the latter stages of the Gulf War of 1991) with A Squadron to its right. B Squadron somehow acquired the nickname of 'The Short Range Desert Group' and, in keeping with this Second World War theme, A Squadron adopted a giant camel spider called Rommel. Perhaps the most welcome innovation was a special cooling-tank designed so that half-a-dozen men at a time could sit up to their necks in water!

The Commanding Officer, with the imminent return to Europe and conversion to tanks on his mind, made several trips to Aden for consultation with higher authority, leaving the Regiment in the capable hands of his second-in-command,

Major George Hodgkinson. On one of these occasions, recalls Lauder,

'We were told there was no regular flight but we were welcome to fly back in a Beverley transport aircraft. We got on board, took off and a few minutes after take-off there was a huge bang. The aircraft keeled over and started to nose-dive. With great skill the pilot landed back at Bahrain Airport and told us to get out quick. We did and to our amazement saw a 6' × 2' hole in the side of the aircraft. I asked what they were carrying and was told warheads for aircraft missiles. Had the explosion blown inwards we would not have survived. We were shaken but lucky. It was later proved to have been sabotage.'

It was not long before Kassem realized that he had overplayed his hand and that, however enfeebled Great Britain may have become, she was still prepared to protect her interests in the Middle East, particularly where a moral issue, the threatened invasion of a small country by a larger one, could be invoked to justify military action. Furthermore, he had little support among the other Arab states and the mighty Nasser was alarmed by Kassem's all too obviously expansionist policy as it did not suit him to have Iraq increasing its wealth and power by annexing Kuwait.

There is no doubt that the arrival of British troops in Kuwait frightened Kassem who feared a pre-emptive strike, particularly after three British soldiers (not 11th Hussars), apparently on a reconnaissance mission on the Iraq side of the border, were captured. According to the British Ambassador in Baghdad, Sir Humphrey Trevelyan, the Iraqis suspected that these men had been sent to create an incident and justify a British attack. At all events, by the late summer of 1961 the 'campaign' began to fizzle out into a war of words. Kassem withdrew his forces from the frontier and tried to pretend that they had never been there. His line was that the whole incident was a British plot to discredit him; if it was, it worked admirably, for he was murdered (probably by Saddam Hussein, among others) in February, 1963.

The 11th Hussars and other British troops withdrew when the Anglo-Kuwait Joint Covering Force, as it had become known, was replaced by troops of the Arab League. Earlier, appreciation for the Regiment's role had been expressed in a letter to Philip Lauder from the C-in-C Middle East, Air Chief Marshal Sir Charles Elworthy:

20 July, 1961

Dear Philip,

Many thanks for your letter from the sharp end. You have done a really first-class job in your vital position out on a limb and to add to your success the excellent relationship that you have established with Sheikh Saleh and his force has been the most important politically, quite apart from the obvious military value.

Unlike the infantry battalions which we can arrange to rotate, the 11th Hussars will have to continue to act as a covering force, but I hope soon to make a substantial reduction in the force deployed forward so that you and your Regiment can get adequate relaxation and rest.

I should have liked to have visited you again but the political issues have been so demanding of my time that I have only been able to see each unit in Kuwait once. I am flying back to Aden today to make a start on reducing the weight of the bumf in my in-tray; but I shall be coming back from time to time.

I am grateful to you for giving George [Captain The Hon George Norrie, his ADC] a bit of real soldiering, most valuable experience for him. I have no doubt that your Regiment, like every other one involved, had profited greatly from this experience.

Thank you all for the fine job you have done. I wish I knew when I could pull you out, but I hope the date will not be too far distant.

S. C. Elworthy

For the short period of the Regiment's tour in the Arabian Peninsula which remained, it returned to duty in Aden, Sharjah and the Protectorate, sailing for home in the TT *Oxfordshire* on 7 November, 1961.

Chapter 12

THE FINAL YEARS – THE UNITED KINGDOM
AND GERMANY 1962–69

Before we embark upon the last phase of the Regiment's history we should pause to remind ourselves of some of the more distinguished members who retired, and in one case died tragically, in the early 1960s.

A sadly premature death was that of Major Sandy Reid-Scott whose Regimental career began in Palestine before the war and continued in North Africa until he was badly wounded outside Bardia in 1940, losing an eye. Prior to this he had been awarded the Military Cross. After recovering from his wounds, he went to India as ADC to the Viceroy, General Wavell, with whom he remained until 1943 when he returned to temporary command of A Squadron at Tripoli. In Italy he served as second-in-command of the squadron under John Turnbull until taking over B, leading that squadron right through to Holland in 1945.

From 1946 to '52 he commanded A Squadron twice with a staff job in between. He is remembered by his subalterns of those days with a mixture of affection and respect tinged with fear. He seldom spoke harshly but a glare from his single eye had greater effect that the most blistering rocket. Had he not been struck down in his prime by leukemia in 1960 he would almost certainly have achieved command of the Regiment.

In 1962, three of Reid-Scott's equally distinguished contemporaries, retired; Tony Crankshaw with two MCs, John Turnbull with one and 'Babe' Roberts, a holder of the French *Croix de Guerre*.

Of even longer service was Sergeant Jack Christie, born in the Regiment and in its ranks for nearly thirty years. A notable all-round athlete, few people had done more for Regimental sports over those years than Jack.

Other notable departures were those of RSM Smith, who was succeeded by RSM (later Major) Hodges; RQMS Johnson, a remarkable survivor who had been wounded no less than three times in the war, and Corporal Wilson. 'Tug' Wilson had, for many years, been a familiar figure in various barracks around the world, his chosen calling being that of Sanitary NCO. Usually accompanied by a ferocious-looking crew of locally recruited ruffians, known as 'Tug's Bandits', armed with rods, plungers and other tools of the plumbing trade, he would stalk the camp, seeking out blocked drains, cracked lavatory pans or over-filled deep drops, urging his bandits forward to their unsavoury tasks in a mixture of many tongues, laced with vivid English expletives. Once asked by an officer how he could tolerate so much of the principal ingredient of his profession, he replied with the immortal words, 'Well, sir, it may be s . . . to you, but it's bread and butter to me!'

To return to more serious matters, the not entirely welcome task now facing the Regiment was that of conversion from armoured cars to tanks, Centurions and Conquerors. At the same time, with the ending of National Service, the Regiment was seriously under strength. In 1962 the last conscripted officer (Second Lieutenant Adlard) and soldier (Trooper Cook) finished their time and the battle for recruits, which has been waged by every regiment of the British Army ever since, was on. 'What we want are men of seventeen-and-a-half to twenty-six years of age, or boys of school-leaving age who are suitable to be trained as junior leaders,' wrote the *Journal*'s editor, Steve Bolton. 'They must be prepared to learn to drive and maintain vehicles from the ¼-tonner Champ up to the 70-ton Conqueror tank. They must have the aptitude to learn signalling or to be a good tank gunner, using all the modern complex fire control equipment.'

The 11th Hussars recruiting area was Berkshire, Buckinghamshire, Gloucestershire, Oxfordshire and the City of Bristol, but 'a man who walks into any Army Information Centre (as Recruiting Officers are now called)' continued Bolton, 'and states firmly that he wants to join the 11th Hussars, must be enlisted for the 11th Hussars.'

Public Relations, hitherto an expression associated mainly with business or politics, began to take on a military significance. Early in 1962, while the Regiment was based at Tidworth, a KAPE (Keeping the Army in the Public Eye) team was formed under Captain Robert Bingley, consisting of a sergeant, two corporals, half-a-dozen troopers and two NCOs from the LAD, equipped with five Ferrets, a Saracen and two 3-tonners which transported the Regimental Mobile Recruiting Display. This team travelled the recruiting area, often accompanied by the Band and, on one occasion, a Centurion tank. Between March and November, 1962, at least a dozen towns were visited and no less than ninety-eight men recruited, bringing the Regiment to a strength of twenty-two over Peace Establishment, a remarkable achievement and a far cry from the depressing state of affairs a year earlier on return from Arabia.

Also in 1962 a Home Headquarters was established at Cirencester under Lieutenant-Colonel (Retd) John Turnbull. The role entrusted to this new organization (in more recent years located at Winchester) was that of safeguarding the interests of the Regiment, its serving members and its Old Comrades, as well as assisting with recruitment, maintaining the historical records and producing a newsletter.

In 1963, as part of the Public Relations exercise, a booklet called *Your Regiment, 11th Hussars* was published, highlighting various achievements of the past. One of these, the capture of eight German guns at Nery in 1914, gave rise to a brisk correspondence in *Soldier* magazine. A Major Smith, then curator of the Middlesex Regimental Museum, protested that these guns had been captured by his Regiment and not the 11th Hussars. However, he may have bitten off more than he could chew as heavier guns than those taken at Nery were turned upon him.

'It was my good fortune,' wrote Lieutenant-General Lord Norrie in reply, 'to have commanded 3rd Troop C Squadron 11th Hussars at Nery. The squadron had been ordered to capture the German battery. Mine was the leading troop and I confirm that we did charge the German guns with drawn swords, capturing eight of them and prisoners as well. My troop sergeant with his sword actually wounded one German gunner who was too slow in shouting "*Kamerad*" and in putting up his hands with the rest of them. There were no other British troops by the guns and the charge was a spectacular one over three hundred yards of open country. I know that both the Middlesex Regiment and the Queen's Bays have claimed the capture of the guns but this was not the case.

'The most probable explanation of the other two claims is that the main body of D Company, the Middlesex Regiment, did not arrive at the guns until 3 Troop had moved on, having handed over the guns and prisoners to the former's advance guard, and possibly the Middlesex had moved on when a party of the Bays arrived.'

Lord Norrie's counter-attack received covering fire from another Regimental heavyweight, Major-General Sir Edward (Louis) Spears.

'Willoughby Norrie's troop supported by fire from the following troops charged the guns and captured or scattered the gunners. Only one stood his ground who was run through by Sergeant Haily. There were eight guns, flanked by two machine guns, the first to be captured in the war.

'While the rest of the cavalry squadron was scouring the fields for prisoners, some companies of the Middlesex appeared. Major Lockett came to a quick understanding with them that they would take over while the cavalry moved on. I think most people would conclude that the cavalry which charged the German gunners and disposed of the gun crews were the captors of the gun.'

Out-gunned, Major Smith displayed humour and dignity in defeat.

'What a broadside from the Nery guns!' he wrote; 'General Lord Norrie's letter is a most courteous and enlightening reply which will help me in putting the record straight. He was there. I wasn't. We often have to adjust old claims and although I like to broadcast Regimental achievements, I never invent them or let inaccurate stories stand.'

Like the Nery guns, both regiments have passed into history, but no doubt, though there can be no survivors of the incident now, one day the controversy will be revived.

But we must bring ourselves back to the latter half of the twentieth century and to Hohne in West Germany where the Regiment found itself in the autumn of 1962.

In less than a year at Tidworth, 121 drivers, 119 gunners and 116 signallers were converted to tanks and the Regiment was ready to join the 7th Armoured Brigade Group, nearly ten years after leaving the then 7th Armoured Division, thus once again becoming entitled to wear the famous Desert Rat.

Of this period, until he handed over command to Lieutenant-Colonel Dick Sutton in November 1963, Philip Lauder writes:

'This was a very testing time for all. Though by now a heavy armoured regiment, we had no operational training. So, Commander 7th Armoured Brigade, Brigadier Ray Leakey, threw us in at the deep end of BAOR training. As the months went by we learnt much and by 1963 we counted ourselves more or less trained. The REME detachment was splendid and never complained (much) about the constant breakdowns and recovery from some awful places.'

The Conqueror was a 'problem' tank and there were many hiccups, but this is not the place to record the technicalities. Human error, however, was not entirely absent and Lauder recalls the occasion when an officer inadvertently set fire to his £500,000 tank, his crew having stowed their bed-rolls incorrectly. At first the offender was led to believe that he would have to foot the whole bill but eventually the long-suffering taxpayer coughed up £499,900, the officer concerned contributing the balance!

Dick Sutton's tenure of command was marked by two notable events, one momentous and the other tragic, the Guidon Presentation Parade and his own death, both in 1965. However, before dealing with these in detail we should glance at one or two important occurrences of the previous year.

On 20 March, 1964, the death took place in Scotland of a man who, although he never rose above the rank of Private (as Troopers were known in his day), was perhaps one of the better-known 11th Hussars of the twentieth century. Patrick ('Mick') Fowler, an Irishman, enlisted in the Regiment in the mid-1890s and thus by the outbreak of the First World War was already an Old Soldier who had spent much of his career as an officer's servant. He went to France with 1st Troop A Squadron and on 26 August, 1914, he and another man, Corporal Hull, found themselves separated from the rest of the squadron behind the German lines. Both were hidden by peasants in the village of Bertry near Le Cateau, but Hull was betrayed and shot by the Germans in 1915. Fowler was more fortunate and remained hidden in a wardrobe in the living-room of Madame Belmont-Gobert and her daughter, Madame Lesur, for four years. The Germans never found him and when the Allies advanced through the village in 1918 he was arrested by South African troops who thought him a spy. But again luck was on his side when, on being sent back for interrogation by the 7th Cavalry Brigade Intelligence Officer, he happened to meet Major F. V. Drake who had been his troop leader in 1914 and was able to identify him.

Not only had the women who had sheltered Fowler and Hull risked their lives for two foreign soldiers but had also suffered acute hardship in the process, having to share their meagre rations with their unexpected guests. After the war, Mesdames Belmont-Gobert and Lesur, together with Madame Cardon, who had tried to hide Hull, and the wife of the local chemist, Madame Baudhuin, were received by the King and Queen and awarded the OBE. Years later it was discovered that these gallant ladies had fallen on hard times and a fund was raised to provide them with annuities. For many years after he left the Army Fowler was employed in Scotland by The Hon Robert

Bruce, a former officer of the Regiment, where he died at the age of 88. In 1993 Mr Len Palmer, the Museum Attendant at The Royal Hussars Museum, traced and visited a living relative of these two brave women. The salver and clock presented to them by the Regiment were produced for his inspection, as were their OBEs. The family were delighted at this renewed contact with Fowler's regiment.

The First World War was again recalled to mind when in June, 1964, at the conclusion of a training visit to Leopoldsburg in Belgium, a party of the Regiment, including Trumpeters, visited the Ypres Salient.

> 'Mr Van de Court, who is Chairman of the Menin Gate Committee,' recalls Major Willie Trotter, 'kindly took us on a conducted tour round the Salient in the afternoon. We started with a visit to the German cemetery, a very dark and gloomy graveyard with nothing but numbers on the gravestones ... From here we were taken to St Julien to see the magnificent Canadian memorial, a single white stone column with the word "Canada" on the base, looking out over the Salient. Another very beautiful cemetery was Tyne Cot with 49,000 names ... We then moved through places which must mean so much to Old Soldiers – Hooge, Sanctuary Wood, Hill 60 ... finally Messines with its rebuilt church, the High Street and the view on La Douvre which 11th Hussars must have known so well, then back to Ypres past Hell Fire Corner. After laying a wreath at the Regimental Memorial the party moved on to Menin Gate. Here at 9 p.m. the Trumpeters sounded the *Last Post* and *Reveille*. Under that great arch it was a magnificent sound and a memorable end to a fascinating day.'

It was also in 1964 that Colonel Trevor Smail was obliged to retire through ill health and was succeeded by Colonel Sir John Lawson as Colonel of the Regiment. Colonel John joined the 11th Hussars at Tidworth in 1933 and served in the Second World War with great distinction, being awarded both the DSO and the MC. At various times he served on the staffs of Generals Patton and Montgomery, the latter appointing him, at the age of only thirty-two, to command the Inns of Court Regiment. At the time Lawson was second-in-command to Bill Wainman, a position which he had no desire to relinquish. A signal was sent to Monty requesting that he, Lawson, should be allowed to remain where he was. The reply was prompt and in character. 'Unless Lawson learns to do what he is told, his chances of promotion in my Army will be negligible,' signed Montgomery. There was no further argument and, in due course, this appointment qualified Lawson as Colonel of the 11th Hussars as no officer is eligible as an Honorary Colonel unless he has commanded a regiment at some stage in his career.

Since 1959 a new Guidon had been ready for presentation but for a variety of reasons the parade did not take place until 13 July, 1965, in the 250th anniversary year of the formation of the 11th Light Dragoons, in fact within nine days of the date of that formation. It was also the 125th anniversary of the Colonelcy of the Prince Consort, Prince Albert of Saxe-Coburg.

A request had been put forward to the Ministry of Defence that the four Guards on parade, each representing a squadron and totalling seventeen officers and two hundred men, should be allowed to wear No 1 Dress, which was not standard issue to troopers, and to carry swords. In the application document an interesting point was made. 'By a unique tradition dating back to 1784, all ranks salute with the sword on the final General (or Royal) Salute at the end of a parade. The Guidon presentation would be the last time, and a most fitting and approriate one, that this manoeuvre would be seen.' Incredibly, it appears that two hundred swords had been 'made available', although it is unclear whence these weapons were to come. However, in the event insufficient No 1 Dress blue tunics could be produced and all four Guards paraded in No 2 Dress (khaki jackets and crimson trousers) and carried rifles.

Preparations for the parade had started in April and, as the editor of the *Journal*, Captain The Hon George Norrie, put it, 'drill had been a mystery to most 11th Hussars until the spring of 1965'. The mystery soon turned into a nightmare when officers and men found themselves being chased round the square, hour after hour and day after day, by two ferocious 'Drill-Pigs' of the Coldstream Guards.

1965 was a wet summer in Germany but miraculously, after twenty-one consecutive days of rain, the sky cleared and the sun came out in time to greet Her Majesty the Queen Mother who was to present the Guidon. In her address, Her Majesty recalled that the late King had been Colonel-in-Chief of the Regiment and, as one of the original Desert Rats, the 11th Hussars 'had helped to turn uncertainty into victory'. She also pointed out that the Parade was a revival of a tradition which had lapsed more than a hundred years earlier and that the 11th Hussars had not carried a Guidon since 1840. In his reply, the Commanding Officer, Lieutenant-General Dick Sutton, noted the long-standing link between the Regiment and the Royal House and remembered that the Regiment's role in the desert campaign had been rewarded by a visit from the late King at Tunis in 1943.

Among other personages who attended the parade were Princess Marina of Kent, the Duke and Duchess of Kent and Field Marshal Lord Harding. Also present were such distinguished 11th Hussars as Generals Norrie, Combe and Spears. But, apart from Her Majesty and the Commanding Officer, perhaps the 'key' figures on parade were the members of the Guidon Party, RQMS R. Hollins, SQMS P. Gillott and Staff Sergeant R. Stones.

The four Guards were commanded by Captain R. Bingley (C), Major W. J. Pinney (A), Major W. K. Trotter (B) and Captain The Hon G. Norrie (RHQ). The Mounted Detachment was commanded by Captain J. Lewis. The RSM was WO1 A. M. Alderton and the Bandmaster WO1 J. A. O'Brien.

After lunch a polo competition, won by the Scots Greys, was played and in the evening a splendid ball, organized by Willie Trotter, for 600 people was held. On the following day the by now exhausted guests and members of the Regiment alike struggled through a programme of demonstrations, sports, lunches and another ball, this time in the Sergeants' Mess. Further dances were held for Corporals and All Ranks on subsequent evenings and by the weekend all concerned must have been in a state of happy and contented collapse.

In the days that followed numerous letters of appreciation were received by both the Colonel and the Commanding

Officer, notably one on behalf of The Queen Mother expre sing her admiration for 'the steadiness and bearing of the Regiment' and thanking all 11th Hussars for 'the magnificent silver cigarette box' with which she had been presented.

These celebrations were continued a few weeks later by an official visit to Coburg, the birthplace of Prince Albert, which was to have disastrous consequences. The visit took place from 4 to 8 August and the Regiment was represented by its Commanding Officer, the Band, the Guidon Party and a small detachment of other officers and men. The Guidon was paraded through the streets of the town and a reception was held in the Town Hall. On the Sunday morning a wreath was laid on the War Memorial and another by Lieutenant Prince Michael of Kent, an officer of the Regiment, on the memorial to his great-great-grandfather, Prince Albert.

The following day, the 9th, Dick Sutton and his wife Sally, driven by Trooper R. Fryer of RHQ Squadron, set out in their staff car to return to Hohne. At about midday near the village of Königshofen, some twenty miles north-west of Coburg, the car, which for some unexplained reason had veered across to the left side of the road, collided head-on with a civilian lorry. First on the scene of the accident was a Munich film producer, Herr Fleischmann, who had been filming the Coburg visit. He enlisted the aid of the German Frontier Police to arrange for an American Army helicopter to fly Colonel Sutton to Würzberg University Hospital. Mrs Sutton remained at Königshofen with a fractured left shoulder and concussion but in no danger. Fryer had been killed almost outright, crushed behind the steering-wheel, while Sutton had been hurled through the windscreen. The German lorry-driver was unhurt.

Under the care of a German brain specialist, Dr Simon, Brigadier Waterstone of the RAMC and a well-known diagnostic physician, Dr Gill, who was the wife of the Commander of the 7th Armoured Brigade, the Colonel at first appeared to be making some progress, at one moment briefly recovering consciousness and speaking to Dr Gill. However, on the evening of 12 August he suffered complications to the brain and it became necessary to operate. The doctors operated continuously from

7 p.m. until 4 a.m. the next morning but to no avail. Colonel Sutton did not recover consciousness again and died at about 7.15 a.m. on 13 August, so far as the present author can ascertain, the only Commanding Officer of the 11th Hussars to die or to be killed while in command of the Regiment. Happily, Sally Sutton eventually made a full recovery and later gave birth to a healthy daughter.

Another officer to die under similar circumstances was Second Lieutenant David Perkins, who had been killed while on border patrol in August, 1963. This may be an appropriate point at which to note that of the approximately forty members of the Regiment who died or were killed in the period 1945-69, over thirty were the victims of traffic accidents.

On 22 August a joint Memorial Service was held for Richard Sutton and Richard Fryer on the Linton Square at Hohne, where so recently the Guidon had been presented at a very different ceremony. Thus Colonel and Trooper were remembered together, a trumpeter sounding the Last Post in their memory.

Dick Sutton, who was only forty-one at the time of his death, had joined the Regiment in Italy in 1943 and had seen much action in France and Belgium in 1944, losing several members of his troop (2 Troop A Squadron), killed and wounded, in a devastating air attack shortly after D-Day. But in September, 1944, he was taken prisoner near the village of St Nicholas in Belgium after his armoured car had been knocked out by a Panther tank and remained 'in the bag' until the end of the war.

In 1950 he was appointed Adjutant and in Malaya commanded first RHQ and then C Squadron. During the Kuwait operation, as we have seen, he commanded A Squadron. There is no doubt that the greatest ambition of this big, cheerful man was to follow in his father's footsteps by achieving command of the 11th Hussars. This he did in November, 1963. His wartime troop sergeant, Nobby Hall, who contributed to his obituary, remembered being summoned to his office and being told, 'I am to command the Regiment!' Hall went on:

'The pride and joy ringing in his voice as he told me this was matched only by the sense of pleasure and of "mission accomplished" that I felt. Some twenty years before, the late Colonel "Squeak" Sutton had given me some pretty tall orders. "Look after the boy (and) keep him out of trouble" were his instructions. With a nod and my thanks for an excellent dinner I took his son off to war.'

Temporary command of the Regiment devolved upon Sutton's second-in-command, Major Tom Hall, who wrote,

'1965 has been a year of triumph and tragedy probably unparalleled in recent regimental history and for those of us who have had the honour to serve in or with the Regiment, a year which will be completely unforgettable.'

Lieutenant-Colonel Peter Hamer had been appointed to succeed Dick Sutton prior to the latter's death but Tom Hall 'held the fort' for seven months until Hamer's return from extra-Regimental employment.

In 1966, under its new Colonel, the Regiment faced the challenge of introducing the untried Chieftain tank to the Army. Of this new weapon, Peter Hamer wrote later.

'For all the criticisms you can read in the Press you might imagine it was antiquated before it came into service. This is the opposite of the truth: it is, in fact, the most advanced fighting machine in the world.

'Ask any light cavalryman what he wants: speed. In spite of all the hullabaloo from the Krauts about Leopard, Chieftain has a good or better acceleration and a better sustained speed.

'Ask a Russian: endurance! We can do better. Ask an Italian: he lacked armour protection in the last war. We have the best in the world, immune to any known tank at very short ranges.

'Ask Trooper Bloggs, he wants the lot and much more; he will agree he has got it and more still. Finally and most important of all, ask any armoured soldier of the desert days what we really lacked and he will tell you: a gun! Chieftain's gun is unbelievable, an 8-inch group at 2,000 yards is pretty good. I believe the 11th Hussars could take on a complete brigade, or more, of anyone else's and see it off day or night, moving or stationary.'

How much substance there was to this high-flown enthusiasm must be left to the judgement of the knowledgeable reader, particularly if he has personal experience of the subject of this hyperbole. Nonetheless, there can be little doubt that the Chieftain contrasted favourably with one of its predecessors, Conqueror, described by Hamer as 'a very expensive failure'.

Coincidental with the introduction of Chieftain, changes were taking place in the tactical management of the armoured brigade. A description of the 'Balanced Brigade' concept was contributed to the 1966 *Journal*.

'In this new experimental organization each brigade has an equal amount of armour and infantry; two armoured regiments and two infantry battalions; the armour and infantry are more closely integrated at all levels than has previously been the case.

'Each regimental and battalion headquarters becomes a Battle Group headquarters with a number of Combat Teams under command plus a supporting gunner battery. A Combat Team consists of a squadron or company headquarters with a combination of tank troops, infantry platoons and a section of armoured engineers. Troops and platoons can be moved from one Combat Team to another. Under this organization, infantry company commanders command some of our tank troops and infantry battalion comanders have one or more of our squadron leaders under them as Combat Team Commanders.'

All this, no doubt, was of great importance and the subject of intense study to those with higher military aspirations, but probably of far more interest to the majority was the victory of the 1966 Regimental football team in the Army Cup. In the competition the team scored 22 goals with only 10 against it and defeated the 1st Bn, The King's Regiment 3–0 in the final at Aldershot. The players were: Trooper Howard (goalkeeper); Lance-Corporal Robertson REME, Bandsman Walton and Sergeant Battye REME (backs); Sergeant Sleep REME, Lance-Corporal Chippendale and Trooper Maynard (half-backs); Cfn Clarkson REME (Captain), Trooper Connell, Lance-Corporal Cotterill, Troopers Tatt and Hepple (forwards). The reserves were Cfn Kirtley REME, Lance-Corporal Coles and Trooper

Partridge. SSM Melles and SSI Charnock played important roles in training and coaching.

As at most other periods of its history, in the mid and late 'sixties we find members of the Regiment scattered throughout the globe in various appointments: Frank Henn at the Australian Staff College; John Woodhouse at SHAPE; Ieuan Davies on the British Military Mission to Libya (pre-Gaddafi); Val Cockle in Washington with the British Joint Services Mission; Paddy Hughes-Young with the Zambian Armoured Car Regiment and, most exotically of all, Nick Muers-Raby flying a helicopter from HMS *Bulwark*.

Writing at the time, Muers Raby described the astonishment of those flying with him on discovering that their pilot was an 11th Hussar. 'If you are surprised you should see the looks on some of my passengers' faces! In fact this squadron (845) must be one of the most 'Joint Services Units' operating today! Twelve from the Royal Navy, nine Royal Marines, three from the RAF and two from the Army'. After training with the Army Air Corps, Muers Raby had hoped to join a regimental flight (see 10th Hussars), which never materialized, but was sent to 7th Armoured Brigade flight in Germany with which he spent two years. 'When I saw the chance of a two-year tour with the Royal Navy I seized it and I can report that there are more exciting places in this world than Hohne Camp and Ranges, and that even Soltau Training Area seems to lose a little of its magic when compared with Singapore, Brisbane, Sydney and Hong Kong!' wrote this modern-day Biggles.

Although the helicopter had been in operation, particularly with the Royal Navy, for some years (11th Hussars first encountered it in Malaya in the early 'fifties), it was not until the 'sixties that its full military potential was realized and perhaps not even then.

In February, 1966, Peter Upton, then serving as DAAG 3 Division at Bulford, sent an interesting memorandum to his GOC (General Blacker) on the subject of a helicopter force, basing his theme on the formation in the 1920s of an 'Experimental Mechanized Force' as recommended to the then CIGS by Liddell Hart. Upton pointed out that, although the British experiment had failed through half-hearted leadership and financial stringency, it had been successfully adopted by the Germans (as evidenced by the campaigns in Poland, the Low Countries and France in 1939/40) and might be used as the basis for an Experimental Helicopter Force, 'only this time galvanized by the right commander and given more reliable support'.

Upton went on to suggest that such a Force might evolve through the setting up of a Helicopter Brigade HQ at Tidworth and assigning to it one infantry battalion and 'an RN/RAF Force of as many Wessex helicopters as could be spared from operational commitments', this force to be built up with a further one or two battalions and supporting arms.

After discussing a possible commander and senior staff officers for the force, Upton realistically concluded that 'the main obstacle would almost certainly be financial' and probably, as in the 1920s, the indifference of the Director of Staff Duties.

General Blacker received Upton's paper appreciatively but without optimism. He too foresaw indifference on the part of the DSD 'as well as considerable inter-service complications', which proved to be the case when the RAF objected to being required to produce the helicopters. Nevertheless, unwilling to dash Upton's enthusiasm, the General concluded, 'the idea could do with development and I am grateful for it'. Ironically, he had recently been appointed DSD himself.

Although Upton had deliberately avoided suggesting a role for cavalry regiments in his proposed forces, he had made this omission for tactical reasons to avoid appearing to have designed his idea for the sake of his own arm of the service. However, the Americans have used so-called Air Cavalry under operational conditions, not least in the Gulf War of 1990, with marked success. Perhaps we have here a repetition of the pre-Second World War situation where a foreign army developed advantageously a British concept which the British themselves chose to neglect. Had some additional role been found for the cavalry in the 1960s, many famous names might have survived and some of the traumatic amalgamations with which the British Army has been plagued since the war might have been avoided.

*

The 1967 *Journal* opened with a sombre message from The Colonel of the Regiment, Sir John Lawson:

'Since the last *Journal* was published many members of the Regiment will have heard with great sadness the news about the amalgamation.

'The Regiment was informed in July, 1967, by the Ministry of Defence that in order to achieve the Government's new man-power ceiling, the Army Board had decided that a reduction in the Royal Armoured Corps would, amongst other steps, be effected by the amalgamation of the 11th Hussars (Prince Albert's Own) and the 10th Royal Hussars (Prince of Wales's Own).

'Dwelling on the sadness of these events which all 11th Hussars automatically and deeply feel, unfortunately serves no useful purpose.

'His Royal Highness the Duke of Gloucester, who is Colonel-in-Chief of the 10th Royal Hussars, has said that he would be proud to serve as Colonel-in-Chief of the new Regiment when it is formed.

'In 1969 the 11th Hussars will return to England enabling all of us at home to see them again and, a short time later, we shall be able to be present at the Amalgamation Ceremony.

'I am sure that all 11th Hussars will agree that these are unpredictable days for their Regiment and indeed for the Army as a whole. Assurances that are given one day are cast aside on the next; standards of honesty in speech are at their lowest ebb. Let us hope and indeed pray that we may now be left alone in our endeavour to create something new out of something old and to be determined that tradition, comradeship and high standards are a very well worthwhile thing.'

Sir John's words have a familiar ring in the early 1990s when another round of amalgamations was to give rise to many of the same emotions, as we shall see in the final chapter of this book. [The author's more pungent comments regarding Sir John's remarks about 'standards of honesty' were excised by the Ministry of Defence.]

The news was received with a variety of emotions ranging from dismay to indifference. Obviously, elderly and retired members of the Regiment felt the forthcoming loss of their spiritual home more keenly than young troopers with a year or

1. Presentation of the Guidon by Her Royal Highness Princess Alice, Duchess of Gloucester, Colonel-in-Chief, with Colonel Sir Piers Bengough, Major M.W. Keats and RQMS Halffman, 30 June, 1990.

2. HM The Queen Mother, met by Colonel Sir John Lawson, arrives at the Guidon Parade at Hohne, 1965.

3. CT headgear and propaganda leaflets 'liberated' by Second-Lieutenant J.H. Harris 11th Hussars, Malaya, 1954.

4. Challenger tank on Soltau Training Area, 1983.

FROM THE ORIGINAL OIL PAINTING BY TERENCE CUNEO

*Colonel Sir Thomas Cerise — Blue Vinney, O.G.M.**
at the charge of Catnip Valley, 1854

*ORDER OF THE GOLDEN MOUSETRAP

5. 'The last Charge of the 11th Hussars' (see p.159).

two's service. In the late 1960s there were still many survivors of the pre-1914 regular army in which the fierce spirit of regimental loyalty burnt more brightly among all ranks than perhaps it does today. In those Imperial days, while officers would 'cut' those of other regiments of which they did not approve, private soldiers would fight to the death in the dives and brothels of Cairo and Calcutta at the hint of an imagined insult to theirs.

From that generation of officers came, for example, General Sir Louis Spears, who, writing to his contemporary, Bobby Hartman, remarked, 'I feel terribly sad about the amalgamation with the 10th, whom I have always considered, perhaps unjustly, as mounted poodle-fakers.' Doubtless there were those on the other side who felt the same.

However, one former officer now takes the view that the amalgamation was not untimely in that the Regiment's fortunes and morale were at a low ebb. 'Hohne for seven years, the longest period in one barracks since before the war and the dreary repetition of the annual training cycle – gunnery on the ranges and exercises on the Soltau Training Area – were beginning to take their toll with an air of boredom together with associated disciplinary problems. One or two soldiers even refused to wear their uniforms!'

So, it may be argued, the prospect of amalgamation at least gave people something novel to look forward to.

Later, after the Regiment's return to England, some of the more boisterous and flamboyant young officers formed the Albert Club, denouncing Shiners and flaunting its own remarkably unattractive tie, crimson, of course, with large yellow balls. But on the whole it was felt that the best had to be made out of a bad job. Brian Osmand, the 11th's last RSM and The Royal Hussars' first, recalls that

'news of the amalgamation was given out in sufficient time for those that felt too strongly about it either to apply for transfer or redundancy [and] of course some did leave. Looking back there was initially the shock as I for one thought we would escape the reductions. Having once accepted the news we all got down to planning the busy days which lay ahead.'

The Regiment's last year in Germany was one of great international tension and 7th Armoured Brigade, which, of course, included the 11th Hussars, was in a sense in the front line.

On the editorial page of the 1967 *Journal* there is reproduced a photograph of Lieutenant-Colonel Peter Hamer and his Adjutant, Captain R. C. G. Gardner, being presented with a scroll by an officer of the 11th Panzer Aufklarüng Battalion of the *Bundeswehr* (West German Army), a reconnaissance regiment with which the 11th were twinned. The ceremony itself may be unremarkable but is linked, albeit tenuously, with those dramatic events which followed a year later, remembered as the 'Prague Spring' and the invasion of Czechoslovakia, an international crisis and potential Hot War flash point not experienced since the Hungarian uprising of 1956.

The military historian Antony Beevor, then a subaltern in the 11th, recalls the occasion and subsequent international events.

'(We) were twinned with the 11th Panzerbattalion and our Colonel was invited to an evening ceremony at their barracks near Munsterlager. Expecting no more than a couple of speeches and a few toasts in the Mess, he and the adjutant were a little taken aback to find themselves facing the whole regiment drawn up on a full torchlight parade.

'Only one of the Panzer officers, a member of a well-known military family, ever came to our Mess at Hohne as a personal guest. After dinner, conversation turned to the recent rise of the NPD neo-Nazi party. He told us the NPD was gaining enormous support within the *Bundeswehr* where its call for the reunification of Germany struck a very emotional chord.

'Not long afterwards the Warsaw Pact forces invaded Czechoslovakia. Over the next weeks, the West Germans concentrated their condemnation on their "*frères ennemis*" (East Germans) whose army had provided the second largest contingent. And the East Germans in turn accused Bonn of having instigated the trouble in the first place. The Cold War had taken a particularly virulent turn.

'For the British Army, however, life returned to normal. Autumn manoeuvres, in the form of Exercise Eternal Triangle, required weeks of preparation, and at the beginning of September, our thoughts focused on the Bad Lippspringe polo weekend.

For spectators and participants, the main attraction that year was the dance to be given by the Royal Dragoons. To my irritation I found I was down for Regimental Orderly Officer on the Friday, which meant little sleep the night before the party.

'When my tour of duty finished on Saturday morning, I handed over to my replacement and went back to the Mess for a late breakfast. Afterwards, as I was leaving to change out of uniform, I passed a rather bemused fellow officer who said that apparently the 2nd Royal Tank Regiment, the other armoured regiment in the 7th Armoured Brigade, had just been put on full stand-by for war.

'The idea seemed so improbable that neither of us could treat it with any seriousness. Quite obviously, the Second Tanks had received the wrong codeword. Whoever sent it must have meant QUICK TRAIN, the codeword for a practice turn-out. I slipped away to pack my dinner jacket and drove off before anyone could stop me.

'On the way south, I began to feel ashamed of such irresponsibility and even considered turning back. But when I arrived at the Lippspringe polo ground soon after lunch and found a number of familiar faces already flushed with Pimms, my guilt immediately lifted. They had heard some rumour, but nobody believed it. We knew from intelligence reports that the Warsaw Pact troops in Czechoslovakia were incapable of offensive action. Out of fuel and short of rations, they were all utterly demoralized because their commanders had told them they would be welcomed by the Czechs as liberators.

'They were also in a state of complete chaos. We had heard from the American sector opposite the Czech border that the day after the invasion a West German patrol in Saladin armoured cars had suddenly sighted a platoon of Russian tanks charging across the open fields in their direction. The sergeant gave the order to load their 76mm main armament and sent back a contact report preparatory to opening fire. At the last moment they saw a figure running across their front waving his arms. He turned out to be a Czech border guard. Fortunately, the Russian commander spotted him and stopped to ask where they were. He did not have a map. With the Russian Army in such a state, the idea of them trying to invade the West as well seemed much more like a bad joke.

'Contrary to our expectations the rumours did not die away.

Soon after the party started, word arrived of more units moving out to their Forward Defence Locations. After much questioning of senior officers, it emerged that the flap had in fact been caused by the opposite of a Russian invasion. A *Bundeswehr* armoured division appeared to have gone rogue and was threatening to invade East Germany. This produced at first a reaction of utter disbelief and then confusion. NATO was supposed to be a truly defensive alliance, and if some crackpots in the *Bundeswehr* were trying to pick a fight with East Germany, then the British Army would surely have to withdraw over the Dutch or Belgian frontier. Subalterns asked majors whether it would actually come down to shooting the polo ponies and chucking the Regimental silver on to 3-tonners as the whole Army pulled out in a hurry.

'Around midnight, news came that the regiments called out had been told they could return to barracks. "Just knew it!" we all said; "Typical bloody panic about nothing!"'

But that is not quite the end of the story. Many years later, having left the Army in 1970, Beevor found himself staying on an estate in Brazil owned by a German family and managed by a cousin of the officer of the 11th Panzer Aufklarüng Battalion who had dined with the 11th Hussars in the 1960s. After dinner one evening, Beevor recounted the story of the 1968 'flap' to his host, who listened with interest and then said, 'But it wasn't just one division, it was four!' His brother-in-law had been on one of the divisional staffs at the time, he explained, and the leading units had advanced to within a few miles of the East German frontier before news of their intentions reached a horrified Bonn government via the British commander of NATO's Northern Army Group whence, presumably, the 'rogue' divisions came. An immediate withdrawal was ordered and, perhaps surprisingly, obeyed and a desperate cover-up instituted, junior officers and men being told that they had simply been taking part in a rapid response exercise.

Such was the uncorroborated story according to Beevor's host, but it does appear that a number of senior German officers were relieved of their commands at about that time. The truth may emerge when relevant British documents are released in 1998 under the Thirty Year Rule – but then it may not.

So, Europe may have been on the brink of a war which might ultimately have obliterated half the world or, paradoxically, have saved the 11th Hussars from extinction!

In the autumn of 1968 Lieutenant-Colonel Clive Robertson took over from Lieutenant-Colonel Peter Hamer as the Regiment's 53rd and last Commanding Officer. He had joined the 11th Hussars in 1947 and was Adjutant in Malaya where he was twice Mentioned in Despatches. In 1957, after several courses at Lulworth, he was selected to go to Australia as a member of a Ministry of Supply trials team to assess 'Malkara', the first anti-tank wire-guided missile which was being developed by the Government Aircraft Factory in Melbourne. This missile, though primitive by today's standards, was extremely accurate and capable of knocking out any known tank of that epoch. Robertson recalls that Woomera, where the trials were held, was an 'exciting and dangerous place', as anti-aircraft missiles such as Bloodhound and Seaslug were being tested at the same time, not a few blowing up or getting out of control. Eventually 'Malkara' was purchased by the British Government and the same team carried out acceptance firing trials in Scotland and subsequently formed the RAC Guided Weapons Wing.

After passing both Staff College and the Joint Service Staff College and a stint at the Ministry of Defence, Robertson returned to the Regiment as second-in-command in 1967. Not only was he to be the 11th Hussars' last Commanding Officer but The Royal Hussars' first. In 1980 he retired from the Army as a Brigadier and was for some years on the staff of the Duke of Edinburgh. In the New Year's Honours of 1992 he was appointed a CVO. His predecessor, Peter Hamer, was rewarded with an OBE for his work in introducing and training with the Chieftain tank.

In the run-up to amalgamation some 150 members of the Regiment retired or were made redundant, including Majors Davies, Addis, Harding and Lewis. The 'Oldest Soldier' of these was Harry Addis who had joined the Regiment in Egypt in 1939, serving with distinction throughout the war in which he was twice wounded and Mentioned in Despatches after Alamein. Commissioned in 1957 as Technical Quartermaster, he was appointed Quartermaster in 1964.

Early in 1969 the 11th Hussars left Germany for England and the final chapter of their history. At the end of his editorial in the last (1968) issue of the *Journal*, Captain Hayman-Joyce wrote, 'Let us hope the breeders will leave us alone for a while so that we can mature and improve the strain.' Now, only twenty-three years later, we know this to have been a forlorn hope indeed.

An unusual event occurred in May, 1969, when Captain Prince Michael of Kent and Captain Eric Westropp took part in the *Daily Mail* Transatlantic Air Race from the top of the Post Office Tower in London to the 86th floor of the Empire State Building in New York and back. Captain Westropp set off on the outward leg at 0911 hours on 9 May proceeding by motor-cycle, power-boat and helicopter to Brize Norton and thence by VC10 to Kennedy Airport. From there he was whisked by motor-cycle (a 750cc model driven by BSA's chief US display rider) in appalling weather conditions through the streets of the Big Apple. Unfortunately his time does not seem to have been recorded. However, Prince Michael, who undertook the return journey by similar means of transport, clocked 7 hours and 45 minutes. Neither time qualified for a prize, but the *Daily Mail* made a special award in recognition of the teamwork shown by the Regiment. Among those playing supporting roles were Captain Fred Barker, Sergeant Humberstone, Corporals Hoste, Allewell and (appropriately) Shuttle, and Mr Robin Seel, a former 11th Hussar living in New York.

Details of the preparation for amalgamation and the ceremony itself, held on the 115th anniversary of Balaclava, are recorded elsewhere in this book. Suffice it to say here that there was a powerful desire on the part of all ranks to build the new Regiment on the strong traditions of its parents, an endeavour in which, as we shall see, they were admirably successful. Brian Osmand recalls the final words of the WOs' and Sergeants' Mess notes in the last *Journal*:

'We request all our many friends to note that as from 25 October, 1969, the goods traded under a different brand name will be of the same high quality one has come to expect of such a good firm. This is a guarantee, with no small print, on which you can rely.'

Among the tributes which have been paid to the 11th Hussars are those from former commanders of 7 Brigade with whom the Regiment was closely associated. General Sir Robert Ford writes:

'I feel that 11H did possess certain special qualities and that they were based on a superficial attitude of cheerful lightheartedness concealing a fierce pride and a belief that only the highest standards were acceptable. I also recall the excellent informal relationship between officers and men, perhaps even a little ahead of its time.'

General Sir Richard Worsley adds:

'The officers and men were highly professional; but combined this with a sure and light touch. Nothing was too much trouble and the attitude of the Regiment was summed up in the phrase "Yes, certainly, of course we will".'

And Major-General I. G. Gill has this to say:

'As their Brigade Commander I spent some of my time in the good company of the 11th Hussars. I never discovered why they were different from other regiments of the British Army but they were . . . An 11th Hussar seems to acquire a selective instinct for what is important and what is not . . . Once it is agreed what is to be done, they raise their game effortlessly with spectacular results.'

The words 'last' and 'final' have, perforce, been used all too frequently in these pages, but we cannot ring down the curtain on the history of a famous cavalry regiment without mounting a 'Last Charge'.

Appropriately, Terence Cuneo's delightful picture, reproduced in this book, was adopted as the 1968 Regimental Christmas card over the caption, *The Last Charge of the 11th Hussars*. 'Last Charge' there was, although not quite as depicted by Cuneo. In the Introduction to his book *Inside the British Army*, after describing the discomforts of Exercise Eternal Triangle in October, 1968, Antony Beevor wrote:

'Our Commanding Officer ordered the last charge of the 11th Hussars, a thoroughly untactical and unchoreographed attack in which two squadrons of Chieftains thundered in line abreast towards an astounded 2nd Panzergrenadier Brigade in a final, self-awarded encore before the Regiment was amalgamated.'

So, after two-and-a-half centuries, the old Cherrypickers went out with a bang, not a whimper.

ICH DIEN

The Royal Hussars

(Prince of Wales's Own)

Chapter 13

FORMATION 1969

The Royal Hussars were born at Tidworth on 25 October, 1969, the offspring of the marriage of the 10th and 11th Hussars, not exactly a 'shotgun' wedding but one imposed upon partners who would have preferred to remain single. But the parents were well bred and conscientious and the child flourished, only to be cut down in early maturity by that same authority which had decreed its birth in the first place. But on that October day, the 115th Anniversary of the Charge of the Light Brigade, hopes were high and thoughts were only of the immediate future.

The Chief Executive, for want of a better title, in charge of the organization of the event itself was the Second-in-Command of the new Regiment, Major Piers Bengough, ably assisted by RQMS Fox, who was responsible for all the equipment required for the occasion, and a team of trusty helpers.

One of the first questions which had to be settled was the actual location of the parade. All the barrack squares in the area were recce'd but discarded for one reason or another and eventually the Tidworth Tattoo Ground was chosen. This choice, however, had its disadvantages, not least that it doubled as the Tidworth Rugby Club Ground and, being grass, could quickly become a quagmire.

'The news that the Regiment was to march on grass,' says the *Journal* of the following year, 'was greeted with anguish by the Old Brigade! No more the crack of boots on tarmac and the easy rhythm of marching on a hard surface; most highly intricate movements were to be made on grass which would more than likely be hopelessly wet.'

In the light of these reservations an elaborate wet-weather alternative programme was planned, but, happily, in the event did not have to be used. As for dress, it had been hoped that No 1 Dress could be worn but as this was no longer official issue, the Regiment had to settle for No. 2 (Service) Dress.

The great day dawned overcast but mercifully dry enough for the outdoor programme to go ahead. Thanks largely to the efforts of Drill Sergeant Groves of the Irish Guards, foot and arms drill, always a problem for cavalry regiments through lack of practice, had been brought to a high standard.

Not only was a new Guidon to be presented by the Colonel-in-Chief, HRH Princess Alice, the Duchess of Gloucester, but the Regiment was handed over by the last Commanding Officer of the 10th Hussars, Lieutenant-Colonel B. C. Greenwood, to the first Commanding Officer of the Royal Hussars, Lieutenant-Colonel C. H. Robertson, who was also the last Commanding Officer of the 11th Hussars.

Apart from those mentioned above and the Colonels of the two parent regiments, Major-General Sir David Dawnay and Colonel Sir John Lawson, the principal personalities involved were the members of the three Guidon Parties, the commanders of the Mounted Escorts and of the four Guards, each representing a squadron. These were: –

The Royal Hussars Guidon Party
RQMS J. Kolaczkowski (Bearer)
SQMS A. Watson
SQMS R. Chatwin
under the command of RSM B. Osmand

The 10th Hussar Guidon Party
WO11 R. E. Courtney (Bearer)
SQMS C. F. Wass
Staff Sergeant R. J. Standley

Formation

The 11th Hussar Guidon Party
WO11 D. A. N. Strike
SQMS A. Day
Staff Sergeant L. W. Knights

10th Hussar Mounted Escort Commander – Captain the Hon
    G. B. Norrie
11th Hussar Mounted Escort Commander – Captain R. E. R.
    Morgan

Guard Commanders
No 1 Guard – Major P. D. Mesquita
No 2 Guard – Major D. J. W. Anstice
No 3 Guard – Major The Hon G. W. M. Norrie
No 4 Guard – Major H. Dawnay

Once the parade had been inspected by the Colonel-in-Chief and handed over to Lieutenant-Colonel Robertson by Lieutenant-Colonel Greenwood, the old Guidons were marched off and the new Guidon consecrated by the Chaplain-General to the Forces, the Venerable Archdeacon J. R. Youens. The Colonel-in-Chief then presented the new Guidon to the Regiment and, after addresses by Her Royal Highness and the Commanding Officer, it was trooped through the ranks with an escort from No 1 Guard under Second Lieutenant P. J. Hall.

The Regiment then marched past its Colonel-in-Chief, No 1 Guard carrying swords and the others rifles. This was followed by an Advance in Review Order and the proceedings were concluded by a March Past of the Old Comrades led by Lieutenant-General Lord Norrie.

Afterwards over two thousand people were entertained to lunch in three centres, the Officers' and Sergeants' Messes and the gymnasium.

At the conclusion of his report on this memorable occasion the *Journal*'s editor, Captain G. J. W. Malet, remarked, 'It was wonderful to see so many people, both past and present, coming to support their new Regiment, though we hope there is no immediate likelihood of our having to run anything on quite the same scale in the near future.' The ceremonial over, The Royal Hussars got down to business.

Chapter 14

TIDWORTH 1969–73

The de facto existence of the Regiment had begun on 2 September, 1969, when the 10th and 11th joined up at Perham Down, although technically it did not become The Royal Hussars until Amalgamation Day, 25 October. Two days later it took over the role of armoured regiment of the Army Strategic Reserve and moved to Bhurtpore Barracks, Tidworth in December.

For former Shiners, particularly those more recently joined, this meant relearning the art of tank warfare after five years in armoured cars. 'Shake-down' exercises were held on Salisbury Plain and it was on one of these that Lance-Corporal Eldridge drew first blood for the Regiment when he inadvertently blew up a cock-pheasant with a 105mm blank!

Within the new Regiment there appeared two new entities: the Administrative Squadron (Major H. Dawnay), replacing RHQ Squadron, and the Command and Support Squadron (Major W. J. Pinney), which comprised the Command Troop, Recce Troop and Guided Weapons Troop.

The Guided Weapons Troop was an interesting but short-lived innovation which disappeared a few years later when GW anti-tank responsibility was temporarily transferred to the Royal Artillery. The troop consisted of eight AFV 438s (tracked launcher vehicles) and two Ferrets. The 438s were usually commanded by junior NCOs and the Ferrets by the troop leader and the troop staff sergeant, who each commanded a half-troop. Its role was primarily long range anti-tank defence of the armoured regiment using Swingfire missiles. Each 438 carried fourteen missiles with a range of 4,000 metres and a flight time of 29 seconds. One officer recalls, 'It packed a big punch – if you hit the target!'

As for the Admin Squadron, perhaps its most notable personality was WOII M. (Paddy) Byrne, BEM, of the ACC, who had been posted to the 11th Hussars some 20 years earlier and had decided it was a pretty good billet. Regrettably, none of the stories related about (or by) this archetypal Irish soldier are suitable for family reading. A famous greyhound fancier, he was also, if only incidentally, an excellent cook.

A tragic early loss to the Regiment was the death in a riding accident of another Paddy, Captain the Hon P. M. Hughes-Young, who had joined the 11th in Aden and quickly demonstrated his leadership qualities during the Kuwait operation and in the Federation. A former adjutant, he was regarded as one of the most promising young officers of his generation.

The first Royal Hussars *Journal* also carried the obituaries of an array of distinguished 10th and 11th Hussars. To name but a few; The Earl of Scarbrough, the author of an earlier history of the 11th; The Earl of Dudley, a First World War adjutant of the 10th and a close friend of the Duke of Windsor; Colonel John Galbraith, who had commanded the 11th in the Palestine campaign immediately preceding the Second World War; and Major Bobby Hartman, another Cherrypicker of the same vintage, distinguished as a writer, wit and horseman.

Although The Royal Hussars was the United Kingdom's Strategic Reserve Armoured Regiment, during the whole tour of nearly four years at Tidworth it never exercised fully in that role, one or more of the sabre squadrons being detached for virtually the whole period. During 1970 A Squadron was based at the Warminster School of Infantry, returning to Tidworth in September. B Squadron, with Major David ('Bassett') Shaw as Squadron Leader, spent five weeks in Hong Kong activating the stockpile of tanks, while in December C Squadron departed for a six-month tour in Cyprus under Major Robin Merton. The squadron took over from C Squadron of the Royal Scots Greys commanded by Major HRH the Duke of Kent and was based at Gleneagles Camp on the perimeter of Nicosia Airport as Recce Squadron to the United Nations Peace-Keeping Force. The other military and police contingents came from Austria, Australia, Britain, Canada, Denmark, Finland, Ireland and Sweden. Although the squadron was kept on a high state of alert there was ample time to enjoy the marvellous sporting and leisure facilities which the island offers – skiing in the Troodos Mountains, water-skiing at Kyrenia, polo and all the usual team games, as well as botany, ornithology and archaeology for the more scientifically and academically minded. This was to be a regular squadron deployment in the years to come and although there were many alarms and excursions in the long running, indeed apparently endless, dispute between Greeks and Turks, The Royal Hussars were never called upon to deal with a major incident.

When the last permanently based armoured squadron left Hong Kong in the 1960s a stockpile of Centurion tanks was maintained at Sek Kong in the New Territories for use by reinforcing troops. The role of The Royal Hussars squadron was to strengthen 48 Gurkha Infantry Brigade in the defence of Hong Kong. This annual exercise was mounted by United Kingdom Headquarters Land Forces to test the reinforcement system and thus three squadrons of Royal Hussars experienced a little of the flavour of the Orient in the early 1970s until the plan was scrapped and the tanks sold to New Zealand early in 1973.

These exercises took place in the autumn and about 120 men flew out in RAF VC10s via Cyprus, Bahrain, Gan and Singapore (all still operating RAF staging posts or bases) to arrive at the world's most dramatic airport, Kai Tak. A base camp was established at Fan Ling which is conveniently placed near a railway station for travel to Kowloon, the Star Ferry and the Wanchai district of Hong Kong Island. The Centurions were kept in immaculate order by an RAOC sergeant and half-a-dozen Chinese fitters. Following a work-up exercise on the small Wanchai training area, including old-fashioned infantry/tank co-operation with a platoon of Gurkhas on each Centurion, the tanks moved by road and sea to Clearwater for open

48. HRH Princess Alice Duchess of Gloucester, Colonel-in-Chief, inspects a Guard accompanied by Lt Col B.C. Greenwood and Major General Sir David Dawnay. Amalgamtion Parade, 25 October, 1969

49. The Colonel-in-Chief, assisted by Major J.A. Hall, hands the Guidon to RQMS J. Kolaczkowski

50. The new Guidon, carried by the RQMS, is escorted by SSM A. Watson and SSM R.C. Chatwin and commanded by RSM B. Osmand

51. Lieutenant General Lord Norrie leads the Old Comrades in the march-past. Canon Lummis is in the leading file on the right

52. The 11th Hussars Mounted Escort commanded by Captain R.E.R. Morgan

53. B Squadron fitters change a Chieftain gearbox in the field, 1969

54. 20 June, 1970. Centenary of the polo match played between 9th Lancers and 10th Hussars on 1 July, 1870

55. Major General Gilbert inspects "A" Force C Squadron accompanied by Major R.B. Merton and Lieutenant M.J.H. Malyon. Cyprus, 1971

56. The Maze Prison Riot, 15/16 October, 1974

57. Aftermath, The Maze Prison Riot

58. The Royal Hussars crew who handed over the first production Challenger to the CGS, General Sir John Stanier, at ROF Leeds. L to R: Cpl R. Taylor, L/Cpl P. Plummer, Cpl R. Brown and Tpr A. Cook

59. Her Royal Highness Princess Alice opens The Royal Hussars Museum 11 June, 1980, with Lieutenant-Colonel P.K. Upton and Major D. Wheyman-Meakins

60. Entertaining the Warrant Officers and Sergeants to Roulette in the Officers' Mess

61. Border Patrol on the Inner German Border. Trooper Curtis with a member of the Bundesgrenzschutz

62. "Where is the other one?" Chieftains on Hohne Ranges. Corporal Lomax on the left. October, 1981

63. The Band at Coburg, 1981

64. The Prime Minister, Mrs Margaret Thatcher, on Hohne Ranges
with Sergeant Penkethman. Chancellor Kohl commands the Leopard 2

65. "Was that the RSM's car?" Cpl Cox and L/Cpl Wild. Fallingbostel,
1989

66. Royal Hussars crewmen bombing-up a Challenger in Saudi Arabia, prior to the attack to liberate Kuwait, 1991

67. D Squadron on the ranges at Pyla, Cyprus, February, 1991

68. 2 Troop D Squadron patrolling in the Western Sovereign Base
Area, Cyprus, July, 1991

69. D Squadron. Lieutenant Harry Upton and his Squadron Leader, Major Robin Bowring, on Exercise 'First Shiner', Cyprus, September, 1991

70. Lieutenant Colonel J.R.D. Kaye, the last Commanding Officer of The Royal Hussars, leaving Swinton Barracks, Munster, on relinquishing command, November, 1992

range firing. 105mm and .30 Browning rounds were fired at a few uninhabited off-shore islands. 'At least they were meant to be uninhabited,' recalls John Friedberger, 'but as the Bay is only a few miles from the world's most populous city, Kowloon, this was not always the case. An Army Air Corps helicopter was therefore deployed to broadcast warnings to fishermen and others. In 1972 the voice behind the 'Sky Shout' was that of Major George Duckett, RH, (GSO2 Public Information HQ British Forces Hong Kong), whose Chinese dialect was more enthusiastic than intelligible! The final exercise took place from October to December, 1972, and Friedberger, the C Squadron Leader, remembers 'that the squadron, having been ferried by LSL from Castle Park to Clearwater Bay, returned on its tracks to Sek Kong in the middle of the night through the newly built Lion Rock Tunnel and past Sha Tin Racecourse, then under construction. Thus ended an enjoyable, if not particularly important, episode in Great Britain's withdrawal from Empire.'

At about this time several other Royal Hussars were serving in the Colony on longer term duty. Lieutenant-Colonel George Hodgkinson commanded the Hong Kong Military Service Corps, Major James Scott was ADC to the Governor and Majors Michael Allenby and Eric Westropp were at different times Brigade Major 51st Infantry Brigade.

Scattered around the world were other members of the Regiment on ERE. These included Brigadier Frank Henn commanding the British contingent in the United Nations Peace Force, Cyprus, during the Turkish invasion of 1974; Major Patrick Mesquita instructing at the Canadian Combat Arms School; Captain Robert Hayman-Joyce was at Fort Knox (guarding the gold reserves?); Captain Oliver Howard was ADC to the Governor of Western Australia; Major Julien Turner was seconded to the Abu Dhabi Defence Force and several Royal Hussars, including Captains Brian Jayes and Victor Seely were similarly on loan to the Sultan of Muscat's Armed Forces during the Dhofar War. Major Glyn Lewis, a Canadian who had joined the 10th after the Second World War and who served in almost every campaign since may have found his posting to the WRAC

College, Camberley, a daunting, if exciting prospect. Lieutenant-Colonel Tony Uloth, in common with many who have served there, has retained an affection for the Sudan and its people as a result of his tour as Military Attaché at Khartoum. Nick Muers-Raby continued his flying career as GSO3 (Air) 19 Inf Brigade, as did Simon Arthur, attached to the 17th/21st Lancers Air Troop in Northern Ireland. Also serving in that troubled province were a number of Royal Hussars in the RAC Para Squadron, including Lieutenants Watt, Howard, Churton and Copeland, Corporals Chafe and Mulley, Lance-Corporals Buffrey and Woodcock and ten troopers. Staff Sergeant Beadle and Sergeant Marshall were with British garrisons in the Gulf, at Bahrain and Sharjah respectively.

On 20 June, 1970, an event of some sporting historical interest took place at Windsor when The Royal Hussars played the 9th/12th Lancers in a 'Centenary' Polo Match. The background to this occasion had been explained in a letter from the Regimental Secretary, Major Archer-Shee, to Colonel Sir John Lawson.

'Polo was started in England,' he wrote, 'by Lieutenant Cheape of the 11th Hussars Depot Troop attached to the 10th Hussars then encamped on the Queen's Parade at Aldershot. This happened in 1869. A letter to *The Field* had been read and Cheape made a suggestion which was readily taken up by the other officers. Borrowing a billiard ball from the Queen's Hotel, Farnborough, and elongating hockey sticks with golf clubs and billiard cues, they started playing on Cove Common, now Farnborough Aerodrome.

'The 9th Lancers at the South Cavalry Barracks took up the game and by 1st July 1870 they were ready to have the first polo match on Hounslow Heath (now Heathrow Airport). The 10th with Lieutenant Cheape in the team beat the 9th Lancers by 3 goals to 2.'

In the 1970 match, played just five days short of the actual centenary of the first one, the result was reversed when the 9th/12th Lancers beat the Royal Hussars with a score which the *Journal*'s correspondent, perhaps out of shame, failed to record.

Both sides fielded eight players from past and serving officers and two chukkas were played. The match, which was staged in aid of SSAFA, was umpired by HRH Prince Philip and Earl Mountbatten, both dressed in tail coats and top hats. The Royal Hussar team was made up of Major-General Sir David Dawnay, Brigadier Roscoe Harvey, Colonels Archer-Shee, Lithgow and Willis, Majors Bengough, Dawnay and Norrie, with Captain Malet coming on as a substitute at half-time. Again our correspondent failed to record the names of the victorious Lancers but does tell us that they were captained by General Prior-Palmer, 'a pre-war six goal player, whose superior tactics won the day and justified his exalted rank and handicap!'

1971 saw the retirement of Colonel Clive Robertson, who had steered the Regiment skilfully through the first two years of its life, and his succession by Lieutenant-Colonel Piers Bengough.

In the same year the Colonel of the Regiment, Major-General Sir David Dawnay, died at the age of only 68 and was succeeded by Colonel Sir John Lawson, previously Colonel of the 11th.

Sir David had been commissioned in the Rifle Brigade in 1924 but within six months had transferred to the 10th Hussars. A keen horseman and polo player, perhaps the highlight of his sporting career had been to captain the British Olympic Polo Team at the Berlin Olympics of 1936, reaching the final only to be beaten by the Argentinians.

During the 1940 campaign in France he led C Squadron, but on the Regiment's return to England he was appointed second-in-command of the North Irish Horse which he later commanded for over two years, including service in North Africa where he was awarded the DSO. Later, in Italy, he commanded an armoured brigade and received a bar to his DSO at the end of the war. He was Commandant of the RMA Sandhurst from 1951 to 1954 and was appointed a Companion of the Bath in 1952. From 1957 to 1969 he was Secretary to the Ascot Authority and Clerk of the Course during which time the new Grandstands and Royal Enclosure Stand were constructed and the Steeplechase and Hurdle Courses were established. In 1968 he was made Knight Commander of the Royal Victorian Order.

As we have seen, he was the last Colonel of the 10th Hussars, from 1962 until amalgamation, and the first of the Royal Hussars until his untimely death.

The career of the incoming Colonel of the Regiment, Sir John Lawson, has been described in the 11th Hussar section.

An unusual event in 1971 was an exchange visit by a composite troop of A Squadron, under Lieutenant Radmore with Sergeant Swinden, to the USA. For administrative purposes the sixteen Royal Hussars were attached to a company of the 1st Coldstream under Major MacFarlane. The exercise was officially described as 'a training and cultural exchange' with an American infantry company and an armoured platoon (troop) proceeding to Tidworth. The destination for the British contingent was Fort Hood in Texas where it was to participate in Exercise Gobi Desert.

The programme, a well-designed mixture of training and entertainment, included driving and maintenance on the M60 tank, gunnery, small-arms practice and simulated patrol tactics with tanks as developed by the Americans in Vietnam. Amusements included a visit to the Texas State Fair at Dallas, an American Football game and a trip to Waco for a dance at which no less than 260 'Chicks' (to use Radmore's word which nowadays would undoubtedly be regarded as Politically Incorrect) were provided as partners for only 176 Guardsmen and Hussars. Clearly the reputation of the British soldier had preceded him!

In the second week there were visits to the NASA Space Centre and the Huntsville Prison Rodeo at which all the performers (except the horses) were convicts. During the final week two very cold days and nights were spent on a field exercise and the visit was concluded with a farewell parade at which the Coldstreamers gave a drill demonstration. The Royal Hussars presented their hosts with a print of the Guidon and received a commemorative plaque in return.

The Royal Hussars probably saw more service in Northern Ireland than any other RAC regiment. In all there were to be three squadron tours in the province in the early 70s (in addition to those members of the Regiment who were attached to the

RAC Para Squadron) and three full regimental tours in 1974, '76 and '78. In April, 1971, a squadron known as the Light Squadron, made up of officers and men from B and Command and Support Squadrons, was based at Gosford Castle near Armagh under command of 16 Para Bde for operation on the border. The Castle was a rambling Victorian edifice with few creature comforts. One troop was detached to Belfast under command of the Parachute Regiment while the remainder of the squadron, less a troop based at Bessbrook RUC Station, operated from Gosford with the Seaforth Highlanders. OPs, patrols, road blocks by day and night were the main tasks. Good intelligence was very limited in those early days of the Ulster 'Troubles' and hard work was rewarded with limited success. A daylight search under all the bridges and culverts in the area resulted in a find of ammunition by Lieutenant Richard East's troop but most of the tour passed without serious incident. However, Trooper Cooper distinguished himself by organizing the emergency services for a bad accident at an RUC road block in the absence of any officers or NCOs. Cooper had been on watch at Squadron HQ when the SOS message came through and when asked by his Squadron Leader the following morning why he hadn't roused him he replied, 'You looked very tired and had only just gone to bed!'

Then, in August, half of C Squadron went to Belfast to run Saracens as operational transport for the infantry battalions; the remainder of the squadron followed later in the month. The Squadron was employed as Armoured Personnel Carrier Squadron equipped with Saracens. It had already undergone conversion from Chieftain tanks to Ferret armoured cars for its role in Cyprus thus a further conversion to Saracens was required and within a fortnight Sergeant Eadie, not without some trepidation, had selected and trained thirty drivers. Some of these tended to underestimate the width of their new vehicles and the Claims Department was kept busy. Movement to Northern Ireland was by ferry from Liverpool to Belfast and the squadron was accommodated on the former RN Submarine Depot Ship, HMS *Maidstone*. She was moored in the Musgrove Channel alongside the Royal Naval Air Yard at Sydenham – 'probably aground on a shoal of empty bottles!' suggests one former inhabitant.

The five Troops each with five Saracens were deployed with battalions stationed in various parts of the city. Squadron HQ was largely superfluous as the Squadron Leader had neither operational nor tactical control over the day-to-day activities of his troops. Their only role was to provide administrative support for the attached troops. 'Belfast was a violent place especially at night,' recalls Robin Merton, the Squadron Leader. 'In certain areas it was not safe to halt at traffic lights and routes had to be chosen with care. The APC Troops supported operations both by day and night and saw their fair share of action. Oliver Howard's vehicle was sprayed with Tommy gun fire one night, the bullets leaving marks on the paintwork. Corporal Eldridge had a lucky escape when a blast bomb landed in the LMG ring behind the commander's position. He was blown to the floor and, although unhurt, suffered from deafness for some time afterwards.'

On arrival back at Tidworth the Squadron prepared to fly to Hong Kong for one of the exercises described earlier. While there Lieutenant Michael Malyon took a party to North Borneo where they were successful in climbing Mount Kinabalu.

The next short tour in Northern Ireland was that of A Squadron from November, 1972, to February, 1973, based at Aldergrove Airport sharing a camp with the RAF and the Military Police. Much of the time was spent in patrolling the rural areas to the north and west of Belfast. Road blocks were manned and searches conducted for arms and ammunition. One troop was employed on urban patrolling and also as 'a quick reaction armoured car force' under command of the local infantry brigade. During the second half of the tour one troop helped man a small base in the Ligoneil area of west Belfast whence it carried out fast mobile patrols. However, in general there was little excitement and it was felt that the IRA were reluctant to take on armoured cars with their good protection and relatively heavy fire power. Conveniently, a few shots were fired at the Ligoneil troop while the Commanding Officer, Lieutenant-Colonel Piers Bengough, was visiting Belfast, but he arrived too late to join in the exchange! Details of the Regiment's principal tours of duty in Ulster and the adventures of some of its members will be covered later.

On 20 November, 1971, one of the most highly decorated 11th Hussars of the Second World War died at his home in Lambourn aged only 65. At the outbreak of war Peter Payne-Gallwey had been a squadron leader and had won two DSOs in the desert. Later he was to be awarded a third and the American Silver Star while commanding the Derbyshire Yeomanry. A man without fear, his troop leaders used to complain that he could not hear shells coming because he was deaf – but, suggested his obituarist, it would have made no difference whether he could hear them or not. Soon after the war he took over command of the Regiment at a time of anti-climax when standards of discipline were slipping, but under him they did not slip for very long or very far. He commanded for four years and retired in 1949 to take up training at which he enjoyed some success. A well-known amateur rider before the war, he had won the Grand Military on a horse called Backsight.

In the following year another distinguished former Cherry-picker, Major J. A. (Nobby) Hall retired. He had joined the 11th as a bandboy before the war, rose steadily through the ranks and was commissioned in 1962, finally retiring as Quartermaster of The Royal Hussars. For the first two years of the war he was Brigadier Jock Campbell's personal operator before returning to the Regiment as troop sergeant of 2nd Troop A Squadron. When his troop leader, John Palin-Evans, was killed, Hall took over the troop himself and stayed as its leader throughout the remainder of the North African campaign and in Italy.

At Ashbridge, prior to the Normandy landings, the troop was taken over by Dick Sutton, a future Commanding Officer of the Regiment, with Hall remaining as troop sergeant. But by the end of the war he had his own troop again and had been Mentioned in Despatches.

In Malaya in the 1950s he was SQMS and then SSM of A Squadron under particularly difficult circumstances and was Mentioned in Despatches for a second time. He served with the Royal Gloucestershire Hussars (the TA regiment affiliated to the 11th) as RSM and then Quartermaster and finally as Quartermaster of both the 11th and Royal Hussars. He was made an MBE in the 1972 New Years Honours List.

In the same year Lieutenant-Colonel Peter Upton retired from the army and succeeded Major Bobby Archer-Shee as Regimental Secretary, while RSM Brian Osmand handed over to RSM F. W. Nicholas. Later Osmand was to return to the Regiment as Quartermaster and retired in 1977 having been awarded the MBE.

Chapter 15

GERMANY AND ULSTER 1973-79

It has been pointed out that as a consequence of the rotation of sabre squadrons, as described in the previous chapter, to Hong Kong, Cyprus and Northern Ireland in varied roles, for some years the Regiment suffered from a deficiency in tank trade skills and armoured tactical training. This was the situation which had to be faced by Lieutenant-Colonel Nigel Winter when he replaced Colonel Piers Bengough in 1973 and took the Regiment to join 6th Armoured Brigade at Sennelager. However, there was little time to ruminate upon, or indeed tackle, the problem as The Royal Hussars soon found themselves having to cope with a role inimical to all soldiers and to cavalrymen in particular, namely that of a prison warder. But we shall come to that in a moment.

On a more personal note, another consequence of these swift rotations was that one officer of the Regiment, Captain HRH Prince Michael of Kent, found himself serving successfully as second-in-command to all three sabre squadrons during one three-year tour at Regimental Duty. He was allowed to serve in Hong Kong and Cyprus but, for obvious reasons, not in Northern Ireland, so each time his squadron was warned for service there he and his faithful Alsatian were transferred to another squadron.

On 18 August, 1973, a 10th Hussar of great distinction died in Northern Ireland, a province of the United Kingdom with which The Royal Hussars were to become very familiar over the next few years. Viscount Brookeborough had joined the

177

10th in 1911 and was awarded both the Military Cross and the *Croix de Guerre* in the First World War. In the Second World War two of his sons were killed serving with the Regiment. Although Brookeborough himself was better known as a politician and was Prime Minister of Northern Ireland for 20 years, his kinsman, Field-Marshal Viscount Alanbrooke, was one of Britain's greatest 20th century strategic thinkers.

The first full regimental tour in Northern Ireland from September to December, 1974, was probably the most eventful and testing episode in the short history of The Royal Hussars.

At the time of writing there is no sign of an end to the 'Troubles' in Northern Ireland but we must assume, perhaps over-optimistically, that the day will come when some kind of settlement will be reached, if only out of sheer weariness. Therefore, although the Ulster problem is all too familiar to the reader of the 1990s, this may not always be the case in the future and thus it is necessary to place the Regiment's role in the province into its historical perspective.

The Republic of Ireland (Eire) is overwhelmingly Roman Catholic, whereas in the six counties of Northern Ireland (Ulster)* the majority of the population is Protestant, mainly of Scottish descent, with a substantial Catholic minority. When the South of Ireland was declared independent in 1922, the North opted to remain as part of the United Kingdom. This partition was never constitutionally accepted by the Republic and was resented by the Catholic minority in the North, who, rightly or wrongly, regarded themselves as oppressed by the Protestant majority. Over the decades various factions of the Irish Republican Army, a terrorist paramilitary movement based in Eire, have taken it upon themselves to 'unite' the North with the South by force. This had been strongly resisted by the Protestant 'Loyalists', both through legitimate political means and by the use of counter-terror, and, with less enthusiasm, by successive British Governments which have always been ambivalent in their attitude to Northern Ireland.

* In fact three of the counties of the old Province of Ulster are in the Republic.

The campaign in which The Royal Hussars were involved had its origins in a series of Catholic 'Nationalist' demonstrations in the late 1960s as a result of which additional British troops (there has always been a British Army garrison in Ulster) were sent to the province to protect the Catholics from Protestant reprisals. Paradoxically, however, the troops soon became targets for the IRA and, as the situation deteriorated, so the British Army found itself drawn deeper and deeper into the sectarian morass.

In 1973 the British Government, for better or for worse, took over direct rule from the local Unionist (Protestant) politicians, but this did little to improve the situation, succeeding only in souring the traditional relationship between the Ulster Unionists and the Conservative Party on the mainland. Nor were British Government efforts to negotiate with the IRA and to ingratiate itself with both the Republic and the Northern Irish Nationalists through the Anglo-Irish Agreement any more successful.

Another fateful decision, taken early in the campaign, was the disbandment of the B Specials, a mainly Protestant part-time police force greatly feared by the IRA but disliked by the Catholic community as a whole.

Meanwhile the army and the police continued their fight against terrorism with their hands tied behind their backs. Legal and operational restraints and an ever-watchful media, often openly hostile to the security forces ensured that the initiative remained in the hands of the terrorists. Worse, the latter's ability to operate across the border with apparent impunity was a further drain on the limited capacity available to the security forces. By 1994 casualties, both civilian and military, had run into thousands. [Once again, the author's opinions on the part played by the Republic were considered unsuitable by the Ministry of Defence and have been deleted.] There was little sympathy from abroad: most European countries and the United States tended, albeit unofficially, to regard British 'occupation' of Northern Ireland as 'colonialism' and the IRA as 'freedom fighters'.

In this situation there is probably no other army in the world which could have maintained its morale and professional integrity as the British Army in Northern Ireland has done over the years.

In his editorial in the 1975 *Journal* Captain J. H. Thoyts wrote: –

'The most significant event of the year (1974) was the Regiment's tour in Northern Ireland from 25th August to 17th December, our first as a complete regiment during the present emergency, and the first time since the Kaiser's War that the Regiment has operated in the infantry role.*

'The Regiment was deployed over a wide area with RHQ, HQ Squadron and a reinforced (with two troops of A Squadron) C Squadron guarding the Maze prison† at Long Kesh; B Squadron based near Enniskillen covering South Fermanagh; A Squadron with one troop looked after a large part of North and South Down; and a troop under command 3 RTR operated initially from Armagh and later Cookstown . . .

'Shortly after we arrived (at the Maze) there was increasing agitation and tension within the prison, manifested by a display of sheets on the wire and the daily ritual of food-throwing by the prisoners. On the night of October 15th this tension exploded into violence and the arson of the prison which became generally known as the 'Maze Ablaze', and on the following day the Regiment, heavily reinforced, took part in the largest operation yet seen at the prison to restore order.'

Here we leave Captain Thoyts' editorial for the moment to recount in greater detail the events of 15/16 October. There had been trouble some weeks earlier in September when a crowd of relatives, probably encouraged by the media, demonstrated in the visitors' car park and broke some windows. Two members of the so-called Prison Visitor Committee had to be forcibly extracted from one of the prison compounds. At the same time the car of one of these men was suspected of containing a bomb and had to be blown up with controlled explosions.

At 6.20 on the evening of 15 October two prison officers were seized by the inmates of Compound 13 who were con-

---

* This is not strictly accurate. The 10th were 'dismounted' on at least one occasion in Italy during the Second World War.

† The Maze contained both IRA and Loyalist Prisoners, detainees and convicted men.

victed IRA terrorists. After some violence, the officers were rescued, but they and several of their colleagues were injured in the process. The Prison Governor decided to arrest those responsible and requested military assistance. At 9.30 pm the inmates of several compounds broke out and started a number of fires, having armed themselves with bed-legs and similar weapons. At 10.15 about fifty prisoners were seen moving towards the prison offices and main gate.

Lieutenant Anthony Trollope-Bellew recalls his troop's (2 Tp, C Sqn) part in the ensuing riot.

'I was watching the prison burn from a water-tower between the troop huts and the Officers' Mess when someone shouted to me that my troop was to go into the prison. I was then briefed that the Governor's office, which was situated inside the prison perimeter fence, was under threat and that my troop was to go in and stop the prisoners reaching the office and the records it contained. The prison main gate was fully four hundred yards away but in true cavalry fashion we climbed into a lorry and drove there!

'An amorphous mass of prison officers was exuding through the main gate but they parted with a cheer to let us in. Our lorry driver, L/Cpl Bird, who had been parking, was less fortunate. He was only 5ft 2in in his boots DMS and had great difficulty in forcing his way through. The prisoners once they spied pattern-clad figures emerging through the throng of Prison Service blue carried out a rapid withdrawal. I was then ordered to put down gas by Oliver Holder; this I was already planning to do. But the memory came back to me of the story of a platoon commander who had ordered gas to be put down before donning gas-masks; result, half a platoon in hospital. So I ordered gas-masks to be donned. The prisoners seeing these preparations withdrew further so I advanced to bring them back in range of my gas guns. After a few rounds of gas cartridges the troop was ordered back to immediately around the Governor's office where we stayed for the rest of the night.

'My troop sergeant, Steve Boulter, had been hit by a brick and went off to be treated. The Band happened by chance to be with us on a morale-boosting tour and so carried out their war role of treating the casualties. He (Boulter) came back singing their praises. I think two or three of the others also got hurt by flying stones and bricks.'

According to the official report, during this period of the riot some 65 rubber baton rounds and 117 CS (gas) rounds of various types were used.

At 10.40pm a large concentration of prisoners was seen at the base of one of the watchtowers and a mass break-out was feared. Authority to fire live ammunition into the ground between the outer fences was given, but in the event only four rounds had to be fired before the situation was stabilized at around midnight. By this time most of the compound huts were burning, except those occupied by Loyalist prisoners who had taken little or no part in the rioting, and the cookhouse and a number of administrative huts were also ablaze. The prison hospital, in the words of the official report, had been 'attached'.

Large numbers of prisoners were still milling about in the compounds. Up to this point the riot had been contained by The Royal Hussars but, in the early hours of the morning of the 16th, large reinforcements began to arrive, including elements of the Royal Anglians, Duke of Edinburgh's Regiment, Royal Regiment of Wales and various other units.

Operations to restore order got under way at 7.40am, in the course of which there was some severe fighting between troops and prisoners, a number of casualties, but none fatal, being sustained on both sides. At one point a soldier of The Duke of Edinburgh's was captured by rioters and rescued by a remarkable assortment of troops, including men of his own regiment, Royal Hussars, 3 RTR and a helicopter dispensing CS gas. According to the official report he had been 'somewhat mauled'.

In one rather bizarre turn of events three Loyalist prisoners approached Colonel Nigel Winter apparently on behalf of some of their IRA enemies who were seeking a peaceful conclusion to the disturbances! The outcome of these negotiations is unclear, but by 10.45am the security forces had regained control of the prison. The rest of the day was spent in carrying out searches, identification and the rearrangement of prisoners in the compounds. By 7 o'clock in the evening most of the troops had left the prison.

Anthony Trollope-Bellew recalls the aftermath:

'When all was finally calmed down my troop had to man the towers. I remember going round and finding one young trooper so totally exhausted that he was quite incoherent and next day could not remember me visiting him, even though I had stayed with him for half an hour! But he, like everyone else, had had no sleep for 24 hours.'

In the course of the riot and the subsequent operation to restore order eighty-two prisoners, seventeen prison officers and twenty-three soldiers had been injured. Additionally, a number of minor injuries had been treated on the spot and were not recorded.

But The Royal Hussars' problems as Guard Regiment were not over. Just after midnight on 6 November a sentry in one of the watchtowers saw movement on the perimeter road and a mobile patrol was ordered to investigate. On its second circuit of the prison the patrol discovered three escaping prisoners in a ditch. Shortly afterwards another was caught coming through a hole in the perimeter wire and then another eighteen emerging from a tunnel. A few minutes later more escapees were spotted as they climbed over the wire. They were challenged a number of times but failed to halt, whereupon a warning shot was fired to no effect. Then a further single shot was fired at a prisoner who appeared to be armed and he fell dead.

Meanwhile an operation to cordon off the prison and prevent further break-outs swung into action. Additional troops from an RE regiment and the Royal Welch Fusiliers were required for this task which involved entering some of the compounds and firing baton rounds and CS gas. By about 3am resistance had ceased and a head-count revealed that three men were still missing, but these were arrested by the police near Belfast that evening. Further trouble broke out in one compound at 7.45 am but had been quelled by about 9.45 am.

In all, thirty-three men had escaped of whom one had been

killed and the remainder recaptured. In the course of the subsequent search no less than three tunnels were discovered, the spoils being hidden among the uncleared wreckage of the October riot.

It is worthy of note that throughout this series of disturbances only half-a-dozen live rounds were fired and only one escaping prisoner shot dead. Almost anywhere else in the world far more violent means of suppression would have been used, resulting in much heavier casualties, probably on both sides. Perhaps the main reason for the relatively bloodless success of the operation on 15/16 October was the saturation of the prison with troops; some 1,700 men, in forty-three platoons with twenty dogs were used, thus deterring resistance on the part of the rioters by sheer numbers. Nevertheless, this kind of duty is intensely disliked by most professional soldiers who often find themselves accused of acting either too harshly or too feebly, or both!

On the day following the break-out, 7 November, in another part of the province the Regiment suffered its only fatal casualty from enemy action when Staff Sergeant Jock Simpson of A Squadron was killed by a bomb in the course of a search for explosives and ammunition. Sergeant Derick Johnson was seriously injured in the same incident and has suffered considerably from his wounds ever since. Simpson had joined the 11th as a National Serviceman at Carlisle in 1958, signing on as a Regular and serving with the Regiment in Aden and Sharjah. He had been a gunnery instructor with the Junior Leaders Regiment RAC and had also served in British Honduras (Belize) and Northern Ireland on a previous tour.*

B Squadron was also kept busy in Fermanagh, being involved in seven bomb incidents, five culvert mines or claymore devices, one mortar attack and a dozen minor incidents in which shots were fired. Considerable quantities of explosives and ammunition were recovered in the course of patrols and searches.

*

* Another former 11th Hussar, Staff Sergeant Lane of the Royal Military Police, was killed in Northern Ireland in 1973.

In 1974 the long-serving Colonel-in-Chief of the 10th Hussars, Field-Marshal HRH the Duke of Gloucester died on 10 June aged 74. Prince Henry had joined the 10th in 1920 and served with C Squadron throughout his active soldiering. Unfortunately, when the Regiment sailed for Egypt in 1928 he was not allowed to accompany it for political reasons, nor was he able to rejoin it in India. However, from 1931 to '33 he served with the 11th. In 1937 he was appointed Colonel-in-Chief of the 10th Hussars and continued in the same role until amalgamation in 1969 when Princess Alice assumed the Colonelcy of The Royal Hussars.

Also in 1974 Colonel Sir John Lawson retired as Colonel of the Regiment, handing over to Colonel Tom Hall.

On returning to Sennelager at the end of 1974 the Royal Hussars, after several months away from their Chieftain tanks, were faced with the challenge of regaining their 'former prowess as an armoured regiment', as the Commanding Officer put it in his 1975 message in the *Journal*.

After a programme of trade training courses and practice on Hohne Ranges, in mid-June 1975 the Regiment, less most of B Squadron, travelled to Canada for Exercise Stradivarius at Suffield as part of a battle group including C Coy 2nd Queens, B Bty 1st RHA and a troop of 26th Engineer Regiment. Suffield boasted a live firing area of a hundred square miles and battle runs over twenty miles long. On arrival in Canada the battle group was greeted with three days of torrential rain followed by tremendous heat and clouds of mosquitos. The temperature in the vehicles often rose to 136°F.

The Suffield Training Area, apart from its obvious advantages from the military standpoint, was a place of considerable natural interest. Formerly the hunting ground of the Cree and the Blackfeet, it teemed with game of many species, including Pronghorn antelope, Mule deer and wild horses.

The battle group took part in four exercises: Chinook, an advance to contact exercise, and a fighting withdrawal somewhat inappropriately named Badajoz. The other two, of unrecorded purpose, were Salamanca and, no doubt in honour of

The Royal Hussars, Balaklava. The visit ended with a three-day holiday, and trips to places like Great Falls, Montana, the Rockies and the Calgary Stampede were arranged by SSM Wass's 'Travel Agency'. Some members of the Regiment stayed on for a further fortnight's adventure training.

In 1975 Lieutenant-Colonel John Friedberger assumed command in succession to Lieutenant-Colonel Nigel Winter. By 1976 elements of the Regiment had served in Hong Kong, Malaysia, Cyprus, the USA, Canada, the West Indies and Belize, not to mention Germany and the United Kingdom, including Northern Ireland. An editorial in the 1977 *Journal* summed up the situation to that date.

> 'In many respects,' wrote Captain Powell, 'the Regiment was fortunate to be based in England for so long. There were, however, penalties. All ranks suffered the spectre of separation; many lived in their own homes and not in army quarters. Thus when we arrived in BAOR in 1973 many were strangers to each other. We wore one cap badge but we tended to see matters from a rather parochial squadron viewpoint. The high standards were there and there was great spirit and determination but there had been no opportunity to harness them and to produce the Regimental sense of tradition and comradeship of which Sir John Lawson spoke.
>
> 'BAOR is not exciting, neither is it adventurous. It does, however, provide a measure of stability in a life of ever-increasing turbulence. When the Regiment takes the field on exercise or in Northern Ireland it does so as a whole. For three and a half years The Royal Hussars have lived and worked together and that spirit of determination which existed at amalgamation and through four years of separation has been harnessed.'

The feelings expressed in this editorial are born out by a letter received by Colonel Friedberger from Sergeant A. G. Adams who transferred to the Army Air Corps in 1976. 'I am very proud to have been a member of Britain's finest regiment,' he wrote, 'and although I will no longer be able to wear regimental dress I shall always remain a Royal Hussar in my heart.'

From August to December, 1976, the Regiment was again deployed in Northern Ireland. Here it was under command HQ 3rd Infantry Brigade with RHQ and A Squadron at Dungannon and Coalisland; B Squadron, HQ Squadron and HQ LAD at Aughnacloy with one troop at Caledon; C Squadron at Cookstown with one troop at Pomeroy. Over the years this central border area of Counties Armagh and Tyrone has experienced some of the worst IRA terrorist atrocities, but the density of troops and the close working liaison with the Royal Ulster Constabulary and the Ulster Defence Regiment* ensured a comparatively peaceful tour of duty.

In general the A Squadron area was quiet although there was an attempt to murder a policeman on traffic duty and a series of incendiary bombs just before Christmas. There were several finds of arms, ammunition and explosives.

B Squadron was responsible for the Permanent Vehicle Check Point at Aughnacloy and the surrounding area, including the village of Caledon. Although the area was quiet throughout most of the tour there were unsuccessful attempts to bomb a garage in Aughnacloy and to assassinate a member of the Ulster Defence Regiment.

C Squadron suffered the only regimental fatality with the death in a road accident of Lieutenant Robert Glazebrook. On 10 November, 1976, the squadron at Cookstown received a request from the RUC to mount an immediate search operation in the north-west of the squadron's area. Returning that evening from the operation, Glazebrook's Saracen left the road and he sustained severe injuries to the chest from which he died four days later. He had joined the Regiment in 1973 and had been actively involved in containing the Maze riots in the following year. At the time of his death he was C Squadron's Intelligence Officer.

The Regiment returned to BAOR at the end of the year and was granted block leave until 20 January, 1977.

Included in the New Year's Honours List was an MBE for the President of the Regimental Institutes, Major Amos Alderton, who was the last of the Regiment's 'wartime' soldiers. He

---

* Now The Royal Irish Regiment.

had joined the 11th in France in the autumn of 1944 and from then until his retirement spent every day of his army career with the 11th and Royal Hussars in a dozen or more stations including active service in Malaya, Aden and Northern Ireland. He had been RSM at the time of the 1965 Guidon Parade and had been commissioned shortly thereafter. Sadly, he died in his early sixties in 1988.

1977 also saw the death of that great Cherrypicker-cum-Shiner, Lieutenant-General Lord Norrie at the age of 83, whose illustrious career has been described elsewhere.

As part of her Silver Jubilee celebrations, Her Majesty the Queen carried out an inspection of the British Army of the Rhine at Sennelager on 17 July, 1977. 4th Armoured Division provided the bulk of the troops and forty of the one hundred and twenty Chieftain tanks on parade were from The Royal Hussars. A Guidon Party consisting of RSM Watson, WO2 Field and Staff Sergeants Bate and Keats was also present and the Band (Bandmaster Jeffs) paraded with the Massed Bands.

The climax of the review was a drive past Her Majesty, in heat and swirling dust, at some 20 mph. Surprisingly now we have entered the video age, no film record of the event exists but the scene is captured in Ken Howard's painting held by the Regiment.

In that year the army was subject to 're-structuring' which temporarily eliminated the brigade level of command. Thus the Regiment's association with 6th Armoured Brigade was broken and it became part of 3rd Armoured Division, itself not much larger (in terms of fighting troops) than the well-tested square-brigade it replaced. A fourth sabre squadron, D, was formed at the expense of the Recce and Guided Weapons Troops. Manpower reductions, ordained by the 1976 White Paper on the subject, meant, as the *Journal* put it, 'less men to do more work'.

At this point a brief description of the Chieftain, which had replaced the Centurion as the British Army's main battle tank, might be in order, although its merits have been mentioned earlier. With a crew of four and mounting a 120mm high velocity gun, the Chieftain weighed 55.8 tonnes operationally loaded and had a maximum road speed of 43.5 kph. It was equipped with an Improved Fire Control System (IFCS) which had four sub-systems. A contra-rotating cupola provided good all-round vision for the commander, enabling him to give rapid target indication to the gunner. Alternatively he could aim the gun himself by means of a sight optically linked to the gunner's sight. Day and night sights were provided for both commander and driver.

Regimental training in Jubilee Year included a visit to Canada for the Recce Troop attached to 4th RTR and they were followed there by B and C Squadrons as part of the 1st Queens Battle Group. A Squadron, with part of HQ Squadron, went to Denmark to train with a Danish brigade. It appears that while there A Squadron taught the Danes to play 'conkers', but what other valuable legacies of British culture they may have bequeathed upon their hosts have not been recorded.

During the year Sergeant David Matthews was Mentioned in Despatches for services in Northern Ireland and Sergeant Douglas Eldridge received the Sultan of Oman's commendation and Distinguished Service Medal for Gallantry. Part of Eldridge's citation read: –

'On 18th December (1975) a patrol of the Imperial Iranian Army, together with a small group of Firqat* were involved in contact with an enemy group of 30. The Firqat became separated and were totally cut off and unable to withdraw. Sergeant Eldridge, hearing this on the radio, immediately drove to their assistance without any infantry protection. The Firqat were withdrawn by the armoured cars whilst under heavy fire. For a period of over three weeks Sergeant Eldridge continually displayed considerable courage and resourcefulness and the actions of this troop greatly helped to reduce the level of enemy activity.'

In 1978 a new Commanding Officer, Lieutenant-Colonel Eric Westropp, took The Royal Hussars on their last tour of duty in Northern Ireland when they operated in Belfast City Centre from June to October. The tour was fairly trouble-free and no casualties were suffered.

* Friendly tribesmen

For a variety of reasons The Royal Hussars as a complete regiment never returned to Ulster. Indeed at about this time the use of RAC regiments in the infantry role in the Province was considerably reduced, but one member of the regiment has estimated that he has spent an aggregate of five years there out of a total of twenty-two years service.

Major Robin Watt was, to say the least, an unorthodox soldier. Within six weeks of joining the 10th he startled his Commanding Officer by forming up and asking to be posted to the Parachute Squadron RAC, a request which was not to be granted for another two years but which led to the first of eight tours of duty in Northern Ireland. He recalls spending the first night of that tour 'in a full-scale riot in the Falls Road, followed by three weeks of gun battles in the centre of the city day and night with hardly a pause.' Later, he lost his troop sergeant (Sergeant D. Cox of the Queen's Dragoon Guards) to a sniper in the Ardoyne.

However, there were moments of light relief. Watt remembers that an armoured fish and chip van, codenamed Codpiece, used to move around in Belfast feeding the hungry soldiery. Following one particularly violent night, this item appeared in the intelligence report which summarized the events of the previous 24 hours: 'At 22.30hrs Codpiece came under fire at junction Falls/Leeson St. One casualty. Cook caught by flying batter.'

Watt, who was Mentioned in Despatches, was to punctuate his Ulster adventures with a six-month tour in Dhofar as part of the British Army Training Team in 1974. A brief description of this campaign (in which Sergeant Eldridge was also involved) has been given in the 10th Hussar section of this book, but one of Watt's experiences in it may not be out of place here.

'I remember one rather exciting moment in Dhofar when one of about a dozen Russian or Chinese mortar bombs landed ten yards from me on the top of a hill plus liberal squirts of heavy machine-gun fire courtesy of the local guerrillas. As the rounds fell I remember flattening myself behind a boulder and thinking that no rock or stone is too small or too insignificant to provide cover! If I had been able to scratch myself one millimetre lower into the ground with my finger nails I would have done so. At that moment I remembered that this was exactly what some boring old sweat on the directing staff at Sandhurst had told me about reaction to enemy fire many years before during a cold, wet exercise on Chobham Ridges when I was still a cadet. Suddenly I believed him!'

Another colourful character with much service in Ulster was Captain Nigel Churton who was awarded the MBE in 1978. Described as 'fearless, fiercely independent, a gifted raconteur and an inveterate practical joker' by a brother officer, in 1974 Churton was based at Aldergrove Airport as a troop leader with the Parachute Squadron RAC when he, or rather his dog, managed one day to bring the airport to a standstill, something the IRA has seldom, if ever, achieved. Jets circled and queued while Churton's labrador occupied the main runway gnawing a bone!

A notable gift to the projected Regimental Museum at Winchester was one of the 10th Hussars two Victoria Crosses. On 13 March, 1900, Sergeant William Henry Engleheart was a member of a patrol making its way through the Boer lines in South Africa. The patrol had to charge an enemy picket and negotiate several deep gullies. At the last of these a sapper's horse failed to get up the bank, leaving its rider in an exposed position. Engleheart turned back to give assistance and under heavy shell and rifle fire managed to extricate the man and his horse from the gully. Previously he had shown great gallantry in charging a group of Boers who outnumbered his party by about four to one. He was the last man to be decorated with the Victoria Cross by Queen Victoria herself.

Born in 1863 he had enlisted in the 10th in 1887 and served with the Regiment until his retirement in 1908. From then until 1936 he was the Lodge Keeper at Windsor Castle. His Cross was presented to Colonel Jack Archer-Shee, representing the Regiment, by Sergeant Engleheart's twin sons, Geoffrey and Hugh, their father having died in 1939.

The 10th Hussars' other VC, that of Sir John Milbanke, was already in the possession of the Regiment.

Although under quite different circumstances, an act of almost equal courage to that of Sergeant Engleheart was performed over three-quarters of a century later by a Royal Hussar, Sergeant John Hutchinson, who received the Commander-in-Chief's Commendation for Bravery. In September, 1978, Hutchinson was supervising the throwing of hand grenades by soldiers under training when one of the men released his hold on a grenade too late. It fell at his feet and Hutchinson lifted him bodily out of the throwing bay as the grenade exploded.

The Commendation read: –

'Sergeant Hutchinson showed great presence of mind and his swift, decisive action, with complete disregard for his own safety, saved a shocked soldier from what might otherwise have been serious injury or even death.'

Chapter 16

CATTERICK AND BERLIN 1979–81

In April, 1979, the Regiment, less one squadron, moved from Sennelager to Cambrai Barracks at Catterick to take over from the Royal Scots Dragoon Guards as Royal Armoured Corps Training Regiment, while D Squadron was detached in Berlin.

As had been the case over twenty years earlier when the 11th Hussars took over as the training regiment at Hadrian's Camp, Carlisle, this role gave an extra work load to the NCOs but left little for troopers to do, thus considerably reducing the 'permanent' strength of two out of the three sabre squadrons at Catterick, leaving B and C Squadrons with three troopers each!

The basic training of recruits was carried out by B Squadron, which had a Coldstream Guards Drill Sergeant on its strength. C Squadron was responsible for the training of potential officers, radio operators, gunners and drivers, while A looked after the vehicles, both hard and soft skinned. It also provided one troop detached at Belize.

The Regiment's tour at Catterick coincided with a period of economic recession, usually a boost to recruiting, and at times there were as many as 600 recruits under training.

Meanwhile, D Squadron under Major Tuck found itself involved in ceremonial duties almost immediately on arrival in Berlin. The Allied Forces' Day Parade was followed by the Queen's Birthday Parade at which The Royal Hussars fired the 21-gun salute.

In the autumn of 1979 the Squadron underwent intensive

training at Grunewald, Hohne and Soltau both before and after changing from Mark 2/3 Chieftains to Mark 8s.

Unfortunately we have no record of the number of recruits who passed through the Regiment's hands at Catterick but the 1981 *Journal* recalls something of the problems and rewards of the training role:

'We know that every fortnight another 48 scruffy, long-haired, ill-disciplined young men will present themselves at the gate, that nine weeks later, their parents will watch proudly from the edge of the square while they march past in slow and quick time, hair clipped, boots gleaming, trousers pressed to razor edges.

'However, civilians don't turn into soldiers at the wave of a magic wand. It requires long hours of dedicated hard work. It is unglamorous, dull, repetitive and full of pitfalls for the unwary. It is greatly complicated by surges in recruiting when at short notice one officer and six NCOs find themselves responsible not just for two intakes totalling eighty recruits, but for two intakes totally a hundred and fifty recruits, rather more than an infantry company . . . There are many more recruits to get into mischief, to be homesick, or to run away; so many more worried mums to pacify on the telephone, so many more reports to write . . . In 1980 the record for the largest intake ever and for the total number of recruits was broken.'

In June, 1980, Lieutenant-Colonel Robert Hayman-Joyce assumed command. In the same month the new Regimental Museum was opened at Lower Barracks, Winchester, by the Colonel-in-Chief, HRH Princess Alice, some eleven years after the project had first been mooted, during which time at least a dozen sites had been considered and discarded for a variety of reasons. Sadly, Mr E. J. Potter, a former 11th Hussar, an invaluable voluntary helper who had put in many hours in preparation for the opening, died the day after he had completed his work.

Chapter 17

GERMANY 1981–88

In February, 1981, D Squadron, now under Major Roe, moved to Lumsden Barracks, Fallingbostel as the Advance Party and the rest of the Regiment followed from Catterick in April to form part of 7th Armoured Brigade. Here it was soon announced that The Royal Hussars had been selected to introduce the new Challenger tank into the British Army, a task similar to that performed by the 11th with the Chieftain many years before, but this would not happen until 1983.

For the next couple of years the even, if somewhat uninspiring, tenor of soldiering in Germany continued undisturbed. In 1982 a new Commanding Officer, Lieutenant-Colonel Euan Morrison, was transferred from the 5th Inniskilling Dragoon Guards but, prior to that, on 22 May the Colonel-in-Chief made a ceremonial visit to the Regiment and the parade in her honour was made up as follows: –

Commanding Officer – Lieutenant-Colonel R. J. Hayman-Joyce
Adjutant – Captain P. R. C. Flach
Regimental Sergeant-Major WO1 C. H. Goy
Guidon Party – WO1 D. G. Ninnim, Staff Sergeants P. J.
   Wilkins and J. C. Binge
No 1 Guard – Major C. P. Thompson, Lieutenant C. S. Fowle
   and 2nd Lieutenant C. D. B. Atkinson
No 2 Guard – Major J. H. Thoyts, Lieutenant A. C. McGregor
   and 2nd Lieutenant E. St J. Hall
No 3 Guard – Major C. R. G. Watt, 2nd Lieutenants C. J. K.
   Yates and D. P. Wiggin

No 4 Guard – Major C. H. Boon, 2nd Lieutenants G. D. S. Lowsley-Williams and M. S. Rogers

Many Old Comrades took the opportunity to visit the Regiment on this occasion but one who was not there was Chelsea Pensioner Frank Martin, the last surviving Boer War Shiner who died the day before his 99th birthday.

The first Challenger tank arrived rather earlier than expected in April 1983, the remaining thirteen following in twos and threes until early September. A Squadron was selected to carry out the troop trials on this new tank and these trials, known as Exercise Crimson Challenge, ran from October, 1983, to February, 1984, and covered some 20,000 kms.

Prior to that, between April and October, each squadron, attached to an infantry battalion, visited the British Army Training Unit at Suffield in Canada. Then, in October, the Challenger made its first appearance on exercise (Exercise Eternal Triangle). The Regiment was completely re-equipped with the new tank by September, 1984.

The Challenger, which is still in service at the time of writing, has much in common with the Chieftain but at 62 tonnes is considerably heavier and faster. Clad in the revolutionary Chobham armour and driven by a Rolls-Royce CV 12 diesel engine, Challenger was found to out-perform Chieftain in most respects. The 120mm gun and 2 × 7.62 MGs were already familiar to crews and gunners needed only a two-day conversion course. Fuel consumption, however, is double that of Chieftain at about three gallons to the mile. There will be more to be said about Challenger when we come to deal with the Regiment's contribution to the Gulf War.

In 1983 Colonel Piers Bengough took over from Colonel Tom Hall as Colonel of the Regiment. Tom Hall had joined the 11th in 1947, was adjutant in Malaya where he was Mentioned in Despatches, had commanded a squadron in Aden and Kuwait and was second-in-command to Dick Sutton in Germany when the latter was tragically killed in a traffic accident. He commanded the Regiment briefly before handing over to Peter Hamer who had already been appointed to succeed Sutton before his death.

Another notable Cherrypicker who retired in 1983 was Major John Lemon who had joined the 11th as a trooper in 1952 and had risen through every rank to become second-in-command of The Royal Hussars.

An unusual Extra-Regimental Employment in 1983 was Major W. R. MacDonald's stint as G3 Ops with the British contingent in the Lebanon. It will be recalled that it was at this time that a large number of French and American soldiers were killed by suicide car-bombers while endeavouring vainly to keep the peace in Beirut. The total Allied force (American, British, French and Italian) was about 5,000 strong of which the British contribution was a single recce squadron of Ferrets. As the whole operation was futile and at the same time fraught with danger, as the terrible casualties to the Americans and French proved, for once the British Government showed some common sense in sending only a token force, which, although it came under fire on numerous occasions, suffered no losses.

In 1984 Lieutenant-Colonel Peter Upton retired from the post of Regimental Secretary and was succeeded by Lieutenant-Colonel Robin Merton. Soon afterwards Major Bob McDonald, who had been in charge of the Museum since its founding, also retired, and the Chief Clerk, Corporal Bob Penfold, who had given several years valuable assistance to the Home HQ despite illness, returned to regimental duty.

The new secretary, Robin Merton, originally a 4th Hussar, had been seconded to the 11th from the Queen's Royal Irish Hussars in 1966 to command B Squadron and transferred permanently to the Regiment in the same year. From 1970 to '72 he commanded C Squadron of The Royal Hussars and was second-in-command of the Regiment from 1972 to '74. During his active career he served in Germany, Aden, Cyprus, Malayasia, Sarawak, Hong Kong and Northern Ireland and qualified as a pilot. At the time of writing he is still Regimental Secretary and although it may be unorthodox for an author to make a personal acknowledgement in the middle of his narrative, the opportunity to do so here is irresistible. Without Robin's knowledge of regimental affairs and personalities, past and present, and his unfailing patience and response to sometimes eccentric requests, this book could never have been written.

A sporting triumph in 1984 was the (apparent) victory of The Royal Hussars Polo Team over the 16th/5th Lancers in the Inter-Regimental Cup. Having drawn a bye in the first round, the team managed to defeat the Royal Navy 5–4 in the semi-final. The word 'apparent' is used above advisedly as the *Journal*'s anonymous Polo Correspondent produced an inspired 450-word description of the final without actually revealing when the match was played or, indeed, who won! However, careful reading between the lines does suggest a Royal Hussar Victory, despite being two down at half-time. The winning team, which perhaps included the writer of that mysterious report, consisted of Majors Rogers and Kaye and Captains Wiggin and Flach.

On 6 June, 1984, three former 11th Hussars attended the commemoration of the 40th Anniversary of the D-Day landings at Arromanches. They were Vivian Esch, George (Skim) Emery and James Rimmer,* all of whom arrived by different routes and without pre-arrangement, but, nonetheless, found themselves representing the Regiment at the March Past by the Queen by well over a thousand veterans of the Battle of Normandy. James Rimmer, wearing his Cherrypicker beret, carried the 8th Army banner.

Vivian Esch stayed on in Normandy for the rest of the week visiting many of the D-Day landing places and two châteaux where members of the Regiment had found comfort and shelter forty years before and whose owners were unchanged since then.

'The two châteaux,' wrote Esch, 'were Madame Humann's Château de Juaye at St Andre, just south of Bayeux (see *The Eleventh at War*, pps. 341–2 and 347–8) and the Princess de Robech's Château de Brumare near Montfort sur Risle, Pont Audemer. We had tea with Madame Humann and her daughter

---

* In 1992 Mr Rimmer carried the 8th Army Veterans Association banner to the altar during the El Alamein Memorial Service in Westminster Abbey and at the ceremony at El Alamein itself marking the 50th Anniversary of the battle.

Madame Frassinet who was thirteen years old when the 11th Hussars sheltered under the trees in 1944. I gave both houses as souvenirs a copy of *The Eleventh at War* and the regimental ice-bucket of the Royal Hussars.'

In the following year Lieutenant-Colonel Sir Christopher Thompson, Bart, succeeded to command, Lieutenant-Colonel Morrison being awarded an OBE and moving to the School of Infantry at Warminster.

As the Regiment was now in its sixth year at Fallingbostel, only ERE could relieve the tedium of soldiering in Germany and several Royal Hussars sought employment around the world in various exotic armies or postings to more exciting places. Among these were Captain T. C. Allen and Sergeant A. J. Kingshott serving with the Sultan of Oman's Armoured Car Regiment, which, wrote Allen, 'started its life less than fifteen years ago as a squadron of Saladins, known simply as the Armoured Car Squadron (ACS). The ACS saw service throughout the counter-insurgency operations of the Dhofar War . . . This squadron is one of three Scorpion-equipped recce squadrons and, along with two squadrons of Chieftains makes up the present day Sultan of Oman's Armoured Car Regiment.'

Sergeant Kingshott found that he was expected to learn Arabic in ten weeks prior to joining the SOACR, a language which normally takes as many years to master. However, an extra £160 'trade' pay compensated to an extent for the effort required. On arrival in Oman Kingshott found another (former) Royal Hussar serving with the Regiment in the shape of Wakeel (WO1) Waite who had left the British Army in 1975 and was now on contract to the Sultan. Kingshott was posted to D Squadron as Training Raqeeb (Sergeant) which entailed teaching in Arabic, no easy task when faced with translating technical words.

In January, 1985, two squadrons, C and D, returned to the Regiment's old stamping ground, the Maze Prison in Northern Ireland, for a short tour of duty of less than three months, but on this occasion there were no untoward incidents.

In November of the same year the death occurred of the oldest Old Comrade, Canon William Lummis, who had joined the 11th as a trooper (then still known as private) in 1904. He had risen to the rank of RQMS when, in 1916, he was commissioned into the Suffolk Regiment with whom he won the Military Cross. After the war he took Holy Orders, spending much of his ministry in Suffolk. A leading expert on the Crimean War, particularly the Charge of the Light Brigade, in 1973 he published *Honour the Light Brigade*, a biographical dictionary of the men who had served with that brigade in the Crimea. When he died he was within seven months of his 100th birthday.

A notable event of 1986 was the visit to the Regiment of the then Prime Minister, Mrs Thatcher, and the German Chancellor, Helmut Kohl. These two dignitaries were given a fair run for their money. In the words of the *Journal*:

'A firepower demonstration took place on Battle Run 9 on the Hohne Ranges. It included a troop of Challengers from C Squadron led by Sergeant Swain; a troop from 3 Company 24 Panzer Battalion; a demonstration of both the British Lynx TOW and the German BO-105P anti-tank helicopters; and finally a demonstration of the simulation equipment SIMFICS. Mrs Thatcher and Chancellor Kohl were then given the opportunity to look over the tanks and fire if they so wished, under the watchful eye of Sergeant Penkethman, who explained the equipment, and Trooper Tyler who was the gunner. Mrs Thatcher fired one round and much to the relief [or more probably the disappointment] of the ninety or so Press who came to watch, she hit the target. In the best traditions of protocol, Chancellor Kohl then fired and he also scored a hit. This was followed by an informal lunch which was attended by the crews who had fired.'

In the Honours Lists of 1986 and '87 several members of the Regiment received a variety of Honours and Awards. Colonel Piers Bengough was made a KCVO; Brigadier John Friedberger a CBE; Lieutenant-Colonel Julien Turner an OBE and Major Peter Flach an MBE, while Lance Corporal N. H. Barnes received the BEM.

One of the more unusual ERE jobs of this time was Captain Ben Adams' attachment to the Mozambique Army as a Training

Officer. As he put it himself, 'The whole situation initially seemed a little bizarre in that we were helping the Communist Frelimo Government train their soldiers using Russian weapons and British military tactics.' Quite why British military personnel were being used to bolster a corrupt, totalitarian and incompetent Communist régime has never been explained, but then it is not for 'simple soldiers' to question the unfathomable policies of the Foreign Office. Suffice to say that Adams and his team, which included several sergeant instructors from the Zimbabwean Army, managed to impart some military knowledge to their pupils, despite serious problems of language and interpretation. Teaching the use of the magnetic compass, for example, was achieved by explaining to the students that the needle pointed to a mysterious figure who inhabited the North Pole and who moved around to a certain extent in search of liquor, thus accounting for magnetic variation!

At last news filtered through that the Regiment would return to England in about November, 1988, over seven years after leaving Catterick. By that time yet another change of command would have taken place with Lieutenant-Colonel Richard Morris replacing Lieutenant-Colonel Sir Christopher Thompson.

During the Regiment's sojourn at Fallingbostel it had seen four Commanding Officers, five RSMs, 67 officers and about 560 other ranks come and go.

Chapter 18

TIDWORTH 1988–90

Towards the end of 1988 The Royal Hussars returned to Bhurtpore Barracks, Tidworth, after an absence of seventeen years. On leaving Germany a message was received from the Commander 1st Armoured Division, General Swinburn, which read in part:

'You have had a tumultuous eight years in 1st Armd Div highlighted by your introduction of the Challenger into the British Army. Throughout your tour you have earned an enviable reputation as an efficient, professional regiment who were ever positive and made many friends. Of all admirable aspects perhaps the most outstanding has been the exceptional quality and ability of your WOs and NCOs. Simply they have no equal and have served the regiment magnificently maintaining high standards through thick and thin.'

The Regiment's return to Tidworth coincided with the arrival of its first female officer, Lieutenant V. S. Collins, WRAC, who was appointed Assistant Adjutant. The move also meant reverting back to the Chieftain from the Challenger and accepting a lower standard of accommodation to that found in most German barracks.

B Squadron (Major Flach) was immediately detached as RAC Demonstration Squadron to the School of Infantry at Warminster and the Recce Troop (Captain Daly) was soon off on a tour of duty in Belize, where it remained from March to September,

1989, working with the Welsh Guards. The Regiment as a whole came under command HQ United Kingdom Mobile Force and in August, 1989, and February, 1990, took part in two major exercises, Crimson Rambler 1 and 11, on Salisbury Plain.

The principal event of 1990 was the Guidon Presentation Parade held at Tidworth on 30 June, but various other items of interest in that year should be recorded before going into the details of this historic occasion.

In March the Regiment was visited by the First Deputy Chief of Staff of the (then) Soviet Union's Armed Forces, Colonel General Bronislav Omelichev, a high-sounding title for a senior officer of an already crumbling empire. Accompanied by a number of British Generals, Omelichev was put through the usual routine of inspecting tanks and fire control systems and was then presented with a regimental plaque and a Royal Hussar beret. The purpose of his visit was, and will remain, a mystery.

In the same month the long-running ambulancemen's strike ended. From the previous September up to thirty-four Royal Hussars had either been on duty or at seventy-two hours' notice to move. These men were deployed across the south and west of the country from Truro to Bournemouth to Stoke-on-Trent and were under the control of the local police, each man spending six days on a twelve-hour shift followed by two or three days' rest. In addition to the medical (mostly bandsmen) support and drivers provided by the Regiment, members of the LAD helped to maintain the ambulances.

In November D Squadron, under Major Bowring, arrived in Cyprus to take over the role of Sovereign Base Areas Armoured Reconnaissance Squadron, equipped with Saladins, Saracens and Ferrets, the former having been regarded as 'ancient' by the 10th Hussars in Aden over a quarter of a century earlier! Later the Squadron's nomenclature was changed to that of Independent Medium Reconnaissance Squadron. With the outbreak of hostilities in the Gulf (with which we shall deal in greater detail later), the dangers of terrorist outrages against the British forces in Cyprus increased considerably and the Squadron was required to have troops on patrol 24 hours a day. Whatever the international situation, Cyprus was and remains a choice posting for servicemen and women, combining a splendid climate with many opportunities for sport and recreation from skiing to scuba diving.

Also in November, according to *The Andover Advertiser*, 'a distressed young Tidworth soldier (a Royal Hussar trooper), who took a Chieftain tank on a joy-ride, did so after the break-up of his parents' marriage.' In the process he managed a good deal of breaking-up himself, inflicting nearly £12,000 worth of damage on MOD property and wrecking a Wiltshire County Council lamp-post valued at £474. His 8½ mile trip, described by his defence as a 'gentle perambulation', was eventually brought to a standstill by a policeman, but in his wake lay a trail of devastation which was to cost him a £450 fine, £10 costs and £473.47 compensation to Wiltshire County Council! The magistrates also ordered 10 points to be put on his driving licence!

The morning of the Guidon Parade dawned windy, and rain threatened, but, happily for the majority, in the event only the VIP spectators got wet as they were placed at the front of the grandstand from whose sloping roof gallons of water ran off onto their heads, causing much merriment among lesser mortals well under cover in the rear.

The parade was to be the last ceremonial occasion presided over by the Colonel of the Regiment, Colonel Sir Piers Bengough, and the Commanding Officer, Lieutenant-Colonel Richard Morris, both of whom handed over to their successors shortly thereafter.

The Guidon was presented by the Colonel-in-Chief, HRH Princess Alice, Duchess of Gloucester, and those taking part included:

The Colonel of the Regiment
The Commanding Officer
Second-in-Command (Major J. J. Rogers)
Adjutant (Captain T. C. Allen)
RSM (WO1 J. Barnard)
Bandmasters (WO1 M. Davidson)
     (WO1 R. D. Williams, Royal Wessex Yeomanry)

Tidworth

The Old Guidon Party
WO2 I. N. R. Stedman-Brown
Staff Sergeant C. A. Attwood
Staff Sergeant C. F. M. Tunstall

The New Guidon Party
WO2 E. M. Halffman
Staff Sergeant P. W. Swain
Staff Sergeant S. J. Wilde

No 1 Guard
Major J. A. F. Howard
Captain J. C. R. de Normann
Lieutenant N. F. V. MacLeod-Ash (Lieutenant of the Escort)
2nd Lieutenant M. E. V. Wakefield

No 2 Guard
Major C. T. R. Hezlet
Captain E. St J. Hall
Lieutenant J. P. Miller
2nd Lieutenant B. W. Gedney

No 3 Guard
Captain S. R. B. Merton
Lieutenant P. A. D. Inkin
Lieutenant M. C. E. Morrison
2nd Lieutenant J. G. Wiggin

No 4 Guard
Captain C. H. D. Danvers
Captain P. J. Wilkins
Captain R. J. Hannay
Lieutenant B. A. Smith

Mounted Escort (Horses provided by the Household Cavalry)
Major N. Grant-Thorold

Armoured Squadron
Major R. A. W. Bowring
Captain J. W. D. Trotter
Lieutenant P. M. E. Clinch

Lieutenant M. A. Ward
Lieutenant J. P. Stevens

Back Drop Tanks
Major R. N. Sweeney, US Army

Quartermaster (assisting the Colonel-in-Chief with the Guidon)
Captain M. Keats

By 10.30 the three thousand spectators were assembled and at 10.40 Trumpet Major Harris sounded the regimental call and the Regiment marched on parade under the command of the Adjutant with the combined bands of the Royal Hussars and the Royal Gloucestershire Hussars leading. Then the Commanding Officer took over the parade and the principal guests, HRH Prince Michael of Kent and the GOC UK Land Forces, General Sir Charles Huxtable, arrived. Meanwhile, a helicopter of the Queen's Flight carrying the Colonel-in-Chief had landed on the polo field to the east of the parade. Princess Alice was then brought up to the parade by landau escorted by the Mounted Troop and, after the Royal Salute, carried out an inspection of the Regiment from the landau. This done, the band trooped in slow and quick time and the old Guidon was trooped through the ranks and marched off to the strains of Old Lang Syne.

For the presentation the Regiment formed a hollow square and a service of consecration was conducted by the Deputy Chaplain-General, the Reverend G. H. Roblin, assisted by several other clergy. Following the consecration the Colonel-in-Chief formally presented the Guidon which was carried on parade by RQMS Halffman.

In her address Princess Alice reminded her listeners that she had presented the Regiment with its first Guidon 21 years before, marking the amalgamation of the 10th and 11th Hussars. She had been connected with the 10th for 88 years of her life, she continued, having had two uncles and two brothers in the 10th (as well as her husband) and a nephew and two great-nephews in The Royal Hussars.

After the Commanding Officer's reply, in which he asked the Princess to convey to Her Majesty the Queen the Regiment's thanks and loyalty, the parade marched past in slow and quick time before advancing in review order and giving the final Royal Salute of the occasion, during which a 21-gun salute by the tanks drawn up at the rear of the parade was fired. Unfortunately, one or two of the blank rounds misfired but this could be blamed on the fact that the tanks were under the command of an American officer!

The Armoured Squadron then drove past, followed by the Old Comrades led by a Sherman tank and a Daimler Armoured Car, two of the principal AFVs of the 10th and 11th Hussars respectively in the Second World War. The Old Comrades Association Banner was carried by a Chelsea Pensioner, Sergeant-Major T. Parnell of the 10th, escorted by Yeoman Warders Hauxwell and Bryant. Over four hundred Old Comrades, led by Brigadier Roscoe Harvey, took part in the march past.

In the course of the parade the gusting wind had removed a few caps, but luckily the rain had been insufficient to dampen the excellence of the marching and drill, a credit not only to those on parade but in particular to Drill Sergeant Humphrey of the Coldstream Guards.

After the parade lunch was served to over 2,500 past and present members of the Regiment and their families. In the afternoon, polo and cricket matches between regimental teams and the Old Comrades were played and there were various military displays in the tank park.

The All Ranks Dance in the evening was perhaps the largest ever such gathering of Royal Hussars and was further enlivened by a spectacular firework display.

On her departure the Colonel-in-Chief issued a Special Order which ran as follows: –

'I know I speak for all past members of our Regiment when I send my congratulations on the magnificent parade today. I have never been more proud of my long association with the Regiment whose interests are very close to my heart.

'The tremendous effort by all ranks to make this historic day such a happy celebration has been deeply appreciated by all those fortunate enough to attend. In these times of uncertainty for you and your families I know that your pride in your Regiment, your professionalism and courage, will see us through the challenging days ahead.'

Shortly afterwards Colonel Sir Piers Bengough retired and handed over to Major-General John Friedberger who was to be the last Colonel of The Royal Hussars.* His ultimate active appointment was Commander British Forces in Cyprus and Administrator of the Sovereign Base Areas. In this task he was assisted by three other Royal Hussars, namely his ADC, Captain Bridge, Staff Sergeant Greenwell and Corporal Hughes.

In his *Journal* notes Bridge sets out the principal character-istics required of a successful ADC (based on 'Advice to Officers of the British Army' 1760). These suggest that he should be 'haughty and insolent to his inferiors, humble and fawning to his superiors, solemn and distant to his equals.' We do not know if Captain Bridge fulfilled these criteria himself but he hastens to point out the hazards of the job as well, reminding us that the great Duke of Wellington had no less than seventeen ADCs killed in action beside him!

Absent from the Guidon Parade was the Recce Troop on service in Belize and one of its members has provided us with a description of that little known country, which was formerly the colony of British Honduras. Since independence a British garrison has been stationed there in order to deter neighbouring Guatemala from prosecuting its claim to the territory by force. This presence seems to have had the desired effect.

'Belize is about the size of Wales', writes our correspondent, 'with a population of about 170,000 most of whom live in Belize City. They are a mixed race of Hispanics, Caribbeans and Mayan Indians. It is a very poor country, reliant on tourism, sugar cane, citrus fruit and the presence of British forces. The northern half of the country is mainly flat terrain with sugar cane, jungle, subsistence farming and swamp. The southern half

* Also the first Colonel of The King's Royal Hussars.

is mountainous jungle and forest except on the coast where it is flat and marshy. There is virtually no industry or natural resources. There are two tarmac roads and therefore transport is reliant on these two roads and helicopters.'

The role of the troop, commanded by Captain the Hon A. E. S. Bathurst, with Lieutenant F. G. Gedney and Staff Sergeant Pearce, was to supply armoured support for the infantry brigade (Gurkhas and Royal Highland Fusiliers) and to carry out patrols in the northern half of the country. These patrols, which consisted of two Scorpions and a 4-tonner, lasted four or five days and averaged about 250 miles. The intention was 'to show the flag', secure the area against drug traffickers and Guatemalan infiltrators, to keep Force HQ informed of what was going on in the area, and, if necessary, to provide a heavy reaction force to counter any enemy (Guatemalan) operation.

Owing to various commitments, Recce Troop held its own Guidon Parade on 2 July rather than 30 June. After the parade, which was inspected by the High Commissioner, who presented Guidon Commemoration medals, various sports competitions were held, including one remarkable event in which nine men had to surmount an assault course while roped together!

On 10 July 1990, Lieutenant-Colonel Richard Morris handed over command to Lieutenant-Colonel Johnny Kaye, who was destined to be the Regiment's last Commanding Officer, and The Royal Hussars entered upon the final phase of their short history when they returned to Germany, less D Squadron to Cyprus, in December of that year.

Chapter 19

MUNSTER AND THE GULF 1991–2

Throughout the Gulf War, to which we shall come in a moment, D Squadron was based in Cyprus, not as part of the UN Peace-Keeping Force but in the British Sovereign Base Areas of Akrotiri and Dhekelia. These two small enclaves in the south of the island had been retained by the British Government when Cyprus became independent in 1960. The role of the squadron was to assist in the defence of the bases and, equipped only with Saladin and Ferret, its deployment to the Gulf was never considered. Instead it operated on a heightened internal security alert for the first few months of its tour. For the rest of the time it was a final chance for Royal Hussars to enjoy the kind of soldiering many of their predecessors had experienced over the years. Sun, sea and sport played a large part but the squadron also earned high praise for its military efficiency as this tribute from Air Vice-Marshal Sandy Hunter, Commander British Forces Cyprus, confirms:

'29th June 1992
To Lieutenant Colonel J. R. D. Kaye RH
I cannot allow the departure of D Squadron to pass without writing to tell you what a really splendid job the Sqn has done during its time under my command. I cannot speak too highly of the way in which all ranks have tackled their duties, nor of the part they have played in our Internal Security effort. They have been first rate in all that they have done and I am hugely grateful to them all. Work apart, the members of the squadron have

210

played a full part in the life of the BFC community and they have done much to add to the reputation of the Regiment.'

In his foreword to the 1991 *Journal* the new Commanding Officer summed up the situation faced by the Regiment and indeed the British Armed Forces as a whole in the light of the tumultuous events which had taken place over the past year or so.

'The Regiment's two years in Tidworth have gone in a flash and it seems only yesterday that we left Fallingbostel. One thing is clear; we have returned to a different Germany to the one we left and we now live in very difficult times. There have been three major earthquakes in our lives in the last 12 months. First our traditional enemy has melted away. Most of us have spent our entire adult life training in order to fight him if necessary.

'Second (and consequent on the first), our government finds itself caught between the jaws of public pressure to achieve the "peace dividend" and a miscalculation about the rate of inflation. As a result of this we now face enormous change in the shape and size of the Army under "Options for Change".

'Third, Saddam Hussein's invasion of Kuwait has resulted in Britain's deployment of a very powerful armoured division to help defeat the fourth most powerful military force in the world.*

'These earthquakes have already resulted in great demands being made upon all Royal Hussars in the last three months: the handover to the 17th/21st Lancers, the arms plot move from Warminster and Tidworth to Cyprus and Munster, the lack of equipment in BAOR to train on, and the requirement to train for possible deployment to the Gulf at short notice. All this has concentrated the mind wonderfully and taught us to remain eminently flexible.'

The first of these 'earthquakes', perhaps one of the most momentous in modern history, namely the collapse of the Soviet Union and its Eastern European empire, requires little elaboration here. In any case, at the time of writing, we are too close to the event to judge anything but its short-term conse-

---

* This was true numerically but not in any other sense.

quences. Among these was Colonel Kaye's second 'earthquake', the ill-famed and reckless 'Options for Change', a euphemism for savage and dangerous cuts to the British Armed Forces, leading to the redundancy (at a time of mass unemployment) of some 40,000 officers, NCOs and men and the abolition or amalgamation of numerous regiments including, of course, The Royal Hussars.

But let us now deal in greater detail with the third 'earthquake', the Gulf War.

As we have seen in the previous sections of this book, since the collapse of the Ottoman Empire at the end of the First World War Iraq has laid claim to its small, but fabulously oil-rich, neighbour, Kuwait. We have recorded how, in 1961, the 11th Hussars played a prominent role in deterring the then dictator of Iraq, Kassem, from invading Kuwait. For nearly three decades the question of Kuwait remained in the pending trays of Kassem's successors, overshadowed by other issues, most notably by the long and inconclusive war which raged between Iraq and Iran throughout the 1980s.

In 1979 Saddam Hussein, an exceptionally ruthless and cunning Ba'ath Party apparatnik, had come to power and rapidly built up a seemingly formidable military machine, including a chemical warfare capability and a nuclear development programme. However, when he embarked upon the invasion of Iran in September, 1980, it was soon to become clear that he, and the rest of the world, had greatly overestimated the competence and battle-worthiness of his armed forces. Despite debilitating purges of their officer corps and the lack of spares for their modern weapons (acquired by the late Shah), over the next eight years the Iranians, many of them ill-armed and untrained teenagers, fought the Iraqis to a standstill. Paradoxically, Saddam had enjoyed both the tacit and material support of both the West and the Soviet Union as well as financial aid from most of his Arab neighbours, including Kuwait, all of these regarding him, perhaps understandably in the light of Iran's 'mad dog' behaviour since the revolution, as the lesser of the two evils.

Both countries emerged from the war in a state of economic

collapse, but, nothing daunted, Saddam proceeded to rebuild his shattered military strength, largely with borrowed money. With his own oil revenues depleted and desperate for more cash, his bloodshot eye soon turned upon the trembling Kuwaitis (who had already written off much of his debt to them), renewing Iraq's claim to their country as a whole and to the Rumaylah oil-fields in particular. Accusing Kuwait of, among other things, stealing $2.5 billion worth of Iraqi oil (presumably the output of Rumaylah over an unspecified period), by the end of July, 1990, Saddam had massed 100,000 men on the border. Then, despite assurances given to most of the leading figures of the Arab World, including King Fahd of Saudi Arabia and President Mubarek of Egypt, on 2 August he ordered his much-vaunted Republican Guard* to invade. There was some resistance, but by the evening of the following day most of Kuwait was in the hands of the Iraqi Army.

What the reaction of the West, and of the United States in particular, would have been had America's principal ally in the region, Saudi Arabia, not been threatened by the large number of Iraqi troops on its border with Kuwait, it is hard to say. However, by the end of the year almost all political and diplomatic efforts to persuade Saddam to withdraw his physical presence from Kuwait and his implied threat to Saudi Arabia had failed. Thus it came about that, with the approval of the United Nations (no longer trammelled by a virtually defunct Soviet Union), the United States and her allies proceeded to construct the biggest sledge-hammer ever designed to crack a rotten nut.

It is difficult to ascertain the precise numbers of men or quantities of materials involved in the Gulf War on the Allied (known as the Coalition) side but, including L of C personnel, probably well over half a million service men and women took part, with thousands of guns, tanks, aircraft and ships. The largest contingent came, of course, from the United States, with

---

* This formation was the subject of astonishingly misleading media hype, constantly referred to as 'élite and battle-hardened'. In fact it was distinguished only for its fleetness of foot and its enthusiasm for massacring civilians.

substantial contributions from Saudi Arabia, Egypt, France and the United Kingdom. It is upon the latter force that we will concentrate.

The British Army's contribution, the main constituent of which was 1st (Br) Armoured Division, amounted to over 33,000 troops. The Armoured Division consisted of 4th and 7th Armoured Brigades and supporting elements. In order to equip and man this division the Ministry of Defence was obliged to strip BAOR of almost all its heavy weaponry and bring all the 'teeth' units up to establishment with drafts of men from other regiments, sometimes in company or squadron strength. The Royal Hussars, for example, found themselves taking over 28 immobile Challengers on arrival at Swinton Barracks, Munster, and six recce vehicles of which two were workable, all engines, gunnery and signals equipment having been removed.

The Royal Hussars had hoped, of course, to take part as a complete regiment, or at least as one or more complete squadrons, and the conversion training of two sabre squadrons from Chieftain to Challenger took place at Lulworth during the autumn of 1990. In the event, however, they had to content themselves with providing under a hundred officers and men, including attached personnel, as Battle Casualty Replacements (see Appendix E), some of whom managed to get themselves up to 'the sharp end' in one capacity or another. Several other members of the Regiment succeeded through arm-twisting and *jeux d'influence* in wangling jobs with the Coalition forces. Among these were Major Robin Watt and Captain Roddy de Norman, some of whose experiences and impressions will be recounted later.

The Coalition air offensive against targets in Kuwait and Iraq started on the night 16/17 January, 1991. The Iraqi Air Force, many of whose aircraft were destroyed on the ground, showed little fight, indeed much of it either defected to Iran or was ordered there for safety by Saddam.

This bombing campaign was undoubtedly the most successful in the history of warfare, in effect deciding the outcome of the war before the launch of the ground offensive. By about mid-February immense damage had been done to Iraq's military capability as well as to industrial and stratetic targets in the Baghdad area and elsewhere. To quote a few statistics, twenty-seven out of thirty-one of the main bridges on the supply routes to the front had been destroyed, as had roughly 2,000 tanks and other armoured vehicles and about 1,200 artillery pieces; all this with relatively minor losses in Coalition aircraft, despite an average of 2,500 sorties per day.

The only significant action on the ground during this period was fought at the Saudi border town of Khafji on 30/31 January, which had been occupied by the Iraqis on the 29th. Although untrained in street fighting, Saudi and Qatari troops managed to eject the Iraqis from the town, killing thirty and capturing 400 for the loss of fifteen of their own men killed and thirty-two wounded.

A serious political, rather than military, problem for the Coalition was presented by the Iraqis' use of Scud missiles, thirty-eight of which were launched against Israel (and about the same number against Saudi Arabia), thus jeopardizing Israel's precarious, but vital, neutrality. Had the Israelis entered the war, the Coalition, which included many Arab nations, might have disintegrated. Though this might not have affected the military situation too seriously, the political consequences could have been disastrous. Fortunately the Scud attacks failed in this objective due to a combination of their inaccuracy, the success of the Patriot anti-missile missiles which destroyed many of the Scuds in the air, and the courage and skill of Special Forces, mostly British and American, on the ground inside Iraq who were able to pinpoint the missile sites and call down air strikes upon them.

The Royal Hussars contingent flew out from Germany in two groups, arriving at Dahran on 22 January and Al Jubail on 29 January respectively. Soon both groups came together at Al Jubail attached to the Life Guards. After a period of training, most of the contingent was placed under command of the Armoured Delivery Group which would supply replacements, either of personnel or vehicles, to the forward (4th and 7th) brigades. Trooper Melvin Tate, for example, went into action as a tank driver within hours of joining 2nd Troop, B Squadron, of the 14th/20th Hussars. Among others who served with forward units during the short, sharp ground operation to liberate Kuwait were Corporals Chandler, Marshall and Foster.

The long period of relative inactivity and uncertainty, aggravated by the nagging fear of chemical attack, had been trying on the nerves and there was some relief when the order to advance was received in the early hours of the morning of 24 February.

Corporal Steve Marshall, commanding a heavy-load supply vehicle with D Squadron of the Royal Scots Dragoon Guards, has given an account of his experiences in letters to Major Sweeney (then commanding B Squadron of The Royal Hussars at Munster) and in a discussion with the author:

'Our push towards Iraq began on the evening of the 24th with a halt called by Brigade in the Neutral Zone. On the morning of the 25th the move continued towards the breach [in the Iraqi defences] and through it. The first thing I saw was a D30 gun position which had been totally destroyed. From the breach the squadron moved into Iraq, about 8kms to FUP [Form Up Point] Yellow. While in the FUP we got information that an Iraqi brigade was on its way. At 14.30 7 Brigade moved into the offensive.

'We pushed about 8 kms before our first contact. Everyone was expecting a bloody battle so anti-climax began to sink in. Shortly before 20.00 hours a man was seen moving to the right of the advancing column and trenches were observed containing about twenty men and six vehicles. This turned out to be an enemy command post with in-depth positions. The tanks turned to face on and our company of infantry [Staffords] moved up.

'The Warriors [armoured personnel carriers] with a tank in support moved to the right of the position. The squadron leader would not let his crew use main armament even before the infantry began to fight through, so machine guns were used. Many Iraqis were killed: some tried to run but were killed also. Two six-man patrols tried to reach the tanks but were destroyed. One man of the Staffords was killed by an anti-tank rocket while trying to accept a surrender. Some Iraqi tanks attempted to outflank the SDGs to the NW but were destroyed by C Squadron. After pushing through the position a halt was called at 23.00

'On the 26th, while advancing in column, we ran into an Iraqi armoured recce screen. These were engaged and left blazing. I remember seeing one Iraqi tank commander lying on the ground blown in half with his arm taken off too. A piece of shrapnel took a chunk out of my vehicle at the front. An Iraqi colonel stood up and encouraged his men to surrender. He was removed by helicopter and the remainder by truck.

'At 12.30 we moved off again but ran through a minefield where one Warrior exploded. At about 15.15 we encountered enemy T55s and MTLB Personnel Carriers, several of which were destroyed. We advanced west then south to recce, then moved north for five or six kms, reaching a building surrounded by bodies with a T55 in it. We advanced on the building with the Staffords in support but without firing and the position was taken without casualties. About 400 POWs had been taken.

'At 12.00 on the 27th we crossed into Kuwait. Groups of Iraqis could be seen wandering about the desert waving pieces of white cloth. Others just waited until the Allies turned up. When caught they would wave to us and smile. It was just as if they had been liberated!'

So ended Corporal Marshall's war.

A ceasefire was confirmed at 0800 on the 28th. During the previous 66 hours the British Armoured Division had advanced 290kms, destroyed the best part of three enemy armoured divisions and taken over 7,000 prisoners.

The aftermath of the campaign has left an indelible impression on the minds of some of the eye-witnesses. Major Robin Watt, whose principal role was that of a war-artist (although he personally dislikes the description) on behalf of the Army Benevolent Fund, took part in Operation Desert Sabre (the land campaign) with B Squadron of the Queen's Royal Irish Hussars. He has very kindly given the author permission to quote from his illustrated campaign diary.

'Went with Major Tim Bidie to the outskirts of Kuwait City. There I saw a scene of destruction the like of which I have never seen before nor wish to see again. Probably a thousand vehicles devastated by Allied air and ground attack on a six-lane highway at the Al Mutla Pass north of Al Jahra on the Basra-Kuwait City road over a distance of about two miles. Artillery pieces, tanks, anti-aircraft guns, military trucks enmeshed and tangled with civilian cars and buses. All had been pushed to the side of the road by military engineers and lay sometimes six deep at every conceivable angle, some hanging crazily on the edge of ravines or down embankments or through fences or upside down on one side. Others were buckled or jack-knifed or blackened by fire. Contents of tanks and trucks were strewn everywhere. Everything from clocks to clothing cascading in a mad jumble from and between tangled wrecks and out across the road itself. Armies of scavengers picked through the devastation like crows on a rubbish tip. Buildings formed the back-drop, gutted and skeletal, but groups of Kuwaitis moved down the highway in cars or on foot apparently grateful to return to this Armageddon. In every direction there was yet more destruction to witness but always too much for the eye to take in or for the brain to register. Probably just as well!

'The background to the carnage at Al Mutla is this: during the final stages of the war, elements of the Iraqi Army fled in large numbers from Kuwait City due north on the Kuwait-Basra road. The Allied Air Force struck in the area of the Al Mutla Pass at escaping Iraqis mounted in any vehicles they could lay their hands on. These ranged from tanks to military lorries to civilian trucks, buses and cars laden to the gunwhales with goods looted from Kuwait City. As the lead vehicles were immobilized near the Al Mutla Police Post by A10 aircraft, traffic piled up behind and became targets for American tanks that now commanded the heights to the west. The Iraqis were unable to deploy to the west of the main road because of an extensive barrier minefield laid down by Iraq engineers. Those who managed to deploy into the desert to the east were cut down. The number of Iraqis who died in this ghastly place is not known.'

Many felt that the Iraqi invaders had received no more, perhaps less, than their just deserts as their treatment of the people of occupied Kuwait had been atrocious. Thousands had been murdered, tortured or abducted, women raped and the city systematically looted, burnt and vandalized. Even the animals in the zoo were shot or starved to death.

This is not the place in which to argue the rights and wrongs of the decision to stop the war before the destruction or overthrow of its principal architect, Saddam Hussein, but it is a curious irony of history that two of his most resolute opponents, Margaret Thatcher and George Bush, were removed from power by (more or less) democratic means while the Iraqi tyrant remained perched on the top of his dung-heap.

With the end of hostilities there came to many members of the Coalition forces and the massive Press Corps attached to them a feeling of let-down and anticlimax. For some the war, at least the ground war, had seemed too quick and easy. Captain Roddy de Normann, whose job had been to accompany and shepherd a team of BBC correspondents, recalls that 'in all honesty, the ground war had been a disappointment from the point of view of the media. All were relieved at the speed and lack of casualties, but one got the impression that they felt they had missed out. As all their emotions flooded out, they levelled some harsh criticisms. After six weeks together these were very hurtful. Still, this was the nature of the beast and one could sympathize to some extent.'

Most of the Royal Hussar contingent returned to Munster in mid-March, relieved that they all escaped unscathed, to the congratulations, not unmixed with some jealous banter, of those they had left behind. Major R. N. (Narge) Sweeney, an American cavalry officer on attachment to the Regiment and commanding B Squadron, had written from Germany to those of his men who were in the Gulf on the day of the Ceasefire:

'I am extremely proud of each and every one of you! Each of you should hold your head high because you have all helped to make and change the course of history by your dedication, professionalism and courage. While not all of you may have been able to fire shots in hostility you were there and were willing to make the supreme sacrifice and to undertake any mission you were assigned. By now you have come to grips with the fact that the months of intensive training, hardships of desert life and being a BCR (Battle Casualty Replacement) who never knows what lies ahead, you have helped to completely destroy the fourth largest army in the world in less than 100 hours.'

The only Royal Hussar to receive any award, in his case the British Empire Medal, for his service in the Gulf was Lance-Corporal Dawson, a technical storeman on semi-permanent attachment to the Royal Scots Dragoon Guards, who, despite ill-health, insisted on accompanying his adopted regiment to the war zone.

Before leaving Germany Dawson worked exceptionally long hours, often spending the night in his store. His citation read:

'Since arrival in the Gulf Lance-Corporal Dawson has spent all his time in the desert and has taken no time off at the Training and Fitness Centre. As an out-of-date Medical Assistant Class 2 he made a determined personal effort to update his techniques and attended a combat medic's course. He then set about organizing the supply of medical stores to the Regiment with a vengeance. By constantly badgering the medical supply chain and keeping close contact with the Medical Officer he ensured that the squadrons were well equipped with every available medical accessory. He planned the distribution of life-saving devices within his own department and issued guidance on their disposition within the echelon. With in excess of twelve years experience in the supply of vehicle spares his uncanny ability to recall part numbers has proven invaluable.

'Due to a vehicle enhancement early in January, 1991, and a corresponding shortage of drivers Lance-Corporal Dawson was requested to solo drive a heavy goods vehicle for which he holds no licence, the latter having been withdrawn due to his medical condition. This he quickly agreed to do as an expedient despite the pain long hours behind the wheel caused him. There were times during the land battle when he could hardly extract himself from his cab but at no time did he complain.

'Throughout the entire operation Lance-Corporal Dawson accepted his fair quota of duties in a cheerful and determined manner regardless of the discomfort he clearly experienced. He displayed great courage and determination at all times and his attitude and example were an inspiration to the younger soldiers around him. There is no doubt that in the circumstances Lance-Corporal Dawson's resolute commitment to carrying out his duty was far in excess of that expected of his rank and station.

His conduct was in keeping with the very highest traditions of his service.'

But at home the patriotic fervour which had been aroused in the early stages of the war quickly faded. General de la Billière's* joyful cry of 'ring out the bells' was almost completely ignored. Largely disregarding the amazing technological and logistical achievements of the Coalition and its minimal casualties (about 250 killed), the media preferred to concentrate on and sensation-alize the less creditable aspects of the war such as the death by 'Friendly (American) Fire' of nine British soldiers.

Roddy de Normann's homecoming was something of a disillusionment. 'No flags, no bands. Back home in England everything carried on as though nothing had happened. Several months later they announced the massive cuts as Options for Change was taken up once more. Never more true were Kipling's words:

'For it's Tommy this and Tommy that, and chuck him out, the brute!

But it's Saviour of his Country when the guns begin to shoot!'

Options for Change was indeed 'taken up once more' and it soon became clear that The Royal Hussars would not escape the net. On 23 July, 1991, it was announced that the Regiment would be amalgamated with the 14th/20th King's Hussars. This news did not come as a bombshell although there had been lingering hopes of a reprieve. Nonetheless, there was a feeling once again of betrayal – that the Army had been sacrificed to Treasury demands for public expenditure cuts, simply using the 'Peace Dividend' as an excuse, and that the military hierarchy had not fought its corner hard enough.

As it had been with his predecessors, Dawnay and Lawson, only 24 years before, it was incumbent upon the Colonel of the Regiment, Major-General John Friedberger, to put a brave face upon a disagreeable and unwelcome prospect. In his Foreword to the 1992 *Journal* he wrote:

* Commander British Forces Middle East

'We had no constitutional alternative but to accept the Government's decision with good grace and the priority is now to work with the 14th/20th King's Hussars to ensure that our new regiment is given the best possible start. The amalgamation will take place in December, 1992, in Munster. As a Guidon for the King's Royal Hussars will take some years to obtain we intend that the inaugural ceremony will be limited in scope. Both our regiments are presently in Munster and this means that much of the domestic upheaval, particularly for families with children, has been avoided.

'We intend that the King's Royal Hussars will continue to recruit from our counties in southern England as well as the 14th/20th's area of Lancashire.

'I am delighted to conclude with the message that HRH Princess Alice, Duchess of Gloucester, has graciously consented to continue her long association with the Regiment by accepting the appointment of Deputy Colonel-in-Chief of the King's Royal Hussars.'*

Some felt that it was extraordinarily magnanimous of this great lady, whose association with the Regiment and its predecessors dated back to Edwardian days, to have accepted this diminished role – a remarkable demonstration of her sweetness of character and absolute loyalty and devotion to the family into which she had married so long ago.

There is little more to be said. However, one may derive some wry amusement and no little admiration for military sang-froid from a document entitled 'The Regimental Diary of Events Oct-Nov 92'. Against the date 27 November appear two items: –

RH Final Parade
Battery Acid Waste Contract Finished

One feels that some of the great military figures of the past, Wellington, Kitchener, Montgomery perhaps, would have approved of such matter-of-fact lack of sentimentality.

* HRH The Princess Royal, having been Colonel-in-Chief of the 14th/20th King's Hussars, assumed the Colonelcy-in-Chief of the King's Royal Hussars on the amalgamation in December, 1992.

During October various social gatherings were held in England and on 4 December a muted and low-key amalgamation parade took place at Munster. But what the future holds for the new Regiment, or, indeed, how long or short their future may be, is anyone's guess.

The end of the Cold War has brought no peace to the world, nor have cries for union, even in Europe, brought any unity. The need for strong national defence is undiminished, except in the minds of politicians. Throughout history an old peril has always been replaced by a new, and one crisis by another, seldom appearing from the directions whence they are expected. This law of nature, or rather of mankind, will not change.

Epilogue

In the near half-century covered by this History immense changes have taken place, not only within the British army but within British society as a whole and to Britain's status in the world. The nation emerged from the Second World War exhausted but with a huge empire still intact of which, forty nine years later, little remains.

Although throughout this period the principal role of the British Armed Forces, and in particular of the Royal Armoured Corps, was the defence of western Europe and the largest concentration of troops was in the British Zone of Germany (BAOR), nonetheless for the first twenty years or so there were dozens of British garrisons, large and small, scattered across the globe. This provided great variety in the lives of regular soldiers and, to some extent, National Servicemen (so long as that excellent institution, compulsory military service, endured).

Imperial campaigns, such as those in Malaya and Aden, provided opportunities for a type of soldiering at troop level which is rarely available to junior officers and men in this last decade of the century. As for overseas garrisons, within the next few years Hong Kong will be gone; Belize and perhaps Cyprus are no doubt already regarded by many politicians and the Treasury as extravagances the nation can ill afford; eventually some kind of settlement with the Argentine will remove the need for anything but a token military presence in the Falklands. BAOR, since the collapse of the Soviet Union and the reunification of Germany, is something of an anachronism and the continued presence of the Second World War allies in western Germany (already sharply reduced) has become more a matter of inertia than of necessity.

Thus, by the end of the century, the British Army is likely to be almost entirely a Home Army, probably still wrestling with the intractable problem of Northern Ireland and occasionally engaged in overseas forays at the behest of NATO or the United Nations. This may encourage future British governments of all complexions to seek further cuts, especially to the Royal Armoured Corps, until, as suggested at the end of the last chapter, some desperate and unforeseen event or series of events forces the whole process into reverse. Already, early in 1993, the Minister of Defence was obliged to admit that the ill-famed Options for Change policy seriously underestimated the infantry requirement for the immediate future and four battalions, earmarked for amalgamation, have been reprieved.

However, the Royal Armoured Corps may be in special danger. As recorded in the 10th Hussar section of this History, a great opportunity was missed in the 1960s with the RAC's failure to develop and enlarge its air role. This chance may or may not come again: if it does not or if it is not seized, the remaining cavalry regiments may wither and die as the tank becomes as obsolete as its predecessor, the horse. This would be especially tragic as, in some intangible way, the spirit of the old British cavalry has lived on, surviving mechanisation, amalgamations and cuts. This elusive quality is lost on the politicians and Civil Service mandarins but is a valuable national asset which should not be allowed to perish.

Before turning to the social aspects of change within the British Army, we must consider briefly the possible effects, should it ever come about, of a United or Federal Europe embracing the United Kingdom. At this time of uncertainty over the development of the European Union, it would be absurd to attempt to predict in detail the impact that such a union or federation might have upon the British Army but who can doubt that it would lead to unprecedented difficulties and tensions within the nation's Armed Forces. To pose but one question, how would the transfer of ultimate loyalty from a national Sovereign, an allegiance strongly held if seldom voiced, to some remote and unloved supra-national entity, be regarded and implemented?

Although many of the Army's best traditions have been maintained, fundamental changes have taken place since 1945, not least in the social aspects of military life. Pay, allowances and conditions of service for Other Ranks in particular, have improved beyond all measure. For example, in 1945 a Trooper's basic pay was 5s (25p) per day, a WO1's 14s and a Lieutenant Colonel's £2-3-0. Although inflation has rendered a comparison in real terms almost impossible, the equivalent rates at the time of writing (1993) are £23.30, £50.45 and £101.27!

Food, accommodation and leisure facilities are as good, if not better, than any available to most people in civilian life and there is far greater emphasis on the importance of the family than ever before, if only because a majority of all ranks are married. But while the standard of living of Other Ranks has risen markedly, that of junior officers has fallen, most notably as the result of the virtual disappearance of the soldier-servant or batman. In 1945, indeed perhaps for another two decades or so thereafter, no officer ever found himself having to clean his own kit, which is far from the case to-day.

Commissioning from the ranks is more frequent than once it was. At the time of amalgamation in December 1992 seven officers had originally joined The Royal Hussars (or the 10th or 11th) as troopers and similarly there were nine such officers in the 14th/20th.

Methods of punishment have changed radically too. Gone the dreaded 'Jankers' so familiar to earlier generations, replaced by a system of fines. All in all the Army of the 1990s is a considerably more friendly and civilised place than it was in 1945. However, the question as to whether it is a better army now than then is probably unanswerable. The average soldier, if there is such a being, is fitter, better fed, better educated and better trained than any of his predecessors but let us hope that the most vital aspects of his qualities as a fighting man, sustained courage and mental stamina, will never be put to the ultimate test of a full-scale and protracted war.

We have given this History a Shakespearean title so perhaps it is fitting that it should end with a Shakespearean quotation. In his Address at the El Alamein 50th Anniversary Service in Winchester Cathedral on 24th October 1992, the Chaplain-General opened his allusions to the roles of the 10th and 11th Hussars in the battle with the most famous line of Henry V's prayer before Agincourt. 'O God of battles, steel my soldiers' hearts!' And he continued: 'As the guns fired the opening barrage on the late evening of 23rd October and thereafter as men and equipment crossed the start line and all the efforts of supply and transport, of engineers and gunners become focused on those who would make the advance, there were among them the men and tanks of the 10th Royal Hussars and the 11th Hussars.

'The 10th were in support of the 51st Highland Division – an arrangement which I can do no other than applaud – constantly in the heat and danger of battle. And here mention must be made of the capture of General von Thoma, commanding the German forces in Rommel's absence, by Captain Grant-Singer, which must have added to the lustre of the Shiners outshining others. And the 11th, who had spent more time continuously in the Western Desert than any other regiment and won more battle honours, were still in the thick of it. In addition to that, they were mentioned nine times in the official history of the German Afrika Korps, the only regiment who can make this unique claim.

'It is this proud record which was brought together with their separate and distinguished histories when in 1969 the two regiments 'The Shiners' and 'The Cherrypickers' merged to form The Royal Hussars. And now to be joined to it are the history and traditions of the 14th/20th King's Hussars on 4th December as The King's Royal Hussars.'

APPENDICES

Appendix A

BATTLE HONOURS

Emblazoned honours are shown in bold type.

10th ROYAL HUSSARS (PRINCE OF WALES'S OWN)

Warburg, Peninsula, Waterloo, Sevastopol, Ali Masjid, Afghanistan 1878–79, Egypt 1884, Relief of Kimberley, Paardeberg, South Africa 1899–1902.

The Great War – Ypres 1914, '15, Langemarck 1914, Gheluvelt, Nonne Bosschen, **Frezenberg, Loos, Arras 1917, '18**, Scarpe 1917, **Somme 1918**, St Quentin, **Avre, Amiens, Drocourt-Quéant**, Hindenburg Line, Beaurevoir, Cambrai 1918, **Pursuit to Mons, France and Flanders 1914–18.**

The Second World War – Somme 1940, North-West Europe 1940, **Saunnu, Gazala**, Bir el Aslagh, Alam el Halfa, **El Alamein, El Hamma**, El Kourzia, Djebel Kournine, **Tunis,** North Africa 1942–43, **Coriano, Santarcangelo**, Cosina Canal Crossing, Senio Pocket, Cesena, **Valli di Comacchio, Argenta Gap**, Italy 1944–45.

11th HUSSARS (PRINCE ALBERT'S OWN)

Warburg, Beaumont, Willems, Salamanca, Peninsula, Waterloo, Bhurtpore, Alma, Balaklava, Inkerman, Sevastopol.

Appendix A

The Great War – Mons, **Le Cateau, Retreat from Mons, Marne 1914, Aisne 1914, Messines 1914,** Armentières 1914, **Ypres 1914, '15,** Frezenberg, Bellewaarde, **Somme 1916, '18,** Flers-Courcelette, Arras 1917, Scarpe 1917, **Cambrai 1917, '18,** St Quentin, Rosières, **Amiens,** Albert 1918, Hindenburg Line, St Quentin Canal, Beaurevoir, Selle, **France and Flanders 1914–18.**

The Second World War – **Villers Bocage,** Bourguebus Ridge, Mont Pincon, Jurques, Dives Crossing, La Vie Crossing, Lisieux, Le Touques Crossing, Risle Crossing, **Roer, Rhine,** Ibbenburen, Aller, North-West Europe 1944–45, **Egyptian Frontier 1940,** Withdrawal to Matruh, Bir Enba, **Sidi Barrani,** Buq Buq, Bardia 1941, Capture of Tobruk, **Beda Fomm,** Halfaya 1941, Sidi Suleiman, Tobruk 1941, Gubi I, II, Gabr Saleh, **Sidi Rezegh 1941,** Taieb el Essem, Relief of Tobruk, Saunnu, Msus, Defence of Alamein Line, Alam el Halfa, **El Alamein,** Advance on Tripoli, Enfidaville, **Tunis,** North Africa 1940–43, Capture of Naples, Volturno Crossing, **Italy 1943.**

THE ROYAL HUSSARS (PRINCE OF WALES'S OWN)

Warburg, Beaumont, Willems, Salamanca, Peninsula, Waterloo, Bhurtpore, Alma, Balaklava, Inkerman, Sevastopol, Ali Masjid, Afghanistan 1878–79, Egypt 1884, Relief of Kimberley, Paardeburg, South Africa 1899–1902.

The Great War – Mons, **Le Cateau, Retreat from Mons, Marne 1914, Aisne 1914, Messines 1914,** Armentières 1914, Ypres 1914, 15, Langemarck 1914, Gheluvelt, Nonne Bosschen, **Frezenberg,** Bellewaarde, **Loos, Somme 1916, '18,** Flers-Courcelette, **Arras 1917, '18,** Scarpe 1917, **Cambrai 1917, '18,** St Quentin, Rosières, Avre, **Amiens,** Albert 1918, **Drocourt-Queant,** Hindenburg Line, St Quentin Canal, Beaurevoir, **Cambrai 1918, Selle, Pursuit to Mons, France and Flanders 1914–18.**

The Second World War – **Somme 1940, Villers Bocage,** Bourguebus Ridge, Mont Pincon, Jurques, Dives Crossing, La

Vie Crossing, Lisieux, Le Touques Crossing, Risle Crossing, **Roer, Rhine**, Ibbenburen, Aller, **North-West Europe 1940, 1944–45, Egyptian Frontier 1940**, Withdrawal to Matruh, Bir Enba, **Sidi Barrani**, Buq Buq, Bardia 1941, Capture of Tobruk, **Beda Fomm**, Halfaya 1941, Sidi Suleiman, Tobruk 1941, Gubi I, II, Gabr Saleh, **Sidi Rezegh 1941**, Taieb el Essem, Relief of Tobruk, **Saunnu**, Msus, **Gazala**, Bir el Aslagh, Defence of Alamein Line, Alam el Halfa, **El Alamein**, Advance on Tripoli, **El Hamma**, Enfidaville, El Kourzia, Djebel Kournine, **Tunis**, North Africa 1940–43, Capture of Naples, Volturno Crossing, **Coriano, Santarcangelo**, Cosina Canal Crossing, Senio Pocket, Cesena, **Valli di Comacchio, Argenta Gap, Italy 1943–45.**

Appendix B

SOLDIERS OF THE 10TH ROYAL HUSSARS (PWO) KILLED IN THE AIR CRASH at AQABA, JORDAN – 17 APRIL, 1957

Sgt Goldstraw W	Tpr Baldwin N
Cpl Patterson R	Tpr Baldwin A
LCpl Worswick N	Tpr Brooke E G
LCpl McHugh J	Tpr Parson S S
LCpl Jewell R J	Tpr Clarke V B
Tpr Hallam E	Tpr Butler A
Tpr Sissons J	Tpr Hughes J
Tpr Johnson R	Tpr Macrow A R
Tpr Bell N W	Tpr Jacklin A K D

REME att 10TH ROYAL HUSSARS (PWO)

Cpl Beattie R	Cfn Mugridge D J
LCpl Gunion J C	Cfn Truss B S

ACC att 10th ROYAL HUSSARS (PWO)

Cpl Liddiard P

Appendix C

CORRESPONDENCE CONCERNING AN AIR ROLE FOR THE ROYAL ARMOURED CORPS

From Major A. C. Uloth 10H

To: Brigadier J. M. D. Ward-Harrison OBE MC
The Staff College
Camberley

November 1966

I hope you won't mind my writing to you but it seems to me that the future of the RAC is not at the moment particularly bright. I would be most grateful if you would allow me to air some purely personal views to you because, in the unlikely event that you accept any of them, you are able to influence matters.

The Problem

I feel that the RAC is suffering from being confined in an 'armour-plated straight jacket' which the RAC itself does not recognise although it will lead to its decline.

The form that this takes is the fact that so much of the RAC is condemned to eternal servitude in BAOR, which produces:

a. Bad effect on recruiting – particularly young officers.
b. Self-hypnosis that the tank is the best and only equipment with which the RAC should fight.

The Answer

The RAC needs to find some form of release from BAOR and I believe there is available now equipment which would enable the RAC to carry out its traditional cavalry role of observation and shock action effectively both in BAOR and also any other part of the world where the army is employed in 'hot' or 'cold' wars.

What is available

As you probably know a trial has been going on here using SS11s mounted on a Scout and although the report is not yet published the results have so far been spectacular. I watched some of the firings and without going into detail I was impressed by the effectiveness of the system. (I believe the overall hit rate will work out at 86% at ranges of between 2,000 and 3,000 yards at static and moving targets).

It seems to me that the Army has available something good and as revolutionary as the invention of the tank. I also feel that no one seems to know what to do with it. In fact I have heard it said that here is a first class new weapon system waiting for some one to man it. It is a matter of time before some branch of the Army adopts this equipment.

Who should man it?

To my mind the proper branch of the Army to operate this equipment is the Royal Armoured Corps who, with a helicopter fitted with a really accurate weapon such as the SS11, could carry out their traditional role more effectively than with their present equipment.

Concept

I feel that a sky cavalry regiment of armed helicopters would have the flexibility to fight in any theatre or type of operation with only minor modifications to its establishment. For instance:

a. In North West Europe it should have three armed helicopter squadrons as part of the anti-tank defence to be used like the old Div Regiment RAC. It would be invaluable in all phases of war.
b. In the Aden type of theatre it should have two armed helicopter squadrons and one assault trooper/SAS squadron to be used as a 'lightning' force unrestricted by terrain. To be employed in the same way as 22 SAS have been recently.

Proposal

I propose that an experimental unit be formed. As this would be beyond the scope at present of an individual regiment, it should be formed with RAC pilots on similar lines to the Para Squadron RAC.

The size of this unit would be nine aircraft each with two pilots, one as second pilot and missile controller. I believe that a troop of three aircraft is a viable tactical unit. The eighteen pilots could be found from the RAC in which there are already fifteen regiments with Air Troops, and quite a large pool of pilots. An experimental squadron on these lines should be developed under the direction of either the BRAC in BAOR or Southern Command. It should be regarded as forerunner to a Sky Cavalry Regiment to be formed when enough experience has been gained and sufficient pilots trained.

Summary

The RAC is suffering from a tank only and therefore a BAOR only mentality.

We have in the missile armed helicopter a possible replacement but certainly a valuable adjunct to the tank.

This equipment offers an extension of the cavalry roles of observation and shock action, therefore the cavalry should man it.

The concept is of Sky Cavalry Regiments equipped with armed helicopters and assault troops with flexible establishments to suit different theatres and operations.

The RAC ought to take up the idea quickly by forming an experimental unit. Delay in doing so may lose it to another arm.

From: Brigadier J. M. D. Ward-Harrison, OBE, MC

To: Major A. C. Uloth, 10H
   Army Aviation Centre
   Middle Wallop

15 December 1966

I was most interested in your letter as it reflects entirely our thinking here.

Since I spoke to you on the telephone I have had an opportunity to discuss the idea with D L/AW and DCD. They confirm my impression that the RAC has said it is not interested.

I enclose a copy of a letter I have written to Jock Holden but do not think it will be very well received. I also intend to send a copy to DASD who I know is sympathetic. We can but hope that it will provoke more interest.

From: Brigadier J. M. D. Ward-Harrison, OBE, MC

To: Major-General J. R. Holden CB, CBE, DSO
   Director Royal Armoured Corps
   Lulworth Camp
   Dorset

15 December 1966

I am writing to ask for your help and advice over a matter which is causing us some concern and heart-searching here at Camberley.

The aspect which worries me personally, as the senior RAC representative in this establishment, is the difficulty of correlating RAC policy with new tactical doctrines and future Combat Development. I have to ensure that, from the point of view of Staff College instruction on tactical doctrine, the RAC 'party line' and that evolving from DCD are both complementary and 'saleable' to Directing Staff and students alike.

In some areas this is easy; for instance, your new pamphlet 'Armour' makes a perfect charter for all arms doctrine in Europe. Mechanised infantry have, indeed, a tremendous amount to learn from that pamphlet alone. There is no conflict in this field, and we make 'Armour' available to all students for this reason.

It is, however, in the field of tank-destruction, direct-fire support and reconnaissance, world-wide that the present dilemma arises. With a major, limited war currently happening in Vietnam, we would be crazy here not to study that war, and the doctrines arising from it, in considerable detail. In fact our newly arrived Australian DS was, just two months ago, actually commanding his battalion there. From this study alone, quite apart from all the other parts of our geopolitical instruction, we are increasingly becoming aware that the air mobile concept is not just an eccentric Texas millionaire's plaything, but a 'quick-reaction', 'value-for-money' way of life for armies in the 1970s.

We must be sensible to keep a proper sense of proportion and not go mad about the concept, and the last thing that we are trying to say is that such a weapons system will replace the tank, or the line of evolution of the tank. What we are saying is that air and ground weapon platforms in the direct fire support and tank destroyer roles are together complementary and the direct concern of the RAC. In fact all our studies here lead us to the belief that as infantry becomes more mechanised and ground/air mobile, so will the roles, characteristics and doctrine of the two fighting corps overlap more and more. We think that it would be wrong to fight this trend, but that we should join it; and by so doing we will ensure a variety of skills, roles and opportunities that would solve most of the present background problems looming for the RAC.

In future doctrine studies here, we are committed to arguing the need for airborne, tank-destroyer and direct-fire support weapons. At the moment we are able to get by with laying this role in the lap of the two direct-fire Corps, Infantry and Armour. There is, however, such a surge of enthusiasm for the doctrine of air mobility in the Ministry of Defence, the Strategic Reserve and Overseas Commands, that the take-over contenders are beginning to line up already. I believe most strongly that the RAC must play a very major part in this new field, otherwise this exciting new role will fall by default into the hands of airborne forces or some other arm.

I do not think that it would be difficult to get this going within the Corps; you only have to talk to regiments like 4/7 DG just back from the Radfan to find that they are convinced that the armoured reconnaissance regiment needs more assault troopers (and helicopters to move them) and a weapon capability for their air squadron. I know that RAC pilots in the Army Aviation set-up are just waiting for a chance to start. I have recently received a long and well-reasoned letter from Tony Uloth pleading for RAC's interest in the highly successful trials of SS11 mounted on a Scout.

My suggestion, carefully considered and discussed both here and with DCD and D L/AW, is that the RAC (from present resources entirely) should form an experimental air weapons squadron to study armed helicopter tactics and techniques. (This could be attached to the 'Trials Brigade' if it is formed). I say from present resources because I believe that by identifying a few Regiments closely with this project we will ensure that we harness in the enthusiasm and brainpower of the young blood in Regiments to-day.

An experimental squadron could be formed, say, from three armoured car regiments with air squadrons. The obvious choices are 4/7 DG with their recent operational experience, 5 Innis DG on return from Libya, and either 10H, QDG or an RTR armoured car regiment. If each provided five aircraft from their air squadrons, with the balance provided by HQ Army Aviation, I believe that we could form an experimental squadron of some eighteen aircraft. Middle Wallop undoubtedly has the best facilities for such a squadron and I am sure that both Army Aviation and D L/AW would want to be involved. I am sure, however, that the bulk of pilots and aircraft should be provided from the outset from RAC resources. I know that 4/7 DG and 5 Innis DG would welcome this role, and I cannot believe that one more Regiment could not be found.

The actual weapons that could be tried out on these helicopters are many. However, the initial step I believe must be to experiment with SS11 in the tank destroyer role. The rest can follow from that.

The eventual formation of an Air Regiment would provide the flexibility to fight in any theatre or type of operation with only minor modification to its establishment. For instance:

a. In North West Europe it could have three armed helicopter squadrons as part of your Light Brigade. It could play a major part in all phases of war.

b. In the Middle or Far East type of operation it could have two armed helicopter squadrons and one assault squadron to be used as a 'quick reaction' force unrestricted by terrain. This regiment could well spearhead a force following up infantry lifted by RN or RAF helicopters in the normal way.

In summary then, I am asking you if you would agree to consider the possibilities of forming such a squadron and of studying the tactics and techniques involved. I am sure we cannot afford to neglect the experience of the US Army in this field, and, as a corollary to the formation of the squadron, I believe we ought to institute an exchange of officers with the US Air Cavalry Organisation. The British component of this exchange could well be an RAC officer who is intensely interested in tactical doctrine, and who would be responsible equally to you and to D L/AW. The US exchange officer could be attached to D L/AW, yourself or to us here at Camberley.

I would be extremely grateful if you would let me talk this over with you in more detail sometime in the New Year. What impresses me, and I am sure you find the same as you visit our Regiments all over the world, is the intelligent and boundless enthusiasm to make doctrine a positive reality that many of the young officers in RAC Regiments show to-day. There are, on the other hand, a number of officers in our Corps who are still suffering from the self-hypnosis that the tank is the best and only equipment with which the RAC should fight. Certainly all of them who come through here as students (and the RAC DS too) have the strong belief that we should miss no opportunity to escape from our 'armoured plated straight jacket'. I do not believe it is a change of role at all – merely a widening of the range of equipment to carry it out. I am convinced that the future of our Corps lies in the complementary evolution of ground (AFV) and air (Helicopter) weapon platforms in the tank destroyer, shock action, direct support and reconnaissance roles.

Author's note
Unfortunately, no reply from General Holden is to be found.

D L/AW = Director Land Air Warfare
DCD = Director Combat Development
DASD = Director Army Staff Duties

Appendix D

THE ROYAL HUSSARS (PWO)
FIRST NOMINAL ROLL

25 October 1969
Regimental Headquarters

Lieutenant-Colonel C. H. Robertson .... Commanding Officer
Major P. H. G. Bengough .... Second in Command
Captain J. R. Turner .... Adjutant
Lieutenant J. R. Powell .... Assistant Adjutant
Lieutenant R. H. East .... RSO
W. O. I. B. Osmand .... RSM

'A' Squadron
S.H.Q. Troop
Major the Hon. M. J. H. Allenby
Captain O. E. V. Holder
Captain P. J. C. Beresford
Lt R. Fearnehough
S.S.M. F. P. Gillott
Sgt R. D. Perkins
Cpl R. C. Aitkinhead
Cpl B. Gibbs
Cpl E. Sheppard
Cpl C. A. E. Townsend
L/Cpl J. C. Binge
L/Cpl R. D. P. Gibbs
L/Cpl P. J. Jones
L/Cpl B. A. Wood
Tpr R. J. Chappell
Tpr P. J. Evans
Tpr E. Suttle
Tpr R. Taylor

Admin. Troop
S.Q.M.S. R. Chatwin
Cpl G. H. Elliott
Cpl J. H. Sykes
Col. D. E. Brooks
Cpl G. Richardson
Tpr R. J. Dean
Tpr P. J. Blake
Tpr K. Carter
Tpr A. E. Gillett
Tpr S. P. Line
L/Cpl D. Powell
Pte B. D. Marriage

1st Troop
2/Lt J. G. Phillips
Sgt E. L. Swinden
Cpl R. McKone
L/Cpl A. Bentley
Tpr S. L. Biswell
Tpr R. J. Bridle
Tpr J. P. Doyle

Tpr J. G. Franklin
Tpr G. J. Frier
Tpr B. J. Heyes
Tpr P. L. Morgan
Tpr J. W. Osland
Tpr R. W. Sly

2nd Troop
2/Lt M. T. Radmore
Sgt B. J. Harvey
Sgt R. H. Howell
Cpl J. Mulley
L/Cpl T. Beck
L/Cpl B. F. Kirk
Tpr I. Aitken
Tpr M. F. Boon
Tpr C. R. Chandler
Tpr D. Matthews
Tpr L. A. Pearce
Tpr A. P. Payne
Tpr P. Whittingham

Tpr R. J. Latham
Tpr S. P. Wragg

3rd Troop
Sgt G. R. Venner
Cpl J. H. J. Green
L/Cpl D. M. McKechnie
L/Cpl J. R. Rix
Tpr D. R. Betteridge
Tpr C. H. Butler
Tpr K. Bradshaw
Tpr A. Harcourt
Tpr T. L. Howell
Tpr B. Porter
Tpr J. P. Phillips
Tpr A. Russell
Tpr L. L. Lawrence
Tpr R. Heslop

4th Troop
2/Lt C. A. A. Forrest
Sgt M. G. E. Hobday
Cpl D. G. Ninnim
Cpl I. Watkins
L/Cpl R. J. Hollands
Tpr R. L. Balch
Tpr D. Cawley
Tpr B. M. Dunnage
Tpr R. S. Foster
Tpr R. H. Hill
Tpr C. R. Hellyer
Tpr F. Lewis
Tpr A. E. Stringer
Tpr R. J. Sylvester

S.E. Troop
S/Sgt R. Wherton
Sgt M. D. Lawrence
L/Cpl L. G. Stagg
Tpr K. T. Bewley
Tpr E. Elliott
Tpr R. Bridge
Tpr A. Worrall

L.A.D. Troop
S/Sgt P. W. Nolan
Sgt R. H. Sleep
Cpl P. Lawton
Cpl M. R. Hammett
Cpl K. Ross
L/Cpl C. F. Berry
L/Cpl J. P. Dorney
L/Cpl R. Donothey
L/Cpl N. W. Grogan

L/Cpl M. O. Latham
L/Cpl R. J. V. Oliver
L/Cpl H. F. Howard
Cfn P. Karkovskis
Cfn D. A. Taylor
Cfn M. Simms
Cfn G. Thacker

M.T. Section
Cpl R. Tulip
Tpr F. J. Graham
Tpr W. V. Knight
Tpr F. D. Young
Tpr A. R. Cornish
Tpr J. W. Hill
Tpr J. Green

'B' Squadron
S.H.Q. Troop
Major the Hon. G. W. M.
  Norrie
Captain G. J. W. Malet
Captain R. E. R. Morgan
Captain H.R.H. Prince
  Michael of Kent
S.S.M. A. Watson
Sgt J. Riley
Sgt B. J. Weston
Cpl S. G. Griffiths
L/Cpl R. J. Holland
Tpr A. R. Nolan
Tpr R. E. Stringer
Tpr J. M. McAnulty
Tpr A. L. Palk
Tpr J. B. Thomas
Tpr P. G. Gabb
Tpr R. T. Hughes
Tpr M. J. Pratt
Tpr M. A. Sulston
Tpr A. C. Weaving

1st Troop
2/Lt M. Reid Scott
Sgt G. Alderson
Cpl G. Waite
Cpl P. Reynolds
L/Cpl J. Welch
L/Cpl D. Mullins
Tpr R. E. Suggitt
Tpr J. F. Sanders
Tpr R. G. Grimes
Tpr I. B. Thurlow
Tpr T. R. Thyer
Tpr M. M. Newell

Tpr M. A. Shrimpton
Tpr K. Gutteridge
Tpr D. Cox

2nd Troop
2/Lt P. J. Allerton
Sgt H. K. Garlick
Cpl C. H. L. Goy
Cpl W. J. Hargrave
L/Cpl R. Hoste
L/Cpl R. J. Campbell
L/Cpl J. W. Durham
Tpr G. Elsey
Tpr P. W. Fox
Tpr A. B. Gass
Tpr V. B. Beasley
Tpr P. W. Evans
Tpr M. L. Bishop
Tpr G. B. Cooper
Tpr I. B. Wright

3rd Troop
2/Lt the Viscount Villiers
Sgt J. H. Cobbold
Cpl J. L. Hannah
Cpl M. W. Keats
L/Cpl R. W. Rowe
Tpr S. Brown
Tpr R. D. M. Hall
Tpr M. Barrigan
Tpr M. G. Pullen
Tpr R. Ward
Tpr M. W. Fahey
Tpr T. D. Morrison
Tpr T. R. P. Scrivener
Tpr D. J. De Heaume

4th Troop
2/Lt J. J. Micklem
Sgt D. D. Gardner
Cpl C. S. Dick
Cpl D. Feltham
L/Cpl A. Smith
L/Cpl K. A. Cronshaw
Tpr K. Nash
Tpr M. G. Smith
Tpr R. Hawkins
Tpr M. J. Buckley
Tpr I. I. Baker
Tpr M. J. Barnard
Tpr M. K. Forsythe
Tpr D. J. Smith
Tpr W. G. Gilroy

Admin. Troop
S.Q.M.S. C. F. Wass
S/Sgt B. Searby
Cpl J. G. Veater
L/Cpl R. V. Stoker
Tpr R. H. Disspain
Tpr M. G. Fowle
Tpr V. C. Whysall
Tpr M. J. Collie
Tpr A. Brown
Tpr R. A. Seymour
Tpr D. F. Coleman
Tpr C. I. Presswell

L.A.D. Troop
S/Sgt Parrot
Sgt E. Green
Cpl T. Fryer
Cpl R. B. MacReadie
Cpl D. Simpson
L/Cpl J. White
L/Cpl J. S. Clark
Cfn J. Langley

'C' Squadron
S.H.Q. Troop
Major P. D. Mesquita
Captain D. G. Dollar
Captain M. P. Capper-
Jackson
S.S.M. F. W. Nicholas,
BEM
Cpl S. L. Bonaqusa
Cpl R. Connolly
L/Cpl R. F. May
L/Cpl L. V. Kennell
L/Cpl K. J. Newton
L/Cpl R. T. Laney
Tpr I. G. Dunn
Tpr T. J. Crossan
Tpr D. T. Wright
Tpr R. King
Tpr A. J. Bessant
Tpr F. Grimmer
Tpr D. S. Essack
Tpr A. J. King
Tpr H. E. Villiger

1st Troop
2/Lt J. E. Herdman
Sgt R. J. Brady
Sgt E. Hurdle
Cpl N. K. Barter
L/Cpl R. V. Wylde

L/Cpl M. M. Eyre
Tpr P. Crutchfield
Tpr R. A. G. Miller
Tpr J. J. Mahoney
Tpr R. M. Strand
Tpr P. C. Hamshare
Tpr D. Preece
Tpr J. Swyer
Tpr N. T. Murphy
Tpr R. G. Morton
Tpr C. J. Kennie

2nd Troop
2/Lt M. J. H. Malyon
Sgt P. J. Stockley
Cpl F. Allewell
L/Cpl H. W. R. Paine
L/Cpl M. W. Tett
L/Cpl J. L. Hewetson
Tpr M. Hewitt
Tpr C. G. Wells
Tpr T. W. Weston
Tpr R. D. M. Pollock
Tpr M. Barrett
Tpr A. R. Esnouf
Tpr M. J. Eaton
Tpr P. P. Millings
Tpr B. A. Smith

3rd Troop
Lt P. J. Hall
Sgt T. J. Gormley, BEM
Cpl R. K. Veitch
Cpl S. C. W. Boulter
L/Cpl G. R. Davis
L/Cpl P. J. Wilkins
Tpr M. F. Scott
Tpr M. W. Collins
Tpr J. Cotterill
Tpr I. Eyre
Tpr T. T. Gill
Tpr D. G. Webber
Tpr R. W. Heath
Tpr W. P. West
Tpr D. R. Hill
Tpr G. J. Slade

4th Troop
2/Lt D. N. V. Churton
2/Lt R. C. H. Boon
Sgt D. Johnson
Cpl D. R. Owen
L/Cpl G. J. Drinkwater
L/Cpl C. L. Rogers

L/Cpl D. J. Eldridge
L/Cpl M. S. Buck
Tpr D. N. Tubb
Tpr M. J. Francis
Tpr R. F. Bird
Tpr E. C. Curd
Tpr R. D. Dormer
Tpr A. D. Cush
Tpr S. Harman

Admin. Troop
S.Q.M.S. A. Day
Cpl A. Tulley
Cpl E. W. Field
Cpl R. A. Saunders
L/Cpl G. R. Hall
Tpr R. A. Peet
Tpr J. A. Greenwell
Tpr P. C. S. Pledger
Tpr R. P. A. Bates
Tpr P. S. King
Tpr P. S. Hawkins

L.A.D. Troop
A.Q.M.S. M. Robinson
Sgt B. Austin
Cpl B. J. Slack
L/Cpl A. V. Denning
L/Cpl J. Hoadley
L/Cpl T. J. Roberts
L/Cpl D. E. McDermid
L/Cpl C. Heaphy
Cfn G. W. Challis
Cfn D. R. Leach

Administrative Squadron
S.H.Q. Troop
Major H. Dawnay
Major D. F. Covill MBE
DCM
Captain M. A. Villiers
S.S.M. D. R. Pierce
L/Cpl M. R. Denholm
Tpr P. J. Lawrence

R.O.R. Troop
O.R.Q.M.S. G. C.
Chappell
Sgt K. A. Laney
Cpl R. K. Mills
Cpl M. J. Ruth
Cpl P. A. Trevett
L/Cpl H. G. Topham
L/Cpl M. S. Taylor

L/Cpl D. J. Walters
L/Cpl A. Wenham
L/Cpl T. Dark
Tpr J. B. Anderson
Tpr E. J. Anson
Tpr H. Penniston

Q.M. Troop
Captain J. A. Hall
R.Q.M.S. J. M.
   Kolaczkowski
Cpl T. Connor
Cpl M. Emery
Cpl A. Fleming
Cpl K. Harrison
Cpl I. McDonald
L/Cpl T. Budden
L/Cpl V. F. Miles
Tpr J. W. Baldwin
Tpr R. P. Speyers

Tech. Troop
Captain T. H. Knight
R.Q.M.S.(T) L. F.
   Osborne-Wakley
S/Sgt L. W. Knights
Sgt W. G. Heather
Cpl R. A. Cotterill
Cpl B. P. Hull
Cpl G. K. Jones
Cpl D. G. Robinson
Cpl T. Walpole
L/Cpl F. W. Dobson
L/Cpl B. Gregory
L/Cpl S. G. Whistlecraft
Tpr R. S. Gaskin
Tpr K. W. Kendry

Admin. Troop
S.Q.M.S. H. McGrath
S/Sgt N. F. Dawson
L/Cpl P. D. Keen
Tpr R. J. Josham
Tpr R. C. Penfold
Tpr D. S. Nightingale
Tpr G. Ray
Tpr A. D. Lyall
Tpr C. P. Cush

Officers Mess
S/Sgt A. McGee
Sgt J. J. Cook
Cpl A. R. Jones
L/Cpl J. C. Pritchard

Tpr J. W. Caswell
Tpr B. Glancey-Hockley
Tpr E. Keill
Tpr E. B. Malone
Tpr R. P. Oxford
Tpr K. Rawlings
Tpr J. A. Sidebottom
Tpr J. Thatcher
Tpr B. M. Sidebottom
Tpr A. E. Waldron
Tpr F. Walton
Tpr F. H. Lynch
Tpr S. W. Durden

M.I. Room
Captain A. R. F. Kerr
Tpr N. A. Mills

– R.A.P.C.
Major M. W. Wadham
S/Sgt L. McNee
Cpl D. J. Hallam
Cpl M. J. Rogers
Cpl D. Stevenson
Cpl M. L. Whitehouse
Pte G. P. Horseman
Pte J. M. Myerscough

Provost Staff
Sgt A. Deverill
L/Cpl J. B. Hutchinson
L/Cpl M. G. Wyatt

P.R.I.
Captain A. M. Alderton
Sgt G. A. Rowles
Cpl M. L. Orchard

Sgts' Mess
Sgt J. H. Johns
L/Cpl D. Price
L/Cpl J. J. Healy
Tpr L. C. Chiverton

Gymnasium
S.M.I. D. C. Sears
L/Cpl N. D. Wright

M.T. Troop
Lieut J. M. Lemon
Sgt R. C. Gough
Sgt G. H. Hickman
Cpl P. F. Feeney

Cpl M. I. Dare
Cpl P. F. Josey
L/Cpl L. Clark
L/Cpl B. Dunn
L/Cpl R. G. Hale
L/Cpl R. G. Hiett
L/Cpl J. M. Price
L/Cpl C. H. Suggitt
L/Cpl M. J. Thomas
L/Cpl G. Tomenson
L/Cpl H. A. Van Der Zee
L/Cpl J. W. Ward
Tpr I. E. Ainsley
Tpr T. E. Atkinson
Tpr R. Bake
Tpr D. C. Brehaut
Tpr A. T. Binding
Tpr G. J. Bushell
Tpr T. Burt
Tpr E. R. Clarke
Tpr P. M. Coltart
Tpr B. A. Cook
Tpr M. D. Cush
Tpr M. Farrell
Tpr P. M. Hannan
Tpr W. J. Henning
Tpr K. M. Howitt
Tpr A. H. Jones
Tpr W. H. Knight
Tpr J. R. Mansell
Tpr J. R. Mace
Tpr R. P. Mead
Tpr A. J. Scott
Tpr W. R. Troke
Tpr M. I. Vaughan
Tpr M. I. Westmacote
Tpr G. N. Wilkinson
Tpr D. K. Wright
Tpr P. W. Young
Tpr K. Robertson
Tpr B. L. Yates
Tpr A. R. Nolan

L.A.D. Troop
Captain R. D. C. Stephens
A.S.M. J. Malone
A.Q.M.S. R. J. Jones
A.Q.M.S. D. W. Wright
S/Sgt W. O. Caley
Sgt M. Allen
Sgt C. C. Hindmarsh
Sgt N. C. Mackie
Sgt J. H. Mortimer
Sgt R. V. Strachan
Sgt G. K. Young

Cpl D. J. Atkins
Cpl G. R. Harrison
Cpl F. A. Holmes
Cpl A. Stewart
Cpl P. A. Smallwood
Cpl T. R. Turner
Cpl T. G. Wright
L/Cpl D. W. Brown
L/Cpl G. Gray
L/Cpl F. Lloyd
L/Cpl D. Lee
L/Cpl P. Laidler
L/Cpl D. R. Paddon
L/Cpl M. Valler
L/Cpl K. F. Willcoxson
Cfn J. K. Blady
Cfn J. W. Boag
Cfn N. Cooke
Cfn D. V. Collister
Cfn G. Foster
Cfn S. Gray
Cfn R. Hallam
Cfn P. J. Hardwick
Cfn R. K. Jarvis
Cfn P. Pangbourne
Cfn S. J. Sanderson
Cfn G. Smith
Cfn D. J. Strong
Cfn K. Roddham
Cfn J. H. Ward
Cfn R. Williams

A.C.C.
WOII M. Byrne, BEM
Sgt C. Richardson
Sgt K. R. Orchard
Cpl E. K. Talbut
Cpl R. M. Rodell
L/Cpl R. S. Lilley
L/Cpl F. Hopkinson
L/Cpl T. E. Walker
L/Cpl P. Whitear
Pte R. G. Corker
Pte A. Devereux
Pte J. K. Finney
Pte I. Mather
Pte R. Smith

Pte D. J. Stewart
Pte D. E. Wylde

**'C' and 'S' Squadron
S.H.Q. Troop**
Major W. J. Pinney
Capt. G. H. Duckett
S.S.M. D. C. Goodman
S.Q.M.S. V. J. Rees-
Oliviere
L/Cpl D. C. Parker
Tpr B. G. Pugh
Tpr K. Walters
Tpr R. L. J. Beechey

Command Troop
Lieut M. I. Scott-Dalgleish
S/Sgt R. Galbraith
Sgt P. S. Copus
Cpl J. T. Reid
Cpl A. J. Hart
L/Cpl R. J. Hall
L/Cpl J. E. Hutchinson
L/Cpl R. G. Packham
L/Cpl P. Truss
Tpr B. F. Crowston
Tpr M. J. Monkcom
Tpr D. G. Rogers
Tpr L. P. Withers
Tpr D. W. White
Tpr C. C. Whitelock
Tpr I. K. Wallace
Tpr L. A. Williams
Tpr I. P. Williams

Recce Troop
Capt. D. E. Roe
S/Sgt R. J. Standley
Cpl J. F. R. Needham
Cpl M. A. Childs
Cpl G. D. Carswell
Cpl R. J. Hall
Cpl W. J. Veater
L/Cpl A. W. Floyd
L/Cpl R. F. French
L/Cpl I. R. Lambert
L/Cpl N. R. McIntyre

L/Cpl R. P. Watson
Tpr D. N. Brown
Tpr J. Croft
Tpr G. F. Murcott
Tpr A. P. Newman
Tpr D. C. Ramsey
Tpr M. E. Richens
Tpr T. D. Rogerson
Tpr G. S. Smart
Tpr T. Tarrant
Tpr R. Whatley

Band
WOI (B/M.) A. R. Jeffs
WOII D. J. Williams
Sgt (T.M.) J. K. Barnatt
Sgt E. A. Slade
Sgt K. F. Bryant
Sgt J. Davies
Cpl R. Black
Cpl J. J. Back
Cpl N. C. D. Best
L/Cpl A. G. Adams
L/Cpl B. Scarlett
L/Cpl R. Coleman
L/Cpl E. Hayles
Bdsm D. J. Anderson
Bdsm K. Byrne
Bdsm M. Capener
Bdsm M. J. Casson
Bdsm P. J. Casson
Bdsm A. Collier
Bdsm J. S. M. Ellis
Bdsm C. P. G. Ellis
Bdsm D. Gasser
Bdsm D. R. Glover
Bdsm D. Griffin
Bdsm B. P. Hallett
Bdsm D. J. Hallett
Bdsm J. Jackson
Bdsm R. T. Maidment
Bdsm D. Ord
Bdsm K. J. Rose
Bdsm W. Scarlett
Bdsm P. R. Smith
Bdsm J. A. White
Bdsm K. Wiles
Bdsm T. J. Wharton

Appendix D

Officers at ERE as at 1st May, 1970

Major General J. M. D. Ward-Harrison, OBE, MC, GOC Northumbrian District.

Col. P. T. I. MacDiarmid, MC, MOD London.

Col. P. D. S. Lauder, Col A. (PS) HQ BAOR, BFPO 40.

Col. F. R. Henn,

Col. G. S. CDS. Briefing Staff MOD

Col. J. B. Willis,

Col. G.S. (W) MGO plans MOD

Col. A. A. V. Cockle, Commandant Armour School, Bovington.

Col. P. M. Hamer, OBE, Col. G. S. ASD 22.

Lieut Colonel G. H. Hodgkinson, RAC Ranges, Castlemartin.

Lieut Colonel J. D. A. Woodhouse, MC, HQ Northern Ireland.

Lieut Colonel B. C. Greenwood, Royal Military College of Science, Shrivenham. GSO 1 (W) DS

Lieut Colonel P. K. Upton, British Liaison Officer HQ Dutch Army, Appeldorrn.

Lieut Colonel H. G. King, MBE, Mons. OCS

Major G. D. C. M. Lewis, WRAC College, Camberley.

Major T. Hope, Tactical School, RAC Centre.

Major R. H. Smyth, MOD (DI).

Major J. K. Courtney-Clarke, ADC to Governor, Hong Kong.

Major R. P. Wilson, Trg. Major, Royal Yeomanry Regiment.

Major A. Uloth, MA Khartoum.

Major W. K. Trotter, RAC Gunnery School.

Major R. B. Merton, DOAE, West Byfleet, Surrey.

Major N.C.P. Winter, B.M. HQ 7 Armd Bde.

Major A. J. W. Gordon, OIC, RAC Publicity Team.

Major D. J. W. Anstice, Joint Services Staff College.

Major J. P. W. Friedberger, MOD GS (OR) 17a.

Major R. N. C. Bingley, MOD, GS (OR) 17

Captain D. C. B. Shaw, Royal Wiltshire Yeomanry.

Captain P. C. C. Kaye. ETW Bovington.

Captain D. C. Edwards, Staff College, Camberley.

Captain (T/Maj.) E. M. Westropp, RMCS Shrivenham.

Captain R. J. Hayman-Joyce, Allied Liaison Division, US Armor Centre, Fort Knox, Kentucky 40121, USA

Captain R. L. Perry, RAF Wittering.

Captain The Hon. G. B. Norrie, GSO3 (Int.), Far East Command, Singapore.

Captain N. J. Muers-Raby, GSO 3 (Air), HQ 19 Inf Bde.

Captain V. R. Seely, Directorate of Military Assistance Overseas.

Captain P. M. Roe, MOD Q (Ops and Plans), Main Building, Whitehall.

Captain R. A. Wilkinson, Defence NBC School.

Captain D. A. Whittlestone, FVRDE Kirkcudbright.

Captain F. C. Hodges, Adjt. 7 Armd Bde Sig Sqn.

Captain J. E. Bent, RAC Ranges Castlemartin.

Captain C. R. Oldham, ADC to GOC Northumbrian District.

Lieutenant N. J. Tuck, RAC Gunnery School.

Lieutenant The Hon. S. M. Arthur, Air Tp. 17/21L. (N. Ireland).

Lieutenant P. V. Scholfield, Long Armour Course.

Lieutenant C. P. Thompson, RAC Gunnery School.

Lieutenant J. H. Thoyts, YLO Western Command.

Lieutenant B. H. Jayes, JLR RAC Bovington.

Lieutenant A. J. Beevor, JTR Rhyl.

Lieutenant C. R. G. Watt, Para. Sqn. RAC

Lieutenant K. B. Bateman, Range Officer, RAC Gunnery School.

Lieutenant J. V. Thirst, AAC Middle Wallop.

Lieutenant R. S. D. Riggall, Cambridge University.

Lieutenant J. J. Rogers, Exeter University.

Lieutenant P. T. G. Copeland, Att. 'A' Sqn. 17/21L., Cyprus.

2/Lieutenant W. R. McDonald, London University.

2/Lieutenant G. A. Awdry, Army School of Aviation, Middle Wallop.

2/Lieutenant O. C. Howard, Att. RAC Para. Sqn.

2/Lieutenant D. N. V. Churton, Att. RAC Para. Sqn.

Warrant Officers, NCOs and Troopers at ERE as at 1st May, 1970

WOI Townsend, RAC Gunnery School.

WOI Melles, FVRDE, Aldershot.

WOI Robertson, Camp Commandant's Office, MOD

WOII Rogers, RAC Publications, Wing. RAC Centre, Bovington,

WOII Strike, Junior Leaders' Regt., RAC, Bovington.

WOII McKay, RYR, Swindon.

WOII Haines, 651 Aviation Squadron, AAC, BFPO 32.

WOII Clifton, ACIO, Bournemouth.

WOII Courtney, HQ RAC 3 Div., Tidworth.

WOII Goodby, 666 Avn. Sqn., Plymouth.

WOII Edwards, 657 Aviation Squadron, BFPO 37.

S/Sgt Cray, MOD (AG17), Stanmore, Middlesex.

S/Sgt Rennie, 21 Combat Supplies Platoon, BFPO 34.

S/Sgt Scriven, FVRDE, Kirkcudbright.

S/Sgt Beadle, HQ Bahrein Garrison.

Sgt Towell, AAC Arborfield.

Sgt James, RAC Gunnery School.

Sgt Dalton, D. & M. School, RAC Centre, Bovington.

Sgt Allsopp, RAC Gunnery School.

Sgt Kemp, AAC Arborfield.

Sgt Kinsella, ACIO Portsmouth.

Sgt Phippard, RAC Centre.

Sgt Simpson, RAC Junior Leaders' Regiment.

Sgt Taylor, D. & M. School, RAC Centre, Bovington.

Sgt Hauxwell, Junior Leaders' Regiment RAC

Sgt McKay, ACIO Bournemouth.

Sgt Gibson, 16. ACF/CCF Training Team, Bicester, Oxon.

Sgt Richardson, 657 Army Avn. Sqn. AAC, BFPO 37.

Sgt Bate, RAC Gunnery School.

Sgt Prebble, RAC Gunnery School.

Sgt Roberts, 19 ACF/CCF Training Team

Sgt Millar, ACIO Hounslow

Sgt Binney, RAC Training Regiment, Catterick Camp, Yorks.

Sgt Humberstone, ACIO Gloucester.

Sgt Boyd, RAC Centre.

Sgt Jones, 'A' Sqn. RYR, Swindon.

Sgt Mansfield, 'B' Sqn. The Royal Yeomanry Regt.

Sgt Dowling, RAC Training Regiment.

Sgt Harvey, RAC Training Regiment, Catterick Camp, Yorks.

Sgt Morris, RAC Training Regiment, Catterick Camp, Yorks.

Sgt Heather, 'B' Squadron, The Royal Yeomanry Regiment.

Sgt Marshall, HQ British Troops, Sharjah, BFPO 64.

Sgt Hodge, HQ UNFICYP

Sgt Hickman, 1 Div. Avn. Regt., BFPO 32.

A/Sgt Owen, D. & M. School, RAC Centre, Bovington.

Cpl Podger, 665 Avn. Sqn. AAC, Colchester, Essex.

Cpl Hunt, RAC Centre, Bovington.

Cpl Robinson, RMCS, Shrivenham.

Cpl Green, HQ UNFICYP

Cpl Coles, AAC, Arborfield.

Cpl Townsend, HQ RAC 3 Div., Tidworth.

Cpl Buckland, RAC Training Regiment.

Cpl Edey, RAC Training Regiment.

Cpl Carey, HQ Northumbrian Area, York.

Cpl Chafe, RAC Para. Squadron.

Cpl Mulley, RAC Training Regiment.

A/Cpl Morriss, Junior Leaders' Regiment RAC

L/Cpl Shelsher, 20 Armd Bde, BFPO 41.

L/Cpl Buffrey, RAC Para. Squadron.

L/Cpl Woodcock, RAC Para. Squadron.

L/Cpl Dicker, 657 Avn. Sqn. AAC, BFPO 37.

L/Cpl Browne, HQ RAC 3 Div.,
Tidworth.

L/Cpl Weatherill, HQ Northumbrian
Area, York.

L/Cpl Andrews, HQ, 1 (BR) Corps,
BFPO 39.

L/Cpl Maynard, HQ Bahrein Garrison,
BFPO 63.

L/Cpl Painter, 666 Avn. Sqn. AAC,
Plymouth.

Tpr Beveridge, 651 Avn. Sqn. AAC,
BFPO 32.

Tpr Summers, 1 Div. HQ and Sig. Regt.,
BFPO 32.

Tpr Courtney, RAC Para. Squadron.

Tpr Ralph, RAC Para. Squadron.

Tpr Warne, RAC Para. Squadron.

Tpr Racjan, RAC Para. Squadron.

Tpr Murdoch, RAC Para. Squadron.

Tpr Corben, RAC Para. Squadron.

Tpr Courtney, RAC Para. Squadron.

Tpr Crawford, RAC Para. Squadron.

Tpr Ward, RAC Para. Squadron.

Tpr Dean, FVRDE, Aldershot.

Tpr Griffin, 665 Avn. Sqn. AAC,
Colchester.

Tpr Stevens, 666 Avn. Sqn. AAC,
Plymouth.

Tpr White, FVRDE, Aldershot.

Tpr Hill, 651 Avn. Sqn. AAC, BFPO 32.

Tpr Kimber, HQ, 1 (BR) Corps., BFPO
39.

Tpr Adamczyk, HQ Rheindahlen
Garrison BFPO 40.

Tpr Tayor, 665 Avn. Sqn. AAC,
Colchester.

Tpr Ames, FVRDE, Aldershot.

Tpr Evans, Army Avn. (Int.) Squadron,
20 Armd Bde, BFPO 41.

Tpr Robertson, HQ RAC 3 Div.,
Tidworth.

Tpr Sly, 663 Avn. Sqn., Perham Down,
Nr. Andover, Hants.

Tpr Torrome, HQ Rheindahlen
Garrison. BFPO 40.

Tpr Taylor, 1 Div. Avn. Regt., BFPO 32.

Tpr Preece, 663 Avn. Sqn., Perham
Down, Nr. Andover, Hants.

Tpr Smith, 666 Avn. Sqn. AAC,
Plymouth.

Tpr King, Att. 'A' Sqn. 17/21L., Cyprus.

Tpr Simmonds, RAC Ranges,
Castlemartin.

Appendix E

THE GULF WAR 1990/91

Officers and soldiers of The Royal Hussars (PWO) who served
in Saudi Arabia, Kuwait and Iraq are listed below

A Sqn

Capt Stevens
Lt Inkin
Sgt Leach
Cpl Perrier
Cpl Smith
LCpl Adams
LCpl Eason
LCpl Green
LCpl Hill
LCpl Rickards
LCpl Thomson
Tpr Armstrong
Tpr Challis
Tpr Childes
Tpr Clarke 293
Tpr Handcocks
Tpr Hill

B Sqn

Sgt Plowman
Cpl Chandler

Cpl Foster
Cpl Marshall
Cpl Robinson
Cpl Thomas
LCpl Humberstone
LCpl Russell
Tpr Bellman
Tpr Tate

C Sqn

Lt Wakefield
Lt Wiggin
Sgt Peachy
Sgt Robinson
Cpl Booth
Cpl Price
LCpl Barley
LCpl Bond
LCpl Burton
LCpl Crowley
LCpl Newton
LCpl Weekes

Tpr Barlas
Tpr Clarke 912
Tpr Lee
Tpr Taylor 616

With The Royal Scots Dragoon Guards

LCpl Dawson BEM

HQ Sqn & Attached Personnel

Capt Morrison RAMC
Capt Tucker
SSgt Weir
Sgt Howard
Sgt Robinson
Sgt Stott
Sgt Surey
Cpl August
Cpl Bingham
Cpl Galloway
Cpl Gowland
Cpl Jones
Cpl Mills
Cpl Noyes
Cpl Whittington

LCpl Carver ACC
LCpl Chamberlain
LCpl Deacon
LCpl Hannah
LCpl Hardman
LCpl Foster RCT
LCpl Higgins
LCpl Law
LCpl Loudon
LCpl Portas
LCpl Sherriff
LCpl Taylor
LCpl Williams
Cfn Catton
Cfn Cooper
Cfn Downton
Cfn Edwards
Cfn Fidler
Cfn Harland
Cfn Helliwell
Cfn Howe
Cfn Hynard
Cfn Ireson
Cfn Joy
Cfn Lavery
Cfn Whitear
Cfn Wilson
Pte Ward ACC

Appendix F

SENIOR APPOINTMENTS 1945–1992

THE 10th ROYAL HUSSARS (PWO)
1945–1969

COLONEL-IN-CHIEF

1937–69 Field Marshal HRH The Duke of Gloucester KG KT
KP GCB GCMG GCVO ADC (P)

COLONEL OF THE REGIMENT

1939–45 Colonel V. J. Greenwood MC
1945–49 Lieutenant Colonel Sir Willoughby Norrie GCMG
GCVO CB DSO MC
1949–56 Lieutenant General Sir Charles Gairdner KCMG
KCVO CB OBE
1956–62 Brigadier C. B. C. Harvey DSO
1962–69 Major General Sir David Dawnay KCVO CB DSO

COMMANDING OFFICER

1943–45 Lieutenant Colonel D. R. B. Kaye DSO
1946–49 Lieutenant Colonel J. P. Archer-Shee MC
1949–52 Lieutenant Colonel A. Abel-Smith OBE
1952–54 Lieutenant Colonel M. F. Morley MBE
1954–57 Lieutenant Colonel A. A. N .Tuck MBE
1957–58 Lieutenant Colonel H. P. Jackson
1958–62 Lieutenant Colonel J. M. D. Ward-Harrison OBE MC
1962–65 Lieutenant Colonel W. S. P. Lithgow

| 1965–66 | Lieutenant Colonel J. B. Willis |
| 1967–69 | Lieutenant Colonel B. C. Greenwood |

SECOND-IN-COMMAND

1946–49	Major A. Abel-Smith
1949–53	Major M. F. Morley
1953–54	Major A. A. N. Tuck
1954–57	Major H. P. Jackson
1957–59	Major R. J. Griffiths
1959–61	Major J. G. Pilsbury MBE MC
1961–63	Major J. de B. Carey
1963–64	Major T. Hope
1964–65	Major R. H. Smyth
1965–66	Major J. B. Willis
1967–68	Major B. C. Greenwood
1969	Major R. P. Wilson

ADJUTANT

1945–46	Captain C. B. Toller
1946–49	Captain J. L. Powles MC
1949–53	Captain J. de B. Carey
1953–56	Captain P. H. G. Bengough
1956	Captain D. A. Harries
1956	Captain J. E. H. Russell
1957–59	Captain J. B. Willis
1959	Captain N. S. M. Delamain
1959–61	Captain D. J. W. Anstice
1961–62	Captain R. P. Cooper
1963–64	Captain A. C. Uloth
1964–67	Captain J. P. W. Friedberger
1967	Captain P. B. de Mesquita
1967–68	Captain The Hon. G. B. Norrie
1969	Captain J. R. Turner

RSM

| 1945–48 | WOI (RSM) K. J. Dunk |
| 1948–50 | WOI (RSM) C. Wass |

1950–57 WO1 (RSM) W. Hedley
1957–58 WO1 (RSM) H. Storer
1958–59 WO1 (RSM) D. Whittlestone
1960–65 WO1 (RSM) T. H. Knight
1966–68 WO1 (RSM) S. T. Murley
1968–69 WO1 (RSM) G. R. Reddish

11th HUSSARS (PAO)
1945–1969

COLONEL-IN-CHIEF

1920–52 HRH Prince Albert Duke of York KG
later HM King George VI

COLONEL OF THE REGIMENT

1945–57 Major General J. F. B. Combe CB DSO
1957–65 Colonel A. T. Smail DSO
1965–69 Colonel Sir John Lawson Bt DSO MC

COMMANDING OFFICER

1945–49 Lieutenant Colonel P Payne-Gallwey DSO
1949–52 Lieutenant Colonel A. V. C. Robarts
1952–55 Lieutenant Colonel P. Arkwright OBE
1955–59 Lieutenant Colonel R. M. H. M. Grant-Thorold DSO
1959–61 Lieutenant Colonel J. A. N. Crankshaw MC
1961–63 Lieutenant Colonel P. D. S. Lauder
1963–65 Lieutenant Colonel R. D. Sutton
1965–66 Lieutenant Colonel T. A. Hall OBE
1966–68 Lieutenant Colonel P. M. Hamer OBE
1968 Lieutenant Colonel C. H. Robertson

SECOND-IN-COMMAND

1945 Lieutenant Colonel R. F. H. P. Stuart-French
1946–48 Major P. Arkwright

1949	Major A. V. C. Robarts
1949–52	Major R. M. H. M. Grant-Thorold DSO
1952–53	Major J. Turnbull MC
1954–57	Major T. I. Pitman MC
1958–59	Major I. M. Davies
1960	Major J. D. A. Woodhouse MC
1961	Major G. H. Hodgkinson
1962	Major A. A. V. Cockle
1962–63	Major G. H. Hodgkinson
1964	Major P. K. Upton
1965	Major T. A. Hall
1965–67	Major S. D. Bolton
1968	Major C. H. Robertson
1969	Major W. K. Trotter

ADJUTANT

1945–46	Captain R. A. K. MacAllan MC
1946–47	Captain R. C. T. Sivewright MC
1948–49	Captain J. R. Ballingall MC
1950–51	Captain R. D. Sutton
1951–53	Captain D. E. V. Sivewright
1954–55	Captain C. H. Robertson
1956–57	Captain T. A. Hall
1958–59	Captain E. V. Farquhar
1960	Captain J. D. Trotter
1961	Captain The Hon. M. J. H. Allenby
1962–63	Captain W. K. Trotter
1964	Captain R. N. C. Bingley
1964–66	Captain D. G. Dollar
1966–67	Captain R. C. G. Gardner
1968–69	Captain The Hon. P. M. Hughes-Young

RSM

1945	RSM (WO1) J. Moore
1946–49	RSM (WO1) H. Hudson
1950–51	RSM (WO1) E. G. Scrivener MM

Senior Appointments

1952–53	RSM (WO1) C. P. Lamb DCM MM
1954–59	RSM (WO1) L. Greensides
1960–61	RSM (WO1) J. Smith
1962–64	RSM (WO1) F. C. Hodges
1965	RSM (WO1) A. M. Alderton
1965–67	RSM (WO1) J. H. Wherton
1968–	RSM (WO1) B. O. Osmand

THE ROYAL HUSSARS (PWO)
1969–1992

COLONEL IN CHIEF

HRH Princess Alice Duchess of Gloucester GCB CI GCVO
GBE

COLONEL OF THE REGIMENT

1969–71	Major General Sir David Dawnay KCVO CB DSO
1971–74	Colonel Sir John Lawson Bt DSO MC
1974–84	Colonel T. A. Hall OBE
1984–90	Colonel Sir Piers Bengough KCVO OBE DL
1990	Major General J. P. W. Friedberger CB CBE

COMMANDING OFFICER

1969–71	Lt Col C. H. Robertson
1971–73	Lt Col P. H. G. Bengough
1973–75	Lt Col N. C. P. Winter
1975–78	Lt Col J. P. W. Friedberger MBE
1978–80	Lt Col E. M. Westropp
1980–82	Lt Col R. J. Hayman-Joyce OBE
1982–85	Lt Col E. C. W. Morrison
1985–87	Lt Col Sir Christopher Thompson Bt
1987–90	Lt Col R. J. Morris
1990–92	Lt Col J. R. D. Kaye

SECOND IN COMMAND

1969–70	Major P. H. G. Bengough
1970–71	Major The Hon. M. J. H. Allenby
1971–73	Major R. B. Merton
1973–75	Major R. N. C. Bingley
1975–76	Major G. J. W. Malet
1976–79	Major D. C. B. Shaw
1979–79	Major R. L. Perry
1979–81	Major J. L. Lemon
1981–83	Major O. F. V. Holder
1983–86	Major A. J. W. Powell
1986–87	Major R. H. East
1987–88	Major O. C. Howard
1988–90	Major J. J. Rogers
1990–92	Major R. C. H. Boon

ADJUTANT

1969–71	Captain J. R. Turner
1971–73	Captain The Hon. S. M. Arthur
1973–75	Captain B. H. Jayes
1975–78	Captain R. H. East
1978–79	Captain W. R. Macdonald
1979–81	Captain C. H. A. Burrell
1981–82	Captain P. R. C. Flach
1982–83	Captain J. R. D. Kaye
1983–85	Captain J. A. F. Howard
1985–87	Captain R. Duckworth
1987–88	Captain A. C. A. McGregor

RSM

1969–71	WO1 (RSM) B. O. Osmond
1971–74	WO1 (RSM) F. W. Nicholas BEM
1974–75	WO1 (RSM) F. P. Gillott
1975–77	WO1 (RSM) A. Watson

1977–79   WO1 (RSM) B. J. Weston
1979–81   WO1 (RSM) B. T. Humberstone
1981–83   WO1 (RSM) C. H. L. Goy
1983–85   WO1 (RSM) M. W. Keats
1985–86   WO1 (RSM) J. W. Durham
1986–87   WO1 (RSM) P. J. Wilkins
1987–90   WO1 (RSM) B. A. Smith
1990–91   WO1 (RSM) M. J. Barnard
1991–92   WO1 (RSM) E. M. Halffman

Appendix G

OFFICERS WHO SERVED WITH
THE 10TH ROYAL HUSSARS (PWO),
THE 11TH HUSSARS (PAO) AND
THE ROYAL HUSSARS (PWO) 1945–1969

Apologies are offered to any whose names have been inadvertently omitted, but the Army Lists of the immediate post-war era are notoriously inaccurate, particularly in respect of National Service officers.

OFFICERS WHO SERVED WITH THE 10th ROYAL
HUSSARS (PWO) 1945–1969

Name on joining the Regiment	Subsequent rank, decorations etc
Abel-Smith A.	Colonel, OBE
Abel-Smith J. W.	
Abel-Smith W. L.	
Allen P.	REME
Anstice D. J. W.	Lieutenant Colonel
Archer-Shee J. P.	Lieutenant Colonel, MC
Archer-Shee R. A.	Major, MC
Arthur The Hon. S. M.	Major The Lord Glenarthur DL
Ashley The Lord	The Earl of Shaftesbury
Awdry G. A.	
Aykroyd M. D.	
Bagshawe M. C.	Lieutenant Colonel, TD
Baird W. S.	Lieutenant Colonel
Ball M. F.	
Baring T. M.	Lieutenant Colonel

Bastin G. A.
Bateman K. B.   Major
Bathurst The Earl   Captain
Bathurst The Hon. G. B.   Captain
Belmont M. J. .K
Bengough P. H. G.   Colonel Sir Piers, KCVO OBE
                               DL

Bennett D. J. C.   Captain
Beresford P. J. C.   Major
Berkeley R. J. G.   Major
Bidgood J. F. S.   Lieutenant Colonel, REME
Bird D. M. G.   Major
Bish R.   REME
Boord O. L.   Colonel, MC
Brooke-Hunt J.   Captain
Brooks M. P.
Brown H. A.
Brown I. W.
Bryant W.   Major
Budd N. B. R.   Major
Bune D. F.   Captain
Canning O. F. C.
Carruthers A. J. E.
Carver W. E.   Captain
Carey J. de B.   Lieutenant Colonel
Castley J. A.   Brigadier, RAPC
Chaplin J. R.   Captain
Charrington N. D.   Major
Childs P. C. F.
Chisnell J. E.
Churchward A. G.
Clode W. A.   Captain
Clowes N. J.   Captain
Combe K. C.   Major, TD
Copper J. B.
Cooper R.
Cooper R. P.   Major
Cory-Wright M. M. G.
Courtney-Clarke J. K.   Major, later J. K. C. Scott
Covill D. F.   Major, MBE DCM
Cowley J. M.   Lieutenant Colonel, OBE

Cox M.	
Craig J. M.	Colonel, TD DL
Cripps A. T. H.	Major
Crosse N. J.	
Cruikshank M. P. D.	Major
Davies R. A.	Major
Davy C. K.	Colonel, MC
Dawnay C. R.	Captain
Dawnay D.	Major General Sir David, KCVO CB DSO
Dawnay H.	Major
Delamain N. S. M.	Captain
Dennis A. J. D.	
Denison-Pender The Hon. J. W.	Captain The Lord Pender of Dudley
Deykin J. D.	Lieutenant Colonel, 10th Light Horse
Drake F. C.	Colonel
Duckett G. H.	Major
Duncan G. A.	
Dundas R. A.	
Duveen A. E.	Captain
Dwerryhouse W. P.	Captain
East R. H.	Lieutenant Colonel
Ednam The Viscount	The Earl of Dudley
Edwards D. C.	Lieutenant Colonel
Elliott S. J.	Captain
Elwes S. V. E. P.	
Erith R. F.	Major, TD
Errington G. H.	Major, MC
Evans L.	Professor, RAMC
Evans M. R.	Major
Fearnehough R.	Major
Fielden E. A.	
Finn R. V.	
Fleming M. W. S.	Major
French C.	
Friedberger J. P. W.	Major General, CB CBE
Frisby W. J.	Major
Gairdner C. H.	Lieutenant General Sir Charles, GBE KCMG KCVO CB

Garcia J.	Major, MBE
Gaskin B. F. P.	Major, TD
Gibb C. O.	Captain
Gladstone C. S.	
Glasse J. J. M.	
Gordon A. J. W.	Major
Gorner R. M.	Captain
Gorsuch M. A.	
Govett F. R.	Major
Govett P. J. R.	
Gray C. R. D.	Colonel
Greenwood B. C.	Colonel
Greenwood V. J.	Colonel
Griffith R. J.	Lieutenant Colonel, MBE MC
Grissell M.	Major
Guild I. R.	
Hanson-Lawson J. G.	
Harries D. A.	
Harriss A. E.	
Harrison S. E.	
Hartigan G. C.	
Hartigan J.	
Harvey C. B. C.	Brigadier, DSO and two bars
Hawkins M. B. C.	Major Sir Michael, KCVO MBE
Haycock M. B.	Colonel, CBE TD DL
Head J. G. F.	Colonel, OBE, Irish Guards
Healey P. T. C.	Captain
Hedley W. J.	Major
Hignett A. D.	
Hignett J. D.	Lieutenant Colonel, DL JP
Hignett J. M.	
Hill D. R.	Captain
Holder O. E. V.	Lieutenant Colonel
Hope A. D. B.	Captain
Hope T.	Lieutenant Colonel
Howard O. C.	Major
Howart J.	Major
Hughes-Reckitt J. B.	
Hughes-Reckitt P. J.	Captain
Ingram J. L.	Major
Inskip L. A.	Captain

Jackson H. P.	Lieutenant Colonel
Jackson M. P.	Captain, later Capper-Jackson
Jayes B. H.	Captain
Jones-Williams D. W.	Lieutenant Colonel, OBE MC TD DL
Kaye D. R. B.	Colonel, DSO DL JP
Kaye P. C. C.	Lieutenant Colonel
Kelsey J. P.	
Knight T. H.	Major
Lacey M. B.	
Landon J. T. W.	Brigadier
Latchford K. W.	Major General, AO RAAC
Leatham P. M.	Captain
Lemieux J. N. V. A.	
Leslie C. L. C.	
L'Estrange F. O.	Captain
Lewis G. D. C. M.	Major
Ley I. F.	Captain
Lithgow W. S. P.	Lieutenant Colonel, formerly RHA
Lloyd E. T. T.	Major
Lloyd H. R. P.	Major
Loney D.	Colonel, RAOC
Low D. C.	
Lyall Grant A. H.	Major, later 16/5L
MacDiarmid P. T. I.	Colonel, MC
MacDonald W. R.	Major
Mace C. T.	Major
Macmullen M. N. E.	Major
Magor E. W. M.	Major, CMG OBE
Mainwaring J. S. K.	
Malet G. J. W.	Lieutenant Colonel, OBE
Malyon B. H.	Major
Malyon M. J. H.	Major
Mander M. G.	
Mander M.	
Manners A. E. R.	
Mason F. O.	Lieutenant Colonel
Maxwell S. M.	The Hon. Simon Maxwell
Mears K. J.	Brigadier, CBE, Intelligence Corps
Mesquita P. D.	Lieutenant Colonel, OBE (Bueno de Mesquita)

Milbanke R. M.	Lieutenant Colonel Sir Ralph Milbanke Bt, MC
Miller C. D.	Colonel
Montagu-Douglas-Scott The Lord G. F. J.	Colonel The Lord George Scott
Montagu-Douglas-Scott The Lord W. W.	Lieutenant Colonel The Lord William Scott, MC DL
Moorhouse S. C. T. W.	
Morley M. D. F.	
Morley M. F.	Brigadier, MBE
Morley T. R.	Major
Morrisey-Paine R. J.	Lieutenant Colonel, later The Life Guards
Murdoch G. P.	Colonel, RAPC
Murray B. C.	
Mylne N. J.	QC
Mylne O. N. P.	Captain
Newman-Burbury J. N.	
Norrie The Hon. G. B.	Lieutenant Colonel
Norrie C. W. M.	Lieutenant General The Lord Norrie, GCMG GCVO CB DSO MC, formerly 11H
North G. E. F.	Major, MC DL JP
Nunes-Carvalho N. J.	
Nunn, J. A. J.	Major
O'Callaghan C. T.	Colonel
Oldham C. R.	Captain
O'Reilly C. V.	
Orr R. S.	Major, MRCVS
Palmer T. B.	Major General, CB, REME
Pernetta M. G.	Captain
Perry R. L.	Major
Phipps C. N.	
Pilsbury J. G.	Lieutenant Colonel, MBE MC
Plomer S.	Captain
Ponsonby C. B.	Lieutenant Colonel
Posnett M.	Captain, MC
Powles J. L.	Captain, MC
Poynder M. F.	Captain
Pugh D.	
Pumphrey M. C. S.	

Radmore M. T.
Ralli R. S. C.   Captain
Ralli S. A.   Major
Raspin K. W.   Captain
Raw R. D.
Reeve C. T.   Major Sir Trevor Reeve QC
Reynolds P. T.
Richards C. R. W. L.
Richardson D. C. H.   Major
Roberts R. G.
Robins J. W. F.   Captain
Robson F. H.   Major, MBE
Roddick M. G.   Brigadier, DSO MC
Rothwell C.
Rothwell F. R.   Major
Rothwell J.
Round C. J.
Russell-Smith A.
Russell J. E. H.   Captain
Russell R. H. E.   CVO
Sampson A. F. W.
Sanderman D. P.
Scholfield P. V.   Major
Sclater J. F.
Scott-Dalgleish M. I.
Scott I. A. G.
Scott J. H.
Scott J. U.
Seymour A. J.
Seymour C. G.   Major
Shaw D. C. B.   Major
Shebbeare R. I.
Shepherd B. T.
Sheppard M. G.
Sloane J. J.   Brigadier, OBE MC
Smoothy R.   Lieutenant Colonel, REME
Smith R. H.   Major
Snow A. E.
Spence C. J.   Captain
Stanley-Smith M. M. G.
Staughton S. D. H. L.

Stirum C. P. M. Van Limburg	Major
Storer H.	Major
Strachan B. L.	Major, CMG, formerly 4H
Strong R. J.	Captain
Stuttaford I. T.	Dr
Stuttaford W. R.	CBE
Sutcliffe W. B.	Captain
Swinden C. E. L.	Captain
Taylor M. J. C.	
Thirst J. V.	Captain
Thoyts J. H.	Brigadier
Toller C. B.	Captain
Toller R. C. R.	Major, MC
Tonks E. E.	
Tremlett R. A. E.	
Tuck A. A. N.	Colonel, MBE
Tuck N. J.	Lieutenant Colonel
Turnbull D. A.	Captain
Turner J. A.	Lieutenant Colonel, OBE
Uloth A. C.	Colonel
Verge J.	Major, MBE
Wakefield E. H. T.	Sir Humphry Wakefield Bt
Walker K. P.	
Wallace J. S.	Captain
Waller D. J. A.	Captain, MC
Wall-Morris G.	
Ward-Harrison J. M. D.	Major General, CB OBE MC, formerly 5 Innis DG
Watson B. B. C.	
Watt C. R. G.	Major
Weatherby J. H.	Captain
Weeber D. R.	Major D. R. Heron-Weeber
White C. A.	
White W. H.	
Whittlestone D. A.	Major
Wiley W. S. F.	
Williams I. M.	Captain
Willis J. B.	Major General, CB
Wilson R. P.	Major
Wilson R.	
Wingfield A. D. R.	Brigadier, DSO MC

Winn The Hon. C. J. F.
Winter C.
Winter W.
Wyatt C. E. N.   Captain

OFFICERS WHO SERVED WITH THE 11th HUSSARS (PAO) 1945–1969

Name on joining the Regiment	*Subsequent rank, decorations etc*
Acland D. A.	
Acland M. A.	
Addis H.	Major
Adlard E. F.	
Ainsworth Sir David	
Alderton A. M.	Major, MBE
Alexander J.	
Allenby The Viscount	Lieutenant Colonel
Allenby The Hon. M. J. H.	Lieutenant Colonel The Viscount Allenby of Megiddo
Alton R. E.	
Arkwright P.	Colonel, OBE
Ballingall J. R.	Captain, MC
Barker F. G.	Captain
Barrie D.	Captain
Bathurst The Hon C. H. L.	The Viscount Bledisloe QC
Beevor A. J.	
Benson J. A.	Captain
Benson J. R.	
Bent J. E.	Major
Bingley R. A. G.	Lieutenant Colonel, CVO DSO OBE
Bingley R. N. C.	Lieutenant Colonel
Birchall P. E. D.	Lieutenant Colonel, TD JP
Bolton S. D.	Major
Bousfield A. W.	
Brett-Smith R.	
Bridge J. W.	
Browne E. K.	
Brown J. J. G.	
Bruce I. N. E.	Captain
Burden W. V.	Major, MC & bar

Burke J. B. A.
Capel W. T.   Captain
Caroe P. R.
Carson M.
Chadwick E.   Lieutenant Colonel, MBE
Champion J. S.   CMG OBE
Chapman P. F.   MC
Churton D. N. V.   Captain, MBE
Churton G. V.   Colonel, MBE MC TD DL
Clarke E. S. N.   Major, MBE MM
Clark M. M. C.   Captain, MC
Clarkson N. R. N.
Clegg T. G.
Coates J. P.
Cockle A. A. V.   Colonel
Combe J. F. B.   Major General, CB DSO & bar
Cooper-Evans M.
Copeland P. T. G.
Copeland R. G. G.
Cowley N. P. T.
Crankshaw J. A. N.   Lieutenant Colonel, MC & bar
Cresswell B.
Crompton J. B.
Crosland C. R. H.
Crosthwaite P. T.
Cunningham W. McG   Lieutenant Colonel, MVO OBE
                                       MC

Currie J. M. B.
Curtis W. R.
Curwen C. R.   LVO OBE
Daly J.
Daniels J. G. U.
Darby A. M. G.
Davies I. M.   Major
de Freville M. G. L.   Captain
de Lisle C. de B.   Colonel
Denison-Pender The Hon. R. C.
Denning C. H. D.
de Sales la Terrière I. C.   Captain
Dexter E. R.
Dier G. E. C.

Dollar D. G.	Captain
Downman T. E.	
Drane J. W.	
Dudley P. J.	
Dunleath The Lord	Hon. Colonel, TD DL
Emery A. G.	Captain, DCM
Esch V. V.	Captain
Faber M. L. O.	
Farquhar E.	Captain
Farrant A. A.	
Fenwicke-Clennell G. T. W.	Captain
Finch J. S.	Major
Flood A. R.	Dr, MC
Forrest C. A. A.	Captain
Forster T. A.	Captain
Friend J. A.	
Galica J. W.	
Gardner J. C.	
Gardner R. C. G.	Captain
Garrard J. W.	
Gibson C. B.	
Glazebrook W. L.	The Reverend
Gormley T. W.	
Gosling H. M.	Captain, J. P.
Goulden J. L.	
Graham J. A.	Brigadier
Grant-Thorold R. M. H. M.	Colonel, DSO
Guymer M. H.	Major
Haig I. R. P.	
Halliday C. A.	MC & bar
Hall J. A.	Major, MBE
Hall P. J.	Captain
Hall T. A.	Colonel, OBE
Hamer P. M.	Colonel, OBE
Hankinson M. J.	Captain
Hardcastle C. P. B.	
Harding J. C.	Major The Lord Harding of Petherton
Harris J. H.	
Hartman T. R.	
Hayman-Joyce R. J.	Major General, CBE

Heneage T. R. W.	
Henn F. R.	Brigadier, CBE
Hodges F. C.	Major
Hodgkinson G. H.	Lieutenant Colonel
Holcroft T. G. C.	Captain
Hopkinson N. H. E.	
Horsfall R. D.	
Horsford T. O'B.	Major, MC
Hughes-Young The Hon. P. M.	Captain
Hunter A. S.	Captain, MC
Hunt W. G. G.	Captain
Innes R. D.	
Jaffray N. J.	Captain
Jenson P. R.	
Jones S. E.	
Kane A.	
Kaye M. R. C.	
Kempe G. M.	
Kent HRH Prince Michael of	Major, KCVO
Keown-Boyd H. G.	
King H. G.	Lieutenant Colonel, MBE
Laidlaw D.	
Lakin R. L.	
Langrishe P. N.	
Lauder P. D. S.	Colonel
Lawson A. S. A.	Lieutenant Colonel
Lawson J. C. A. D.	Colonel Sir John Lawson Bt, DSO MC
Leetham A. I.	
Leetham W. I.	
Leigh The Hon. B. C.	
Leigh The Hon. W. R.	
Lemon J. M.	Major
Lewis J. H. P. S. B.	Major
Lewis M.	
Lister J. A. D'A.	
Lloyd D. P. J.	Major, MC
Loch The Lord	
Loehnis A. D.	
Lovett G. J.	
Lowsley-Williams D.	Colonel, TD DL

Lutyens L. A.	
Lyster P. H.	
MacAllan R. A. .K	Major, MC
MacAlpine-Downie R.	
MacLean A. D.	
Maddock J. F.	
Markham C. J.	Sir Charles Markham Bt
Meade R. J. H.	OBE
Merton R. B.	Lieutenant Colonel, formerly 4H and QRIH
Metaxa P. A.	
Miller A. G.	
Mitchell J. de C.	Major, TD
Mitchell W. A. M.	
Morgan R. E. R.	Captain
Muers-Raby N. J.	Major
Muir J. R.	
Nation-Tellery G. L.	
Newall The Hon. F. S. E.	Captain The Lord Newall
Newnham P. A.	MC
Newsome A. J.	Major
Norrie The Hon. G. W. M.	Major The Lord Norrie
O'Neill The Lord	Hon Colonel, TD DL
Oppenheimer A. E.	
Orton S. R.	
Osborne K. L.	
Parker C. R.	Major, DCM
Paton A. W.	MC
Paul G. C. P.	
Payne-Gallwey P.	Colonel, DSO & 2 bars
Payne-Gallwey P. F.	Sir Philip Payne-Gallwey Bt
Pearson F. E.	
Penny E. W.	Major
Perkins D.	
Petch H.	Major, MC DCM
Peter-Hoblyn G. H.	
Phillips J. G.	
Pinney W. J.	Major
Pitman T. I.	Major, MC
Ponsonby The Hon. T. M.	Colonel, TD DL
Porter P. J.	

Powell A. J. W.	Lieutenant Colonel
Queckett C. E.	Captain
Rapp R. A.	
Rayner N. C.	
Reid-Scott A.	Major, MC
Reid-Scott M.	
Richmond J.	Captain
Ridley-Day N. S.	
Riggall R. S. D.	
Robarts A. V. C.	Lieutenant Colonel
Robertson C. H.	Brigadier, CVO DL
Roberts H. C.	Major
Robinson N. F.	
Roe D. E.	Lieutenant Colonel
Roe P. M.	Captain
Rogers J. J.	Lieutenant Colonel
Scarbrough The Earl of	Colonel, DL
Seely V. R.	Major
Sivewright D. E. V.	Captain
Sivewright R. C. T.	Colonel, CB MC DL
Smail A. T.	Colonel, DSO & bar
Smail S. T.	Major
Soames A. N. W.	The Hon. Nicholas Soames MP
Soames R. H.	Lieutenant Colonel
Sowerby W. H.	
Spencer G. R. C. M.	
Spicknell C. J.	
Staughton S. T. J. T.	The Rt. Hon. Lord Justice Staughton QC
Steel A. E. W.	
St Johnston K.	Sir Kerry St Johnston
Stockdale H.	
Straker I. C.	Major
Stratton V. G. L.	
Stuart-French R. F. H. P.	Lieutenant Colonel
Sutton J.	
Sutton R. D.	Lieutenant Colonel
Sykes N. C. M.	
Thimbleby N. T. L.	Captain
Thompson C. P.	Lieutenant Colonel Sir Christopher Thompson Bt

Thomson D.
Todhunter M. J. B.
Trotter W. K.   Major, CBE DL
Trotter J. D.   Captain
Troughton J. C. M.   Captain
Turnbull J.   Lieutenant Colonel, MC
Upton P. K.   Lieutenant Colonel
Venner G. R.   Captain
Villiers The Viscount
Villiers M. A.   Major
Wainman W.   Lieutenant Colonel, DSO MC
Ward F.
Warren R. S. R. de W.   Captain
Waters W. B.
Watson W. S.
Wentworth-Stanley O. M.   Major, MC
Westropp E. M.   Brigadier, CBE
Wheeler, J. R. G. C.
Whistler R. A.
Whitley P. A.
Wiggin G. D. H.
Wiggin M. P.
Wiggin P. M.   Lieutenant Colonel, JP
Wild H. N. H.   Colonel, OBE
Wilkinson R. A.   Major
Wills F. H. P. H.
Wingfield-Digby R. E.   Captain, MC
Winlove N. H.
Winter N. C. P.   Lieutenant Colonel
Woodhouse J. D. A.   Lieutenant Colonel, MC
Wood P. H.   Major (later Haselden-Wood)
Writer W. H.
Young E. A. I.   Major

OFFICERS WHO SERVED WITH THE ROYAL HUSSARS (PWO) 1969–1992

Name on joining the Regiment	*Subsequent rank, decorations etc*
Adams B. J.	Major
Ainsworth A. T. H.	
Alderton A. M.	Major, MBE

Alers-Hankey D. G.	
Allenby The Hon. M. J. H.	Lieutenant Colonel The Viscount Allenby of Megiddo
Allen T. C.	Major
Allerton P. J.	
Allfrey C. J.	Captain
Anstice D. J. W.	Lieutenant Colonel
Archer R.	Captain, RAMC
Arkwright M. P. V.	
Arthur The Hon. S. M.	Major The Lord Glenarthur DL
Ashton-Johnson P. J.	Royal Wessex Yeomanry
Ashton The Hon. T. H.	
Atherden T. L.	
Atkinson C. D. B	
Awdry G. A.	
Axellby L.	Captain, RAEC
Barclay R. D.	Captain
Bateman K. B.	Major
Bathurst The Hon. A. E. S.	Captain
Baugh D. M.	Captain, RAPC
Beevor A. J.	
Bengough J. F.	
Bengough P. H. G.	Colonel Sir Piers, KCVO OBE DL
Bent J. E.	Major
Berchem N. P. F.	
Beresford P. J. C.	Major
Bingley R. N. C.	Lieutenant Colonel
Blair J. W.	The Reverend, RAChD
Bolton C. T. G.	Major, later Grenadier Guards
Boon R. C. H.	Major
Boulter S. C. W.	Major
Bowring R. A. W.	Major
Bridge S. T. W.	Captain
Brodey A. C.	2 RTR
Brudenell-Bruce The Lord Charles	
Budgett J. F.	
Bueno de Mesquita N. P.	Captain
Burell C. H. A.	Major
Capper-Jackson M. P.	Captain, formerly Jackson
Carter	Captain, RAPC

Chesney D.	Major, RAMC
Churton D. N. V.	Captain, MBE
Clarke J. A.	Captain, RAMC
Clinch P. M. E.	Captain
Coates O. H. F.	Captain
Collins V. S.	Captain, WRAC
Cook J. R. B.	Colonel, R Signals
Copeland P. T. G.	
Corbett R. J.	Lieutenant Colonel, RAPC
Covill D. F.	Major, MBE DCM
Cray R. V.	Major
Crewdson W. A. H.	
Daly D. C.	Captain
Dann N. C.	Army Air Corps
Danvers C. H. D.	Major
Darell C. H. D.	Lieutenant Colonel
Darke J. M. J.	
Davenport O. J.	
Dawnay D.	Major General Sir David Dawnay, KCVO CB DSO & bar
Dawnay H.	Major
Delamain C. M.	
de Normann A. L.	Captain
de Normann J. R. C.	Major
Diggens D. A. L.	Captain
Dixon R. S.	REME
Dollar D. G.	Captain
Drapper C. J.	Captain, REME
Duckett G. H.	Major
Duckworth R.	Captain
East R. H.	Lieutenant Colonel
Edwards D. C.	Lieutenant Colonel
Erith R. F.	Major, TD
Evans G. D.	Captain, RAMC
Evetts R. M. I.	Captain, 16/5 L
Farquhar P. C. E.	
Fearnehough R.	Major
Flach P. R. C.	Lieutenant Colonel, MBE
Foot V. H.	Captain, RAMC
Forrest C. A. A.	Captain
Forrest P. A. A.	

Fowle C. S.	Captain
Freedman R. E. J.	Captain
Friedberger J. P. W.	Major General, CB CBE
Frostick P. C.	Captain, REME
Gatehouse M.	Captain
Gedney B. W.	
Gedney F. G.	Captain
Gibson-Fleming J. R.	
Gillott F. P.	Lieutenant Colonel
Glazebrook R. W.	
Godfrey-Faussett C. B.	
Gordon A. J. W.	Major
Goy C. H. L.	Captain
Grant-Thorold N.	Major
Greenwood B. C.	Colonel
Grimston R. J. S.	Captain The Hon Robin
Guthrie B. G.	
Hall E. St J.	Captain
Hall J. A.	Major, MBE
Hall P. J.	Captain
Hall T. A.	Colonel, OBE
Hamer P. M.	Colonel, OBE
Hamilton P. A.	
Hannay R. J.	Captain
Hayman–Joyce R. J.	Major General, CBE
Hazel J. F. T.	
Henderson M. G.	Captain, RAMC
Herdman J. E.	
Hezlet C. T. R.	Major
Hodges F. C.	Major
Hodgkinson G. H.	Lieutenant Colonel
Hodgson C. C.	Captain, REME
Holder O. E. V.	Lieutenant Colonel
Holford-Walker E. A.	Captain
Hope T.	Major
Howard J. A. F.	Major
Howard O. C.	Major
Hubbard N. G.	Captain
Hudson D. D.	Royal Signals
Hughes-Young The Hon. P. M.	Captain
Humberstone B. T.	Captain, MBE

Hunter N.	Captain
Ingram H. R. M.	
Inkin P. A. D.	
Jayes B. H.	Captain
Jones G. L.	Captain
Jude B. M.	Major, RAMC
Kaye J. R. D.	Lieutenant Colonel
Kaye P. C. C.	Lieutenant Colonel
Keats M. W.	Major
Kent HRH Prince Michael of	Major, KCVO
Kerr A. R. F.	Dr, RAMC
King H. G.	Lieutenant Colonel, MBE
Kitson C. H. M.	Major
Knight T. H.	Major
Lane M. G.	Major, Director of Music, WRAC & Irish Guards
Langhorne C. J.	2 RTR
Lawson P. J.	Major
Lemon J. M.	Major
Lewis G. D. C. M.	Major
Lindsay K. B.	Captain
Loveday J. M.	The Reverend, RAChD
Loweth J. R.	Captain, REME
Lowsley-Williams G. D. S.	Captain
MacDiarmid R. P. A.	
MacDonald W. R.	Major
MacLeod-Ash N. F. V.	Captain
Malet G. J. W.	Lieutenant Colonel, OBE
Malyon M. J. H.	Major
Marcus R. B.	Captain
McGimpsey	Major, RAPC
McGregor A. C. A.	Captain
Merton R. B.	Lieutenant Colonel, formerly 4H and QRIH
Merton S. R. B.	Captain
Mesquita P. D.	Lieutenant Colonel, OBE (Bueno de Mesquita)
Micklem J. J.	
Millais H. M.	Captain
Miller J. P.	Captain
Moir J. D. S.	Major

Morgan R. E. R.	Captain
Morrison E. C. W.	Brigadier, OBE ADC
Morrison M. C. E.	Captain
Morris R. J.	Colonel
Muers-Raby N. J.	Major
Mundy A. H.	
Norrie The Hon. G. B.	Lieutenant Colonel
Norrie The Hon. G. W. M.	Major The Lord Norrie
Nunn J. J.	
Offer H. M. J.	
Oldham C. R.	Captain
Orton S. R.	Captain
Osmand B. O.	Captain, MBE
Paskell C. W.	Captain, REME
Perry R. L.	Major
Phillips J. G.	Captain, REME
Phillips P. D.	Captain, REME
Pinney W. J.	Major
Powell A. J. W.	Lieutenant Colonel
Price P. M.	
Prickett M. J.	16/5 L
Radmore M. T.	
Reid J. E.	Captain, Lord Strathcona's Horse
Reid-Scott M.	Captain
Rigall R. S. D.	Captain
Robertson C. H.	Brigadier, CVO DL
Robertson I. P. J.	R Signals
Roe D. E.	Lieutenant Colonel
Roe P. M.	Captain
Rogers J. J.	Lieutenant Colonel
Rogers M. J.	Captain
Rogers M. S.	Captain
Rome D. P.	Captain
Roulstone A. R. M.	Captain, REME
Scholfield P. V.	Major
Scott-Dalgleish M. I.	
Scott J. K. C.	Major, formerly Courtney-Clarke
Seely V. R.	Major
Selby M. P.	Colonel, REME
Seymour R. A. T.	Captain
Shaw D. C. B.	Major

Smith B. A.	Captain
Smith D. W.	Lieutenant Colonel, RAMC
Smith J. S. W.	Captain, REME
Smyth R. H.	Major
Soames A. N. W.	The Hon. Nicholas Soames MP
Spencer M. J. B.	The Reverend, RAChD
Stevens J. P.	Captain
Stevens R. W.	The Reverend, RAChD
Sutcliffe J. M. B.	Captain
Sweeney R. N.	Major, United States Army
Swinden C. E. L.	Captain
Taylor J. C.	Captain, RAPC
Thackeray J.	Captain, RAPC
Thimbleby N. T. L.	Captain
Thirst J. V.	Captain
Thompson C. P.	Lieutenant Colonel Sir Christopher Thompson Bt
Thorpe D. A. R.	Captain, REME
Thoyts J. H.	Brigadier
Tilley G. A.	Army Air Corps
Topp A.	Captain, REME
Townsend D. A.	Captain
Trollope-Bellow A. H.	
Trotter J. W. D.	Captain
Trotter W. K.	Major, CBE DL
Troughton E. T. A.	
Trubody R. T.	Captain, RAPC
Tuck N. J.	Lieutenant Colonel
Turnbull M.	
Turner J. R.	Lieutenant Colonel, OBE
Uloth A. C.	Colonel
Uloth A. M. C.	Captain
Upton P. K.	Lieutenant Colonel
Upton R. H.	Captain
Vale E. H.	
Venner G. R.	Captain
Verghese	Captain, RAMC
Vernon J. C.	The Reverend, RAChD
Villiers The Viscount	
Villiers M. A.	Major
Wadham M. W.	Major RAPC

Wakefield M. E. V.
Ward M. A.   Captain
Wass C.
Watson A.   Captain
Watt C. R. G.   Major
Westropp E. M.   Brigadier, CBE
Whelan T. R.   Dr
White The Hon. L. R.   Captain The Lord Annaly
Whittlestone D. A.   Major
Wiggin D. P.   Captain
Wiggin J. D.   The Reverend, RAChD
Wiggin J. G.
Wilby T. D.
Wilkins P. J.   Captain
Wilkinson R. A.   Major
Williams C. J. M.
Willis H. J.
Wilson R. P.   Major
Winter J. H. P.
Winter N. C. P.   Lieutenant Colonel
Woodhams M. G.   Captain, RAPC
Woodhouse J. D. A.   Lieutenant Colonel, MC
Wood P. H.   Major (later Haselden-Wood)
Yates C. J. K.   Captain

Bibliography

Barber, Noel *The War of the Running Dogs* (Collins 1971)

Beevor, Antony *Inside the British Army* (Chatto & Windus 1990)

Brander, Michael *The 10th Hussars* (Leo Cooper 1969)

Brett-Smith, Richard *Berlin '45 – The Grey City* (Macmillan 1966)

Brett-Smith, Richard *The 11th Hussars* (Leo Cooper 1969)

Clarke, Brigadier Dudley *The Eleventh at War* (Michael Joseph 1952)

de Normann, Major J. R. C. *The Gulf War* (Unpublished ms)

Dexter, E. R. *Ted Dexter Declares* (1966)

Henniker, Brigadier M. C. A. *Red Shadow over Malaya* (William Blackwood 1955)

Lunt, James, *Imperial Sunset*, (1981)

Watt, Robin *A Soldier's Sketch-book* (National Army Museum 1994)

The 10th Hussars in World War II
The 10th Hussar *Gazettes* 1945–69
The 11th Hussar *Journals* 1945–69
The Royal Hussar *Journals* 1970–92
The Army List
Ministry of Defence Library Records

Index

Index

Index

Index

Index

Index

Index

Index

Index

Index

Index

Index